Before the Deluge

Parisian Society in the Reign of Louis XVI

By the same author
The World of Fanny Burney

Evelyn Farr

Before the Deluge

Parisian Society in the Reign of Louis XVI

PETER OWEN
London & Chester Springs

PETER OWEN PUBLISHERS
73 Kenway Road London SW5 0RE
Peter Owen books are distributed in the USA by
Dufour Editions Inc. Chester Springs PA 19425–0449

First published in Great Britain 1994
© Evelyn Farr 1994

*The endpapers show contemporary engravings of
(left) Notre Dame de Paris, spiritual heart of the
French capital, and (right) Hôtel de Ville, its
bureaucratic nerve centre*

A catalogue record for this book is available from the British Library

ISBN 0–7206–0893–7

Printed and made by Biddles of Guildford and King's Lynn

For Marcelle Vernon-Powell

Acknowledgements

I am very grateful to Librairie Droz S.A. of Geneva for permission
to quote and translate material from the *Journal (1780–1789)*
of the Marquis de Bombelles (2 vols, 1977, 1982).

Contents

Acknowledgements   vi

Chronology   ix

Pre-revolutionary French Currency   xii

Introduction   13

1. Life in Paris   15

2. The Court of Versailles   35

3. Le Beau Monde   68

4. Trysts and Tragedies   92

5. Age of Miracles?   117

6. Towards the Precipice   144

7. 1789: Year of Reckoning   167

Biographical Notes   193

Notes   202

Bibliography   214

Chronology

1770   May. Marriage of Dauphin of France (future Louis XVI) to Archduchess Marie-Antoinette of Austria.
Dec. Dismissal of Duc de Choiseul, architect of Franco–Austrian alliance.

1774   May. Louis XVI becomes king at age of twenty after death of Louis XV from smallpox. Comte de Maurepas becomes prime minister. Turgot, as Controller-General of Finances, attempts to introduce economic reforms, but is forced out of office in 1776.

1776   July. American Declaration of Independence.
Dec. Benjamin Franklin arrives in Paris.

1777   Visit of Emperor Joseph II to France. Lafayette leaves to join American forces against Britain.
Jun. Necker becomes Director of Finances.

1778   Feb. France enters American War of Independence against Britain.
Dec. Birth of Louis XVI's first child, Marie-Thérèse-Charlotte, Madame Royale (d. 1851).

1781   Feb. Necker publishes *Compte-rendu au roi* detailing state of French finances.
May. Necker resigns.

1781   Oct. Birth of first Dauphin, Louis-Joseph-Xavier-François (d. 1789). British forces under Cornwallis surrender to combined French and American army at Yorktown.
Nov. Death of Maurepas.

1782   Mar. Publication of *Les Liaisons Dangereuses*.
Oct. Bankruptcy of the Prince de Guéméné for thirty-three million *livres*.

1783   Jan. Treaty of Versailles concludes peace between France, Britain, and the USA. American independence established.
Jun. First balloon flight by Montgolfier, Annonay.
Nov. First manned balloon flight, Paris. Calonne appointed Controller-General.

1784   Apr. First public performance of *The Marriage of Figaro*.

1785   Mar. Birth of Louis-Charles, Duc de Normandie (Dauphin from 1789, presumed dead in prison, 1795).
Aug. Arrest of Cardinal de Rohan over Diamond Necklace Affair.

1786   May. Rohan acquitted at conclusion of Necklace Trial in Paris.
Jul. Birth of Princesse Sophie (d. 1787).
Sep. Anglo-French Treaty of Commerce signed.

1787   Feb. Assembly of Notables convened to discuss fiscal reform.
Apr. Calonne dismissed. Loménie de Brienne appointed Controller-General.

1788   Jan. Full civil rights granted to Protestants.
Jul. Severe storms destroy crops across France. Orders given for the convocation of the States General.
Aug. Necker returns to office as Controller-General.

1789   5 May. Opening session of States General at Versailles.
27 June. Formation of National Assembly after revolt of the Third Estate.
11 July. Necker dismissed and ordered into exile.
14 July. Storming of the Bastille.
16 July. Emigration begins with flight of the Bourbon princes.
20 July. Necker recalled to office.
4 Aug. Noble privileges and feudal dues abolished by the National Assembly.
5 Oct. Paris mob marches to Versailles. Louis XVI accepts the Declaration of the Rights of Man.
6 Oct. Royal family and National Assembly forced to move to Paris.

1790   Sep. Necker resigns and emigrates.

1791   Jul. Unsuccessful attempt by royal family to flee France. Stopped at Varennes and escorted back to Paris.
Sep. Louis XVI accepts the Constitution.

1792   10 Aug. Storming of the Tuileries. Royal family imprisoned.
22 Sep. France declared a republic.

1793   21 Jan. Execution of Louis XVI.
16 Oct. Execution of Queen Marie-Antoinette.

Pre-revolutionary French currency

Since French coins during the eighteenth century had many different names, and units of account were different from the coinage, a table of equivalents is given below. The *franc* was a coin, the *livre* a unit of account.

$$1 \textit{ franc } = 1 \textit{ livre}$$

$$1 \textit{ franc/livre } = 20 \textit{ sous/sols}$$
$$1 \textit{ sou/sol } = 4 \textit{ liards}$$
$$1 \textit{ liard } = 3 \textit{ deniers}$$

$$\textit{petit écu } = 3 \textit{ francs/livres}$$
$$\textit{gros écu } = 6 \textit{ francs/livres}$$
$$\textit{louis d'or } = 24 \textit{ francs/livres}$$

N.B. Most historians give the *écu*'s value as three *francs*, but Frénilly writes of '*gros écus de six francs*' and Madame de La Tour du Pin speaks of an '*écu de six francs*'. There are many references to the '*petit écu*'. It seems therefore that there were two *écu* coins, one worth three *francs* and the other worth six.

French/British Currency

During the reign of Louis XVI, the exchange rate varied between twenty-two and twenty-three *francs* or *livres* to one pound sterling. According to the calculations of the agriculturalist Arthur Young, in 1789 the exchange rate was 22.85 *francs* to £1.00. The *louis d'or* was therefore roughly equivalent to one guinea.

Introduction

For many people, the French Revolution summons up a few recurring images, nearly all of them gory: starving *sans-culottes*, arrogant aristocrats, the storming of the Bastille, the grimly efficient guillotine. Such images, reinforced by two centuries of art, literature and drama, can be neatly arranged to provide a simple explanation of the cause and progress of the Revolution, in which the oppressed populace is seen throwing off its chains and wresting power from a tyrannical king and his dissolute Court to the stirring tune of the Marseillaise. The truth, of course, is far more complex.

It is hard to disagree with Louis-Sébastien Mercier's assertion that 'Paris made the Revolution', but it would be wrong to assume that he refers only to the Paris of the *sans-culottes*. In fact, although the *sans-culottes* undoubtedly pushed the Revolution to its bloody conclusion, it was largely the Parisian nobility who set it in motion. It was not a ragged mob, baying alternately for bread and democracy, who first promoted the doctrine of liberty and threw down a challenge to absolute monarchy, but well-fed, elegantly attired aristocrats who enjoyed all the privileges and pleasures their rank could afford. Yet in books on the *ancien régime*, Parisian high society is usually dismissed in a few paragraphs as a frivolous, voluptuous and decadent élite, doomed to fall with the monarchy to which it clung parasitically – a cause of revolution rather than a catalyst for reform.

This book is written with the hope of throwing new light on this often neglected but very important section of society in Louis XVI's France. I have tried to show pre-revolutionary Parisian high society in all its moods – not only in its dependence on a Court which it nevertheless mocked and scorned, in its amusements, love affairs, mysteries and scandals – but also in its active support for liberty and equality long before the words became part of a Jacobin slogan.

What emerges is a portrait of a society which, rather than collapsing as a result of decadence, brought about its own destruction through supreme and unshakeable self-confidence coupled with a complete absence of self-criticism. Nowhere is this dangerous complacency more apparent than in the many interesting memoirs I have drawn on for this book; but as the work of eyewitnesses, if they sometimes lack objectivity, they provide a wealth of information, anecdote and entertainment which is unsurpassed for bringing the period and its fascinating characters to life.

All quotations are reproduced exactly, which accounts for eighteenth-century idiosyncrasies in spelling and punctuation.

1

Life in Paris

'Paris', declared Louis-Sébastien Mercier in his portrait of the city in the 1780s, 'does not trouble itself about any place on the globe.'[1] During the reign of Louis XVI, Paris indeed considered itself supreme among the capitals of Europe. A confident, bustling metropolis, it had almost completely recaptured the power and prestige it had lost to Versailles in the seventeenth century, and 'followed only its own ideas, having received none from the Court since the days of Louis XIV'.[2]

Such independence was not thrown away on a city which thrived on rivalry with the Court and gloried in its status as an acknowledged arbiter of taste. If some writers are to be believed, Paris set the tone not only for the whole of France, but for the entire Continent as well. The centre of French artistic and literary life, it was also the undisputed home of high society. Unlike eighteenth-century London, Paris was not seasonal. Only a few anglophile noblemen chose to spend the summer months in their country châteaux, and even then, far from abandoning urban life for a pastoral idyll, they 'lived as in Paris', taking care to provide music, theatricals, fêtes and amours to entertain those guests who could be lured away from city pleasures.[3] It was a common joke that for a true Parisian even a short excursion beyond the city gates entailed a month's preparations and heartbreaking farewells of friends and family. This is not perhaps as ridiculous as it sounds when one learns that

15

the Baron de Frénilly, born into a very wealthy family who could certainly have afforded to travel, never ventured farther than the Bois de Boulogne or Vincennes as a child, and considered 'everything originating from the suburbs as provincial, and everything beyond the Île de France as foreign'.[4]

To the eighteenth-century Parisian, Paris was the hub of the universe; but what was it really like during the reign of Louis XVI? A very different city indeed from the one which emerged after the depredations of the Revolution and the demolition and reconstruction carried out by Haussmann in the nineteenth century. In Arthur Young's opinion, though 'one-third at least' smaller than London, Paris in 1787 was still 'a vast city'.[5] It was in fact continually expanding westwards from its ancient centre, and new buildings were going up in the Faubourgs Saint-Germain and Saint-Honoré on the very eve of the Revolution. The current *arrondissements* one to six mark the site of the city boundaries for much of the eighteenth century, though the customs barrier which was virtually complete by 1789 took in a large swathe of surrounding land. This barrier, universally detested by the Parisians, was on the site of the modern outer boulevards and the Péripherique. With its fifty-five impressive gates, through which all goods and traffic were obliged to pass, it was a veritable monument to the *ancien régime*'s fiscal injustice. It also enabled the city to be completely closed, although when he authorized the barrier in 1784, Louis XVI could hardly have envisaged it being frequently used by the revolutionaries to turn Paris into a prison!

For the majority of its inhabitants, however, eighteenth-century Paris lay within the confines of the inner boulevards, which had been built by Louis XIV on the former ramparts. In the east were twisting medieval streets, too narrow even for full-sized sedan chairs; to the west, magnificent new *hôtels particuliers* and the growth of development along the Champs Elysées, which had been laid out by Le Nôtre in 1670 and largely neglected thereafter. Louis XV's contribution to Paris, the Place de la Concorde, was designed as a grand entrance to the city from the Champs Elysées. Then known as the Place

Louis XV, with a statue of the monarch duly occupying a prominent position next to the gardens of the Tuileries, its neoclassical lines were widely admired. The Pont de la Concorde which was to have been named Pont Louis XVI, was not completed until 1791, much of its stone coming from the demolished Bastille.

Royal Paris clung mainly to the Right Bank of the Seine. Though abandoned to officials and largely consisting of grace-and-favour apartments, the Tuileries remained a royal palace, and was to see kings and emperors in residence once more before it was burnt to the ground by the Communards in 1871. The Louvre housed not only the royal art collection, but also the Académie Française and the Académie des Sciences; when necessary it offered shelter to the temporarily homeless Comédie-Française and the Comédie-Italienne, though it was most frequented by Parisians during the annual 'Salon'. The third royal palace, very much occupied and almost a constant feature of gossip in the 1780s, was the Palais Royal, owned by the King's cousin the Duc d'Orléans. The Left Bank, home to the Sorbonne and the educational establishment, had a royal presence in the Palais Bourbon (residence of the Prince de Condé) and the Palais du Luxembourg, though in the eighteenth century it was better known for its large *hôtels*, built by aristocrats who had forsaken the medieval Marais for the more spacious Faubourg Saint-Germain.

The greatest difference between pre-revolutionary Paris and its later incarnations, however, was the huge number of religious buildings. In 1768, in addition to fifty-one parish churches, there were forty-seven monasteries and other institutions for male religious orders, fifty convents for women, twelve seminaries, and numerous small chapels – all clustered within the first six *arrondissements*.[6] Many convents had extensive gardens, and the largest belonged to the Carthusians, just south of the Luxembourg; the kitchen garden alone comprised nearly thirteen acres, and whether by design or accident, was situated uncomfortably close to the devil on the rue d'Enfer (Hell Street).[7]

Modern shoppers on the rue de Rivoli, which was not built

until 1811, would hardly be aware that the street was cut
through the grounds and buildings of the former convents of the
Feuillants and Capucines, not to mention the famous Jacobins –
nor that to this day, Madame de Pompadour lies buried beneath
the rue de la Paix. She had been laid to rest in the cemetery of the
Capucines, which like the convent, was disposed of and destroyed during the Revolution. Workmen digging a drain in the
rue de la Paix in 1864 uncovered the grave of the Duchesse de
Guise. Madame de Pompadour was known to be buried nearby,
but it was deemed too dangerous to try to find her tomb – and
so Louis XV's brilliant marquise still lies beneath the traffic.[8]

Despite the large area of central Paris they occupied, religious
establishments boasted few inmates; most only just survived by
running schools and taking in boarders, and their decline made
them easy targets for revolutionary speculators, who made for-
tunes from nationalized church property in prime locations. No
exact figures exist for the population of Paris as a whole during
the reign of Louis XVI, and estimates range from 600,000 to
900,000. When all fluctuations are taken into account, 700,000
seems a probable number.[9] There were 3,000–4,000 noble families, although the wealth of the Parisian bourgeoisie may be
deduced from the fact that almost 18,000 families employed
servants. They were also the principal providers of labour for
many other Parisians. Mercier calculated that 6,000 lackeys engaged solely in the art of hairdressing were reinforced by 2,000
visiting *coiffeurs*, while the city's 1,200 wigmakers employed a
further 6,000 workers.[10] The legions of milliners, tailors, cooks,
coachmen and grooms can only be guessed at, but what is
certain is that the Parisian economy depended almost wholly on
luxury trades and the professions of the law, finance, and the
church. There was very little manufacturing industry, which
made life for casual labourers at the bottom of the social hierarchy extremely hard; on the fringes of the prosperous centre
was another, much poorer Paris, inhabited by what was often
contemptuously called *le bas peuple*.

As the English society hostess Mrs Thrale noted on her visit
to the city with Dr Johnson in 1775, 'the Extremes of Mag-

nificence & Meanness meet at Paris'.[11] Vincennes was then, as it is now, a popular venue for race meetings, but to reach it fashionable society had to drive through the insalubrious Faubourg Saint-Antoine, its skyline dominated by the menacing towers of the Bastille. On the left Bank, the Faubourgs Saint-Marcel and Saint-Marceau sheltered an ill-fed and abominably housed populace, whose dissatisfaction was habitually ignored. After all, it was nothing new. Louis XV detested journeys through Paris because of the inhabitants' propensity to riot, and Louis XIV had settled the entire Court at Versailles to escape his uproarious subjects in the capital. Few people in the reign of Louis XVI heeded Rétif de la Bretonne's predictions of a disastrous revolution born out of the lower classes' growing spirit of insubordination, or noted, like Mercier, the air of 'melancholy constraint' about the *petit bourgeois*, indicating 'a painful and hard struggle for life'.[12]

This unhappy struggle was often viewed with a great deal of scepticism by those in more fortunate positions. The American lawyer Gouverneur Morris, liberal in his politics and generally a very shrewd observer, had little sympathy for Parisian beggars even in the cruel winter of 1789.

> They all ask for the Means to get a Morsel of Bread, and shew by their Countenances that by the Word Bread they mean Wine. . . . Among the numerous Objects which present themselves doubtless some are deserving of Charity, but these are scarcely to be noticed in the Crowd of Pretenders.[13]

Mrs Thrale, attending a race meeting on the Plaine des Sablons, was astounded to witness the methods employed by Parisian fishwives to extract some tokens of compassion from the young Queen Marie-Antoinette.

> Fortythree Fishwomen . . . surrounded the Queen, & with the loudest Voices and frantic Gestures uttered a thousand Gross Obscenities in her Ears till she was forced to give 'em Money to be rid of them. When I expressed my Astonishment at such

Things being permitted; Ah, says a French Gentleman with great Composure, *que ces Gens là sçachent bien la Méthode d'attraper les Ecus!*[14]

It is difficult to decide which is more revealing about French society at the time – the fishwives' successful aggression, or the gentleman's sang-froid. Had the Parisian mob been less fierce in the past, their well-orchestrated violence at the beginning of the Revolution might not have been so readily dismissed as trivial by a government inured to displays of popular discontent.

In fact, high society rather enjoyed singing the latest anti-government songs in *poissard* dialect – *poissard* being a generic term for all Parisian low life. Parisians daily murdered the French language anyway; they pronounced *français* as *françoué*, and transformed the king into a rake as *roi* became *roué*. The liquid *ll* in Versailles or *bouillon* proved impossible for the Parisian tongue to master, and *r*'s had to be rolled for the full metropolitan effect. 'What is more,' wrote Mercier of his fellow citizens, 'they do not notice this fault in their actors, and should the latter fail to be endowed with this particular talent, they make haste to acquire it so as to please the public more.'[15]

The people were not to be trifled with, even at the theatre, for a Parisian crowd was an ugly beast, and very difficult to control. Rétif de la Bretonne illustrates this in a report of how two dandies looking for some amusement on a walk in the Tuileries managed to gather a large crowd around a pretty girl merely by ogling her and dogging her footsteps. When a riot nearly ensued (though only 'genteel' and well-dressed people were supposed to be permitted to enter the gardens), her father had to draw his sword to fight a way out of the mêlée![16] The pleasures of *le bas peuple* were not, therefore, disdained by those who claimed superiority over them.

Even the more affluent quarters of Paris were subject to their own social stratification in the 1780s, as the Baron de Frénilly explained.

In those days, with the exception of the high nobility, which occupied the Faubourg Saint-Germain, and the law, which had

entrenched itself in the austere quarter of the Marais, all the good society of Paris, and above all the financial class . . . was grouped near the Palais Royal and the Tuileries.[17]

'Good society', comfortably ensconced in its richly decorated salons, in mansions separated from the street by large court-yards, seldom had occasion to visit the run-down outer faubourgs; but for all classes in Paris, certain fundamentals of life were similar. The air they breathed was the same, and if Mrs Thrale is to be believed, must have been beneficial to their health. 'The purity of the Air in a Metropolis so crouded is truly surprizing; no Sea Coal being Burned, the Atmosphere of the narrowest part of Paris is more transparent & nitid than that of Hampstead hill.'[18]

The agriculturalist Arthur Young also found the atmosphere exceptionally clear, but the same, alas, could not be said for the water. In 1765, the Revd William Cole, another English visitor to Paris, described the river Seine as:

thick & muddy . . . so that to drink such Water is not practicable: besides they say it is very unwholesome, creates Gravel, & is very purgative, especially to Strangers: so that they carry clear Water about in Pails & Vessels, & sell it by the Quart or Gallon, at a very extravagant Price.[19]

The French passion for bottled water and their talent for selling it to the gullible English have a respectably ancient his-tory! Reservoirs at Chaillot were fed by water pumped from the Seine by two huge steam pumps on the river bank, which remained part of the city's water supply until 1902, but mineral water from Passy was preferred in the eighteenth century. Paris also had thousands of wells, though many were contaminated by the open sewage drains.

Nearly all commentators are agreed on the deplorable state of the sewers, which surely played a significant part in the small-pox epidemics which ravaged the city at regular intervals. Only one sewer (the 'Great Sewer', which ran from the Bastille to

Chaillot) was vaulted over, having been channelled underground by the financier Joseph de Laborde to facilitate a property development. The rest of the city discharged sewage directly into the street, where it collected in a central gutter; by means of open drains and cesspools the noisome sludge was carried down to the Seine. This made walking in any part of Paris a hazardous business indeed, as Arthur Young soon discovered. 'The streets are very narrow, and many of them crowded, nine-tenths dirty, and all without foot-pavements. Walking . . . is here a toil and a fatigue to a man and an impossibility to a well-dressed woman.'[20]

Another danger for the pedestrian was the habit Parisians had of relieving themselves even in the middle of busy thoroughfares. 'The Women', reported Mrs Thrale, 'sit down in the Streets as composedly as if they were in a Convenient House with the doors shut.'[21] The few public conveniences available were, in Young's opinion, 'temples of abomination', which might explain this lack of decency. Rétif de la Bretonne thought the filthiness of Parisian streets entirely unnecessary, and proposed a complete reform of public sanitation, but it is doubtful that he could have changed French attitudes to bodily functions. Spitting was common, even in the highest ranks of society, and a detailed description of the various infirmities suffered by an absent guest might form an unwelcome hors-d'oeuvre at the grandest dinner. William Cole, who found all these aspects of Parisian life distressing, and had a delicate stomach to boot, considered the butchers' shops also in need of reform (the food was displayed on the street). He had no quibble, however, with the quality of produce available, pronouncing game, fish, meat, bread, and fruit as 'excellent'; chicken was exceptionally good. Surprisingly, Arthur Young was equally enthusiastic about French roast beef. Mrs Thrale did not share his opinion. She found bad meat too often disguised by garlic and vinegar, and food generally very overpriced. During his stay in Paris, Cole made use of the *traiteur*, or cook, opposite his hotel, 'from whence I had any Thing I had an Inclination for, & in the best Manner'. There were about 1,200 *traiteurs* in Paris, who had developed an early form of the take-away, preparing meals to

order and delivering them to customers' homes. Cole fortunately chose a good cook; the Marquis de Bombelles, diplomat and diarist, wrote that he would rather go hungry than risk being fed 'by the *traiteur* who is poisoning my sister'![22] According to Mercier, the true gastronomical centre of Paris was the Hôtel d'Aligre on the rue Saint-Honoré, which stocked delicacies from the whole of France – for those who could afford to buy them. The thousands of rats who 'enter the cellars when the river rises, and gnaw everything they find' doubtless found their way to any leftovers in wealthier households along the *quais*.[23]

Rats were certainly not the only form of animal life in Paris. Mrs Thrale was highly diverted to see a *grand seigneur* taking his tiny dog for a walk in the Jardin du Luxembourg, and noted that 'Dogs indeed live very happily here . . . everybody appears to me to keep a Dog, & the smallest are in the highest Estimation.'[24] Songbirds kept in cages were favoured by workmen, probably because they were cheaper to feed. Evidence of a general love of animals runs counter to the usual portrayal of Parisians as totally urban in outlook. Many actually came from the provinces, though if they wished to succeed, they soon adopted Parisian manners and looked down on new arrivals as country bumpkins.

In order to avoid the damning title of 'provincial', the aspiring young lawyer, financier, or ensign would have been well advised to lay in a good stock of linen and buy himself a carriage. Plenty of shirts were necessary owing to the unmerciful pounding they suffered at the hands of the Seine washerwomen. In Mercier's opinion, 'there is no town where more linen is used than in Paris or where it is more badly washed', and Cole bears him out: 'your Linen comes back torn to Pieces, dirtier than when it first went there, & just of the nasty dirty yellowish Colour of that beastly River.'[25] The washerwomen's tyranny affected noble and bourgeois alike, although it is to be hoped that 'fine gentlemen' put on clean shirts more than once a fortnight, as Mercier claimed! Of course, numerous perfumes were used to compensate for any deficiencies in hygiene.

Having solved these sartorial problems and had his hair

dressed in the latest style ('the Parisian . . . needs a hairdresser every day'), it was time for the hopeful provincial to sally forth with appropriate Parisian *élan*. There was no surer way to succeed than to attempt to knock down as many of his fellow citizens as possible in a spanking new carriage. 'Mind the carriages! Here comes the black-coated physician in his chariot, the dancing-master in his *cabriolet*, the fencing-master in his *diable* – and the Prince behind six horses at the gallop as if he were in open country.'[26]

Only a foolish pedestrian stopped to identify the prince's arms as they flashed past. Arthur Young, who stoutly defied snobbish custom and travelled throughout France on horseback, reported that in Paris:

> The coaches are numerous, and, what are much worse, there are an infinity of one-horse cabriolets which are driven by young men of fashion and their imitators . . . with such rapidity as to be real nuisances, and render the streets exceedingly dangerous . . . I saw a poor child run over and probably killed, and have been myself many times blackened with the mud of the kennels. To this circumstance also it is owing that all persons of small or moderate fortune are forced to dress in black, with black stockings.[27]

French driving habits do not appear to have altered much in two hundred years, but there was a method in this traffic madness. Since a *fiacre* ('squalid and forlorn' according to Cole) was no fit conveyance for those aspiring to make their way in society, and white silk stockings (obligatory wear in polite circles) would not remain white if one had to go on foot, a carriage was essential – whether the 'young man of fashion' could afford it or not. It was a key weapon in the constant war waged by the Parisian male on the opposite sex.

> A bachelor who owns a carriage is a valuable man . . . women, since their husbands have grown inattentive, have adopted the system of considering only bachelors who own a carriage, and, taking it all in all, they are right. For how can a woman exist

without horses? In a space of twelve hours must she not have
visited the opera, a play, a fair, have attended a ball, and gambled
at Faro?[28]

Since Parisian social life straddled both banks of the Seine,
journeys between engagements were sometimes lengthy. The
carriage-owning man was thus provided with ideal opportunities for furthering his romantic ambitions; as Gouverneur
Morris and a host of gallant Frenchmen testify, tête-à-têtes in
carriages not infrequently yielded the fruits of victory. After all,
there was no danger of intrusion when one was galloping from
the Faubourg Saint-Germain to the Marais.

Given the generally filthy condition of Parisian streets and the
city's unprepossessing appearance, perhaps amorous dalliance
was the best way to pass a carriage ride. Louis XVI's Paris did
not flaunt her treasures, as a disappointed Mrs Thrale soon
found out. 'Their great Houses are all shut from the Street in the
manner of Burlington House & are said to be princely. I have
not yet seen any.' Morris described the narrow streets as 'very
crooked' with houses consisting of 'four to five stories of stone
walls', while William Cole (possibly still suffering from dyspep-
sia) was roundly scornful of the French capital's visual attractions: 'upon the whole, it is one of the most dreary & gloomy
Cities I have been in.'[29] Arthur Young airily damned the Louvre
as a building not worth his attention because it did not have a
flat roof, so foreigners' comments on the Paris cityscape have to
be treated with caution!

Notwithstanding adverse criticism, Paris continued to attract
visitors from the whole of Europe. Italy was for art and knowledge, London for business – and Paris for pleasure. Gouverneur
Morris declared: 'I have seen enough to convince me that a Man
might in this City be incessantly employed for forty Years and
grow old without knowing what he had been about.'[30] Nearly
devoid of both industry and industrial traffic (the ports of
Rouen and Bordeaux were far more important commercial cities
than Paris), the French capital relied heavily on its prestige as an
important cultural and artistic centre. As a showcase for French

luxury goods, it made wealthy foreigners especially welcome, for apart from Parisian nobles and financiers, they were the principal buyers of Sèvres porcelain, Aubusson and Gobelins' tapestries, furniture, clocks, watches, and numerous objets d'art which were made in and around Paris.

Visits to the Sèvres factory often figured on tourists' itineraries, and could be fitted in comfortably with a trip to Versailles. Those determined to 'see Paris' would almost certainly also have visited the Louvre, which housed the King's paintings, the Tuileries, and the superb art collection amassed by the Duc d'Orléans in the Palais Royal.[31] The Bibliothèque Royale, to which scholars had free admittance, attracted men of letters from all over the Continent, and was the direct antecedent of the present Bibliothèque Nationale. The Invalides, then in a rural setting, was admired as a piece of imposing modern architecture, but old churches, convents, and Notre-Dame itself were considered mere medieval curiosities, seldom worth more than a cursory glance. William Cole, who visited countless Parisian religious establishments in his quest for historic monumental inscriptions, found much of medieval Paris so caked in dirt that discerning its esoteric beauties was decidedly difficult – which might account for most tourists' indifference.

It was only when satiated with sights and suitably refreshed (or poisoned) by the *traiteurs* that the visitor ventured where native Parisians in search of entertainment went first – the boulevards. These wide, spacious thoroughfares planted with elms were built over the old city ramparts by Louis XIV, and extended on the Right Bank from the Porte Saint-Antoine in the east to the Porte Saint-Honoré in the west. The boulevards on the Left Bank never achieved the same popularity, largely because by the time they were complete, *le Tout-Paris* was flocking to a new playground at the reconstructed Palais Royal. For much of the eighteenth century, however, the Parisian *bourgeoisie* and *petite bourgeoisie* passed their leisure hours in the cafés, street theatres and booths on the former ramparts. High society also frequented the boulevards, particularly on Thursdays, when the avenues would become jammed with splendid equip-

ages, all vying for pre-eminence and constituting something of a show in themselves.

Gouverneur Morris soon decided that 'pleasure' was 'the great Business' of the French capital. 'A Man in Paris', he wrote, 'lives in a sort of Whirlwind which turns him round so fast that he can see Nothing.'[32] English visitors were rather surprised to see that the many amusements available were not confined to the monied classes. In 1789, the Earl of Clarendon noted somewhat dourly that: 'In England a man of common rank would condemn himself as extravagant and culpable, if he permitted his family to partake of amusements more than once or twice a week. In France, all ranks give themselves up to pleasure indiscriminately every day.'[33]

Where better to see this whirlwind of pleasure than on the boulevards? Mrs Thrale described them as 'Places of publick Amusement for the ordinary Sort of People', consisting of 'rooms, Arbours, Walks &c. filled with Fiddles, Orgeat, *Lasses and other Refreshments*.'[34] Her italics lead one to conclude that male as well as female prostitution flourished on the boulevards, since she goes on to state that 'no Wine, Beer or Spirits are sold'. William Cole also encountered 'Rope-dancers, Mountebanks, Sleight-of-Hand People', while Arthur Young visited one of the theatres and found 'music, noise, and *filles* without end', as well as 'mud . . . a foot deep' and no street lighting.[35]

The plays, or *parades* which were performed at boulevard theatres were crude, indecent and extremely popular. Though by the 1780s censorship had wrought a considerable improvement in this area, the new Comédie-Italienne which opened on the boulevards in April 1783 was built facing away from the road to avoid contamination by its raucous neighbours. Earthy boulevard theatre, which was much appreciated by the aristocracy, had originated in the famous Paris fairs. The Foire de Saint-Germain on the Left Bank was a magnet for all Parisians, high and low, but declined after a serious fire destroyed its permanent site in the grounds of the Abbaye de Saint-Germain.

Whether held on religious or secular premises, entertainment in Paris could be found seven days a week. On her second visit

to the capital in 1784, Mrs Thrale was shocked by the lack of religious observance. 'They leave their little wretched Shops open on a Sunday, & forbear neither Pleasure nor Business on account of the Sabbath.'[36] It was possibly the only way for *le bas peuple* to survive their enforced leisure, for as Mercier remarked, 'a feast-day is for these classes still a day when there is no money to spend'.[37] For those of little means, a stroll in the various public gardens cost nothing, although shoe leather was likely to suffer from the gravel walks.

The Jardin du Luxembourg was favoured by the lower classes, who gathered to listen to the 'newscasters' who recounted the day's events (with suitable embellishments) for those unable to afford newspapers. Entry to the garden of the Tuileries was forbidden to soldiers, servants and 'ill-dressed persons'. The Marquis de Bombelles had nothing but praise for 'this masterpiece by Le Nôtre', full of 'such superior beauties that one never tires of admiring them'.[38] Mrs Thrale strongly disagreed; for her, the Tuileries exemplified the collision of 'magnificence and meanness' which she observed everywhere in Paris.

> Today I walked among the beautiful Statues of the Tuilleries, a Place which for Magnificence most resembles the Pictures of Solomon's Temple, where the Gravel is loose like the Beach at Brighthelmstone, the Water in the Basin Royale cover'd with Duck Weed & some wooden Netting in the Taste of our low Junketting Houses at Islington dropping to Pieces with Rottenness & Age.[39]

Even such mixed delights as these were best on a sunny day. When it was raining, hours could be spent reading the newspapers, playing chess or gossiping in a café. Mercier estimated the number of cafés in Paris at six to seven hundred, so they must have been well patronized, although by the 1780s it was 'no longer the thing to linger on at a café', because it showed 'a complete ignorance of good society'.[40]

Good society was naturally never without ways of amusing itself; in addition to private suppers, dinners and balls, there

were the theatres, the Opéra, the Comédie-Italienne, horse-racing, masquerades, country picnics in summer and the Carnival in winter. But summer or winter, fair weather or foul, there was nowhere else in Paris which drew such large crowds from all levels of society, or aroused such violent passions as the stronghold of the Duc d'Orléans – the Palais Royal.

Built on a princely scale by Cardinal Richelieu in the seventeenth century, the Palais Royal was known as the Palais Cardinal until his death, when it passed to the crown. Louis XIV gave it to his brother Philippe, Duc d'Orléans, bestowing it on the cadet branch of the royal house in perpetuity. Yet the palace seemed in some way inextricably bound up with the character of its first owner, his ambition reflected in its very location. Richelieu, a cunning politician and subtle power-broker, satisfied his vanity by building as close to the royal Louvre and the Tuileries as possible, yet also protected his flank by keeping a watchful and repressive eye on the rebellious nobility in the Marais. The brawls between the Cardinal's musketeers and their counterparts in the King's service were perhaps a portent which Louis XIV would have done well to heed. In the reign of Louis XVI the Palais Royal was to become a hotbed of intrigue, espionage and conspiracy. It was the home of printing presses which spewed out invective against the monarchy in general and horrible libels about the Queen in particular, and the power base for a prince who, even if he did not wish to seize the throne himself, was guided by those who wished to set him on it as a puppet king.

But things had not always been this way. Frénilly looked back nostalgically to the Palais Royal's days of splendid innocence, which lasted right through to 1781, when a huge commercial development gave the palace and its garden an entirely different and more dangerous character during the latter years of Louis XVI's reign. The old Palais Royal had little indeed in common with its later incarnation. Frénilly particularly recalled the gentle attractions of its 'vast garden', in which he regularly took the air.

It was divided by straight avenues, fountains and flower beds, and to the south reigned that grand avenue of chestnut trees,

unequalled in France for its age, breadth and superb canopy,
impenetrable by the sun. . . . From the days of Anne of Austria
this immense gallery of verdure formed the common salon of all
good society in Paris, without distinction of *quartiers*. Evening
was the time for promenades, and in summer – for in those days
one lived in Paris all year round – no one left the Opéra without
going to the Palais Royal. It was a promenade of luxury, gaiety
and ceremony. There were plumes, diamonds, embroidered
clothes and red heels; a *chenille*, that is to say, a frock coat and a
round hat, would not have dared to appear there . . . the Palais
Royal was the heart and soul, the centre and the core of the
Parisian aristocracy. . . . This is what the Duc de Chartres one day
undertook to destroy.[41]

The Duc de Chartres, possibly better known as the Duc
d'Orléans (he inherited the title on the death of his father in
November 1785), was to go down in history as 'Philippe Égalité', the prince-turned-republican who voted for the execution of
his cousin Louis XVI and was himself guillotined in 1793. In the
early 1780s, however, he was known principally as a fashionable
playboy, fond of expensive women and equally expensive
horses, and consequently forever in debt. This was despite the
fact that he was probably the richest man in France; Arthur
Young quoted his pre-revolutionary income as seven million
livres per annum (£306,250 in 1789), with a further four million
livres per annum (£175,000) in reversion on the death of his
father-in-law, the Duc de Penthièvre.[42]

Comte Alexandre de Tilly goes so far as to declare that
Orléans deliberately led his brother-in-law the Prince de Lamballe into the excessive debauchery which resulted in his early
death, in order to inherit the Penthièvre fortune. Tilly, a former
page to Queen Marie-Antoinette, was naturally no friend to the
man who did so much to bring her down. In a *caractère* of the
Duc d'Orléans, he wrote that the duke made up for a lack of
intelligence by his 'excellent taste and a sharp and light humour
which never betrayed his moral depravity'. As a free-thinker,
Orléans 'cared for none of the things of this world. . . . Crime
and virtue were one and the same to him, discredit or considera-

tion were but creations of the mind, all human actions a matter of indifference.'[43]

Grace Dalrymple Elliott, an Englishwoman who was probably at one time Orléans's mistress, takes a more charitable view of the duke's failings. She called him 'a man of pleasure, who never could bear trouble or business of any kind'.

> The Duke of Orléans was a very amiable and a very high-bred man, with the best temper in the world, but the most unfit man that ever existed to be set up as the chief of a great faction. Neither his mind, his abilities, nor indeed his education, fitted him for such an elevation.[44]

Man of pleasure, free-thinker and roué (Talleyrand hints strongly at sexual perversion), Orléans was nevertheless endowed with a keen commercial sense.[45] And, caring nothing for public opinion, he was not afraid to go into trade – a move which inspired greater indignation among the nobility and *haute bourgeoisie* than all his other defects combined. 'The Palais Royal became what it is today,' wrote a horrified Baron de Frénilly, 'its verdant salon was transformed into a bazaar ... and the reign of democracy began in this capital of Paris.'[46]

No longer was the garden of the Palais Royal reserved for aristocratic promenades. The grand old avenue of chestnuts was felled, the fountains and parterres made way for booths and side-shows, and shops were built under the colonnades which lined the large new buildings enclosing the garden. A year after its completion in July 1784, the inquisitive Marquis de Bombelles found much of the new development empty save for prostitutes. One wit at Court commented that he could not understand why such opprobrium was being heaped on the mercantile Duc de Chartres – '*il n'a rien fait qui ne soit à louer*'.[47]

Little by little, however, the new Palais Royal began to acquire its reputation as 'the capital of Paris'. Mercier even grew rhapsodic in his description of its many attractions. 'This enchanted spot is in itself a little town of luxury ... it is the very

temple of pleasure, where vice is so bright that the very shadow of shame is chased away.'[48] There were shops of all kinds to tempt the crowds who soon flocked to this enormous 'bazaar' – jewellers, haberdashers, silk merchants, fan makers, tobacconists, bookshops, even grocers. The numerous cafés became a meeting place for the disaffected *philosophes* of Paris, and political clubs were established in this centre of opposition to all that emanated from Versailles. Since it was a royal palace, the police had no right to patrol the garden, and this undoubtedly led to the huge increase in crime; stealing and vandalism were daily occurrences, fights were common, and according to Mercier, respectable women were safe in the palace precincts only at 11 a.m. and 5 p.m.! They were quite likely to be accosted or even assaulted at other hours, for the new Palais Royal was quite notorious for vice. 'Here it is that the tyranny of libertinage exercises its sway over the unchecked youth of society who display a hitherto unknown indecency in their conduct.'[49] On a visit to the garden in 1785, Bombelles was appalled to see what 'the sordid greed' of the Duc d'Orléans had done to the former 'salon' of the nobility. 'At eleven in the evening all the lights are extinguished; then the most indefensible debauchery follows the habitual indecency of this nasty place.'[50]

Though ineffectual in controlling the disorder in the Palais Royal, the Parisian police force nevertheless prided itself on its efficiency, and many of the thieves, pickpockets and prostitutes who frequented the garden were probably also police informers. Mrs Thrale, however, dismissed the superiority of the French police as an idea put forward to delude foreign visitors about safety.

Nothing is so false as the Notion of the French Police being so excellent as to prevent disturbance in the Streets. I have from my Window seen more Quarrels, Overturns & Confusion in the Rue Jacob, where I have now lived a Month, than London will exhibit in a Year's walking the Street at decent Hours only.[51]

Despite this criticism, her overall opinion of the citizens of Paris was entirely favourable. 'The good behaviour of the

people', she declared, 'deserves to be commended ... you are sure to meet no Insults from the Populace of Paris, where every Man thinks himself the Protector of every Woman. This Species of Gallantry goes through all ranks of People as far as I have been able to observe.'[52]

Three years later, in 1778, the young Mozart spent a very miserable time in Paris; his mother died during their visit, and in contrast to Mrs Thrale, he found the Parisians most unwelcoming. In his opinion, they had lost their wonted politeness and grown coarse and boastful.[53] He was, of course, a mere male and a musician, so of considerable less value in Parisian eyes than a wealthy *dame anglaise* who would be expected to repay any attentions in gold coin.

What is revealing about eighteenth-century memoirs is the extent to which travellers (and indeed, Parisians themselves) based their opinions on the whole French nation solely on its representatives in the capital. Arthur Young was amazed to find provincials meekly accepting the domination of a metropolis most had never even seen. At Nancy in the tumultuous days of July 1789, he found no one willing to venture an opinion on the crisis facing France: 'they are as nearly concerned as Paris; but they dare not stir; they dare not even have an opinion of their own until they know what Paris thinks.'[54] This was a somewhat worrying state of affairs, since Parisians could not be trusted to think rationally – least of all about their own city. 'Some woman', reported Mercier, 'said that she would rather be buried at Saint-Sulpice than be alive in the country.'[55]

The Parisian, even if he were a downtrodden pauper in the outer faubourgs, considered himself infinitely superior to any provincial; but whereas a talented provincial might earn a tomb at Saint-Sulpice, the arrogant Parisian's mortal remains suffered a fate which truly levelled the score.

There was, on the rue Saint-Denis, a very old church with an equally ancient burial ground and charnel house – the Cemetery of the Innocents. William Cole stumbled across it by mischance in his search for ancient inscriptions. His horror at this 'most stinking, loathsome & indecent' place extended to a full four

pages of his journal. Bodies, even those of smallpox victims, were placed in flimsy coffins which were stacked one on top the other in shallow graves and open tombs above ground, with no regard to the rank of the dead or the health of the living. The charnel house was the repository for the bones of all Parisian cemeteries, and by 1785 it and the cemetery were deemed such a hazard to the occupants of nearby houses and the water supply, that Louis XVI signed a decree abolishing this gruesome city of the dead. The bones of over one million Parisians were removed, at night, to the natural underground passages now known as the Catacombs, in an operation which lasted three years. There lie the duke and the beggar, the countess and the *grisette* – perhaps a little resentful that no one thought of creating a Père Lachaise for them. Paris, in the end, always seemed much mightier than her citizens.

2

The Court of Versailles

Paris, for all her grandeur and self-importance still endured painful moments of inferiority and unease; she had a rival. A rival whose power Parisians both feared and despised, whose brilliance could cast even the brightest of the capital's monuments into the darkest shade, and whose activities invariably drew the envious gaze of the entire Continent – the Court of Versailles.

'There is none of his subjects, be he far or near,' declared Mercier, Parisian to the core, 'who does not want news of the Court, and whose eyes do not constantly turn towards the King.'[1] The fact that this news was mainly collected and disseminated by malicious courtiers and adventurers has a great deal to do with the distorted picture that has emerged of Versailles during the final years of the *ancien régime*. It is a picture which could benefit considerably from a little restoration work.

The defeat of absolutism in France of necessity implied the destruction of the Court, seat until 1789 of all power and much of the wealth of the country. An official opposition being out of the question in a state which had no elected ministers or parliament, the only way to wrest power from the Court was to undermine its authority, and the weapons employed to this end prove that the pen was indeed mightier than the sword. The King's Bodyguard was totally ineffectual against the flood of slander which circulated daily in Paris about life at Versailles

during most of Louis XVI's reign. In the end, it became all but impossible to distinguish fact from fiction; unfortunately for the King and Queen, the populace seemed to prefer fiction.

One fact, however, remained uncontested throughout: the supremacy of Versailles. If Paris considered herself the capital among capitals, Versailles was the acknowledged sovereign of all European courts. From Stockholm to St Petersburg, from Potsdam to Vienna, emperors, kings and princes vied to reproduce the splendour and éclat of Louis XIV's creation. The British monarchy alone seemed immune to the contagion.

No one could behold Versailles, created on the site of a minor royal hunting lodge in marshland some fourteen miles to the south-west of Paris, and not be struck by Louis XIV's vanity. The whole palace embodies his famous dictum: '*l'état, c'est moi.*' One might say that the palace of Versailles was the very temple of absolutism: its magnificence, the constantly reiterated *roi soleil* motifs in the decoration, its architectural and artistic references to rulers and conquerors of myth and antiquity, all served to emphasize the supreme power of the king – and the corresponding lowliness of his subjects. The luxury was not without purpose. Versailles was to become the glittering cage for nobles who had made the early years of Louis XIV's reign so bloody and turbulent. *Frondeurs*, encouraged by generous tax privileges, built new mansions in the environs of the palace, subdued their pride, and accepted Court offices and pensions instead of political reform. But who cared for politics when all was wealth, pomp and gaiety? The Court become a magnet for anyone with a title and a favour to ask of the King. Only poorer provincial nobles remained in the country to run their estates, while the rising class of the *bourgeoisie*, denied the right to appear at Versailles on an equal footing with the old aristocracy, set up their own satellite courts in Paris.

It was chiefly members of the *haute bourgeoisie*, lawyers and financiers, who supplied Paris with the talent and the money to beat off the challenge from Versailles. By the time Louis XVI ascended the throne, they were fairly confident of having succeeded. Lawyers and financiers alike enjoyed both titles and

prestige, owned splendid mansions in the Faubourg Saint-Honoré and the Marais where they gave suppers and balls to which *le Tout-Paris* was eager to come, and hosted salons for wits and philosophers. But they remained unwelcome at Court, even if they succeeded in marrying their sons and daughters into the Court nobility. The *noblesse d'épée* made no secret of its disdain for the *noblesse de robe*.[2]

The nobles who thronged the corridors of Versailles in a ceaseless quest for both profit and amusement perpetuated an image of Court life which, if certain contemporary witnesses are to be believed, bore little relation to reality. Admittance to both the gardens and the palace was granted to anyone in suitable attire, and foreign visitors naturally took advantage of this fact to see the marvel of Versailles for themselves. Many returned decidedly unimpressed to Paris. Arthur Young considered that

> The palace of Versailles . . . is not in the least striking. . . . From whatever point viewed, it appears an assemblage of buildings; a splendid quarter of a town, but not a fine edifice. . . . The whole palace, except the chapel, seems to be open to all the world; we pushed through an amazing crowd of all sorts of people to see the procession, many of them not very well dressed.[3]

William Cole visited the palace during the Court's absence (it moved to Fontainebleau every autumn), and found it crawling with workmen because a refurbishment programme was in progress. 'The Apartments', he declared, 'are all very royal & magnificent', but it was a 'dirty magnificence'.

> At Versailles, even under the Palace Walls, nay even on that very stone Staircase which leads into the Gardens, & under the Windows of the Royal Apartments, people were suffered to lay their Nastiness in such Quantities, that it was equally offensive to the Sight & Smell.[4]

Cole was unable to discover whether this highly unpleasant custom was permitted when the Court was in residence, but he was neither prejudiced nor untruthful. The French themselves,

when not trying to dazzle their audience with their own self-importance by revealing the latest Court scandal or *bon mot*, could be equally critical. Madame Roland visited Versailles in the early 1770s, and was 'fortunate' enough to be offered a lodging in the palace.

> Mme Legrand, one of the Dauphine's ladies . . . lent us her apartment. It was under the tiles, opening onto the same corridor as those of the Archbishop of Paris, and so close to his that the prelate had to be careful lest we should hear him talking, and the same applied to us. There were two rooms meanly furnished . . . with an approach rendered horrible by the darkness of the passage and the smell of the latrines.[5]

It was hardly what one expected of the grandest royal residence in Europe – but at Versailles, as in Paris, filth and opulence seemed inextricably intertwined. Opulence in the state apartments and general design was probably intended to blind the visitor to any minor defects; it was too bad if one had a sensitive nose. The Marquis de Bombelles, who lived in the town of Versailles during the 1780s because his wife was *dame d'honneur* to Louis XVI's sister, Madame Elisabeth, was at Court almost every day, and did not consider the poor sanitation at all offensive.

> Nothing in all the quarters of the world offers the vast and beautiful ensemble of the interior of the Château of Versailles and the magnificence of its gardens. Foreigners, forced to admit it, fall to criticizing the dirtiness of the common passageways, but though it would be possible to remedy this more than is done, they are obliged to agree that a palace which lodges twelve thousand persons cannot be tended like the boudoir of a pretty woman.[6]

Twelve thousand pairs of feet gliding across the polished parquet, twelve thousand deferential courtiers, officials, guards and flunkeys, all performing a synchronized ballet whose arcane rules were never questioned: Court etiquette. The degree to

which the French monarchy was enslaved by etiquette is almost inconceivable to the modern mind. In the words of one devoted royal servant, Madame Campan, the royal family were 'martyrs to decorum'.[7] Their whole day was marked by a series of rituals which gave employment and purpose to the twelve thousand. Like the sun, the King had his *lever* and his *coucher*, and neither event took place without the appropriate number of attendants to pass his nightshirt. His clothes had to be put on in a strict order, and he was not even allowed to help himself by so much as fastening a button. The sight of an able-bodied man being dressed and undressed in a room full of people is silly enough, but when one considers that although a monarch 'he could not dismiss from his apartments those whose privileges and office gave them the right to remain', it becomes ludicrous.[8] 'Speaking here of etiquette,' says Madame Campan, 'I mean those minute ceremonies that were pursued towards our kings in their inmost privacies, in their hours of pleasure, in those of pain, and even during the most revolting of human infirmities.'[9]

These 'minute ceremonies' doubtless provided ample topics of conversation, sneer and conjecture for the retailers of Court rumour who dined out in Paris on the strength of their information, but the question remains: why enforce such rigid etiquette? It was an etiquette that could see the Queen shivering naked in her apartments while princesses, duchesses and maids disputed over who should hand her her shift; or threaten her life in childbirth as all those who had the right to witness the birth insisted on filling her chamber to bursting point; an etiquette which actually seemed to benefit the servant rather than the master.

The fault originated with Louis XIV's strategy of subduing all his more powerful and rebellious subjects by offering them places at Court; this was so successful that it entailed the creation of countless posts with imposing titles but minimal practical purpose. Many courtiers during the reign of Louis XVI actually fulfilled their functions on a rota system; ladies-in-waiting, equerries and chamberlains usually spent only one week out of every three or four in attendance at Court. The rest

of the time they could be found at leisure in Paris, trading on their connections at Versailles. The attractions of a post at Court were real enough; duties were far from arduous, and the financial rewards could be considerable. It was this which made the reform of etiquette and ceremonial so difficult to achieve. Marie-Antoinette's early efforts to loosen the constraints of Court routine gave rise to a hostility she was to endure for the rest of her life, and Louis XVI's tardy attempts to slim down the royal household in 1787 only made him enemies among those who should have been his most loyal subjects.

The root of the problem can be traced to the rather peculiar way in which Court posts (like many official positions under the *ancien régime*) were filled. Very few courtiers were personally chosen by the royal family. Most posts could in fact be bought, and carried tax privileges and numerous perks. They were also often hereditary, and were jealously guarded by the same families, who frequently succeeded in appropriating any newly created post for distant cousins and younger sons. Hence the heavy battalions of the Noailles, the Rohans, the La Rochefoucaulds and the Montmorencys who so often appear in the annals of Versailles, and the outrage caused when, contrary to custom, the obscure and penniless Polignacs were granted high office at Court. Tilly condemns 'the belief that court favour is family property' as 'stupid', but stupid or not, it was a belief most fervently held, and had an enormous impact on royal finances.[10] In his *Compte-rendu au Roi* of 1781, Necker put the cost to the Treasury of royal pensions alone at twenty-eight million *livres* a year! It was hardly surprising, then, that courtiers clung tenaciously to their rights and privileges, engaged in petty intrigue to acquire the perks of office (there was nothing at Versailles which could not be sold for profit, from candle ends to the remains of a royal banquet), and were equally determined to ensure that on death or retirement their post passed to a *survivancier*, or heir, they had personally chosen. Despite this, according to the Marquise de La Tour du Pin, *dame d'honneur* to Queen Marie-Antoinette, 'it was the height of fashion to complain of one's duties at Court, profiting from them at the

same time and often even abusing the advantages they brought'.[11]

Under such a system the royal family was undoubtedly very ill-served, but revenge could only be exacted in the manner they adopted to greet, or pointedly ignore, courtiers who had incurred their displeasure. The Marquis de Bombelles became an expert in the gradations of esteem or dislike which appeared on royal countenances as he patrolled the galleries of Versailles in a two-year quest for a diplomatic posting. Merely 'to pay one's court' meant that the expectant courtier was given just a glance; if he was 'well treated' he received a few words from royal lips, while 'wasting one's time' was a polite way of saying one had been snubbed.

'Saturday evening and Sunday were Court days in full dress', Sunday notable as a day when, in the words of the Prince de Ligne, 'all the most illustrious bores of France pay their court to the Queen, after dinner, at the Polignacs'.[12] Paying one's court was a strenuous business for both courtiers and courted. After a morning audience in the Queen's apartments, the King and Queen walked to Mass with their retinue, stopping to speak to individuals in the crowd which lined their passage; their return from the Royal Chapel was followed by *le grand couvert*, or public dinner, which saw them solemnly eat in front of numerous spectators. The Queen, who heartily disliked this custom, seldom ate anything. The meal over, courtiers gathered their strength, skirts and swords for a race to the apartments of the rest of the royal family – 'Monsieur', the Comte d'Artois, the King's aunts, Madame Elisabeth, and even the little Dauphin, all received the homage of loyal subjects. According to Bombelles, only with the rather shy and pious Madame Elisabeth was one sure of being 'well treated', while Madame de La Tour du Pin and other young ladies preferred the lively reception they were given by the Comte d'Artois. Those on a more intimate footing with the royal family would often find the Queen, and occasionally the King, in the apartments of the Duchesse de Polignac, who held an open salon in the evening, and the customary card table in the Queen's own apartments after 7 p.m. drew some of the heaviest gamblers in Paris.

The Sunday courtiers gone, Versailles was very quiet during the week, and it became easier to capture royal attention as the King and Queen passed through the Hall of Mirrors on their way to Mass. It was not necessary to have been officially presented, but Court dress was obligatory. Uniforms could never be worn except by the Garde du Corps on duty; officers were permitted to present themselves in uniform only on the day they left Court to join their regiments. This regulation, according to Bombelles, was designed to encourage the French cloth industry, and Madame de La Tour du Pin testifies to the rigour with which it was enforced. When the French seized Grenada during the American War of Indepedence, her cousin Dominic Sheldon was given the mission of bringing captured British standards to Versailles. He travelled post-haste to Court after landing back in France, but on arrival at the War Ministry, was surprised to find he could not proceed directly to an audience with the King. He was told that '"Mr Sheldon could not be received in uniform"'! The dress in which he had captured the standards was improper for their presentation!'[13] Before news of victory could be delivered, Sheldon had to borrow full Court dress – a richly embroidered suit, buckled shoes, dress sword, and a tricorne.

This immutably rigid ceremonial ceased the moment the royal family left Versailles, and it is no wonder they preferred the informal atmosphere of the smaller private establishments they had set up elsewhere. During the 1780s, Madame Campan reported, 'Versailles became, in the estimation of all the royal family, the least agreeable of residences'.[14] The Queen would spend days at a time with only a handful of attendants at the Petit Trianon, usually while the King was absent hunting. Louis XVI's brothers, Monsieur and the Comte d'Artois (later Louis XVIII and Charles X respectively), each entertained at private residences in the Île de France, and the first thing their sister, Madame Elisabeth, did on attaining her majority was to furnish the house bought for her by the King in the town of Versailles. The purchase of the châteaux of Rambouillet and Saint-Cloud in 1784 added greatly to the disorder in royal finances, but like

many of their subjects, the King and Queen were addicted to home improvements.

More absences from Versailles would probably have helped the poor Dauphin (born 1781), who was almost literally a 'martyr to decorum'. As heir to the throne, he was whisked off to his own apartments on the day of his birth; surrounded by a bevy of female attendants, he seldom saw either his parents or any other children, and was rarely permitted to leave his palatial accommodation. The Queen created a furore among the nurses and governesses in 1782 when she insisted on keeping her daughter with her for 'a part of the morning, without under-nurses'. This was 'an event at Court because it has never happened before', noted the Marquis de Bombelles, adding that it spread great alarm among the royal governesses (his mother-in-law, Madame de Mackau, was one of them), who feared for their posts.[15] Some were in fact abolished, but by the time a slightly more humane regime had been introduced at the Queen's insistence, the Dauphin's health was suffering. With almost no exercise other than walks along the insalubrious terrace outside his apartments, it was little wonder that he developed tuberculosis. Medicine did the rest. By June 1788, though moved to the fresher atmosphere of the Château de Meudon, the young prince was 'bent like an old man, his dying eyes opening in the middle of a livid complexion. He fears people, he is ashamed to be seen.'[16] The Dauphin died at Meudon on 4 June 1789, to the general indifference of a populace by now hell-bent on the destruction of the monarchy. The King and Queen deeply mourned their son, but met with scant sympathy. Royal children were always known as 'the Children of France'; France created them, and France could destroy them, whether by an etiquette carried to extremes or by revolution. The intricate web of ceremony dreamed up by Louis XIV to subjugate *frondeurs* and fill regal coffers in the end served only to enmesh his own descendants, who became the impotent victims of a vast, pointless and uncontrollable Court bureaucracy.

Louis XVI was not the man to tame this monster. Great hopes were expressed when the twenty-year-old King ascended the

throne in 1774. More upright courtiers, knowing his honest, serious character, believed that fresh leadership would sweep away the abuses which had flourished during the reign of his grandfather, Louis XV. Immediate satisfaction was obtained by the banishment of Madame Du Barry and her cohorts, but although the new King was good, he was weak-willed and lacked innovative ideas. A sober, conscientious and rather gauche young man, he wanted to implement financial and political reforms, but he was too easily persuaded to betray his liberal instincts. He was also a very poor judge of character. Many people might well have preferred the petticoat government of Louis XV's favourite Du Barry to the *laissez-faire* approach of the Comte de Maurepas, who was to be prime minister for seven years.

Maurepas's appointment is in itself illustrative of Louis XVI's weakness. The Comtesse de Boigne quotes the King's aunt, the redoubtable Madame Adélaïde, as her authority for declaring it an accident! Louis XVI had wanted Machault (former Keeper of the Seals to Louis XV) to be prime minister, and had summoned him to Court to attend his first Council of State. Unfortunately he had also sent for Maurepas on an unrelated matter, and Maurepas arrived at Versailles before Machault, who was delayed by bad weather. Maurepas had held office over twenty-five years previously, but was dismissed by Louis XV for having written a song lampooning Madame de Pompadour. In 1774, a septuagenarian, his wit was as light and frivolous as ever, though it did not dull his keen political sense. As the young Louis XVI emerged from his apartments, he found the elderly ex-minister awaiting him in an antechamber; they began a conversation. An equerry arrived to summon the King to the Council of State. Machault failed to appear. Maurepas deferentially accompanied the King to the door of the Council chamber, and after a moment's fatal hesitation on the King's part, followed him into the room. He came out as prime minister, the reins of office having fallen effortlessly into his hands.[17]

In the opinion of his brother-in-law, the Emperor Joseph II of Austria, Louis XVI was an absolute monarch only in his

ability to choose his ministers who, once in office, were complete masters of a government which they ran purely for their own personal benefit.[18] Of the King himself, he wrote: 'this man is a little weak, but not an imbecile. He has ideas and a sound judgement, but his body and mind are apathetic.'[19] A somewhat mixed appraisal, though far more polite than French comments on the King. His childhood hobby and adult passion for mechanics earned him the nickname 'the locksmith' from an early age, although later he generally went by the unregal appellation of 'the fat pig'.[20] His hesitancy and indecision in affairs of state were characteristics shared with Louis XV, as was his inordinate fondness for hunting, but he had none of his grandfather's good looks and charisma. Louis XV's expressive eyes and noble features still drew admiration from his censurers, whereas even Louis XVI's friends found it very difficult to praise his personal appearance.

'The features of Louis XVI were noble enough, though somewhat melancholy in expression,' wrote a guarded Madame Campan. 'His walk was heavy and unmajestic; his person greatly neglected.' In compensation for these shortcomings, he was 'a good husband, a tender father, and an indulgent master'. Well-read in history and skilled in geography, he also 'knew the English language perfectly' and loved drama and literature.[21] The fourteen-year-old Comte de Tilly, newly arrived at Versailles to join the School of Pages, was extremely disappointed when he first set eyes on the King: 'his face did not answer to what I had expected; it was simple and kindly, I should have liked it strongly cast and majestic.'[22] Simplicity, kindness, goodness: these were not the attributes to be desired in a *roi soleil*. More damning still is the Marquise de La Tour du Pin, who speaks with the prerogative of one of the prettiest women at Court. The King was far from being her *beau idéal*.

He was so short-sighted that he could not recognize anyone at three paces. He was a stout man, five-feet-six or seven inches tall, high-shouldered, with the worst shape one could imagine and the appearance of a peasant waddling along behind his plough; there

was nothing haughty or regal in his bearing. Always embarrassed
by his sword, never knowing what to do with his hat, he was
very magnificent in his dress, to which (to tell the truth) he paid
not the slightest attention, since he always took the first suit
handed to him without even looking at it.[23]

According to Bombelles, the King's blue eyes functioned
perfectly well, and his myopia was often diplomatic, though the
Prince de Ligne had reason to believe otherwise. 'Louis XVI was
very imprudent when hunting. I once heard one of his bullets
whistle past my ear at the death of a stag, but one day as he
turned round, he killed a partridge between the Queen and
me.'[24]

The King probably found the prince's alarm amusing, for as
Ligne rapidly discovered, he 'used to love playing practical
jokes. . . . The Queen managed to cure him of that.'[25] Ligne,
suave, urbane, cosmopolitan, very handsome, and a *grand seigneur* in every sense, was a chamberlain at the Imperial Court in
Vienna, and consequently far more attached to the Austrian
Marie-Antoinette than to her clumsy French husband. Although
he recognized Louis XVI's many good qualities, he found him
physically 'the ugliest and most disgusting of men' – a remark
possibly occasioned by jealousy, since Ligne's self-esteem was
considerable, and his feelings for the Queen very warm.[26]

Unbiased foreign observers were often more favourably disposed towards the King. Mrs Thrale thought he looked 'well
enough – like another Frenchman'.[27] 'Well enough' was high
praise indeed; her overall opinion of French looks was not
calculated to flatter the male ego! The English found Louis
XVI's unaffected manners attractive, more in tune with English
informality, whereas in France elegant insincerity would have
made a better impression. Nor was the King so wanting in
majesty as the French claimed. Gouverneur Morris, attending
the opening of the States General in 1789, was somewhat surprised by the regal way in which the King addressed the assembled deputies. Morris had been regaled with countless tales
about his *gaucherie* and inadequacies by (and here's the rub)

highly placed courtiers, but instead of a 'waddling peasant' he found a monarch who delivered 'a short Speech, very proper and well spoken, or rather read. The Tone and Manner have all the *fierté* which can be desired or expected from the Blood of the Bourbons.'[28]

Nothing Louis XVI did, however, could save him from being deemed boring, a capital crime in the eyes of pleasure-loving, dissipated high society both at Court and in Paris. His mildness was despised, his sobriety scorned, and he became the target of ridicule. His children alone adored him. People instead looked elsewhere for the glamour and brilliance they expected from the most magnificent of courts, and they found it in the Queen.

Marie-Antoinette, Archduchess of Austria, Queen of France: beautiful, frivolous, kind, charming, or stupid, capricious, cruel, vicious, spendthrift, lesbian, nymphomaniac, paedophile, intriguer, 'the modern Messalina'.[29] What does one believe of a woman so vilified during her lifetime that her image stubbornly remains sullied, no matter how great the efforts to set it in perspective? One could be forgiven for thinking she was the King's strumpet, for rarely is she accorded her title. '*Putain!*' screamed the crowd as she was marched to her trial from the grim Conciergerie. To others she was merely '*l'Autrichienne*', the Austrian they had never wished to see as wife of the King of France, who for twenty-three years endured probably the most sustained and virulent campaign of libel in history. Poor 'Toinette', as she would always be to her mother; it killed her, and she never knew what she had done to deserve her fate.

Events surrounding the Queen were disastrous and distorted from the very beginning. So huge was the crowd which gathered to watch a fireworks display held on the Place Louis XV to celebrate her marriage to the Dauphin on 16 May 1770 that a stampede ensued. Most memoir-writers quote the number of dead as 600, when in fact Parisian police records show it was 130.[30] Did Marie-Antoinette recall that fatal day when she met her end on the same spot in 1793? Does anyone remember any of it now in the swirl of traffic on the Place de la Concorde?

The Baronne d'Oberkirch, who watched the arrival in

Strasbourg of the fifteen-year-old Austrian archduchess, youngest daughter of the Empress Maria-Theresa, could never have foreseen her metamorphosis into 'the modern Messalina' and her horrid end. Already married by proxy to the Dauphin, and on her way to Versailles, Marie-Antoinette was received with all the pomp and honour France could muster. She responded by conquering the hearts of her new subjects. Madame d'Oberkirch wrote ecstatically of 'her queenly carriage, the elegance and grace of her whole person!'[31] She was not alone in her raptures. The new Dauphine was almost universally considered to have all the majesty her husband lacked.

For the Comte de Ségur, 'Queen Marie-Antoinette, endowed with all the charms of her sex, united that dignity of deportment which commands respect, and grace which softens the pride of majesty'. The Comte de Tilly found that she had 'the face of a Queen of France even at those moments when she most tried to appear only a pretty woman', while Horace Walpole, who saw her at a Court ball in 1775, quite lost his cool critical head in describing her. 'It was impossible to see anything but the Queen! . . . She is a statue of beauty, when standing or sitting; grace itself when she moves. . . . They say she does not dance in time, but if so it is certainly the time which is at fault.'[32]

Tall and majestic, with ash-blonde hair, blue eyes, aquiline nose, and the Habsburg lip (a fateful inheritance), the Queen aroused envy or admiration among women. 'She is wonderfully pretty', commented Mrs Thrale approvingly, later adding, 'the Queen is far the prettiest Woman at her own Court'.[33] Men always seemed more struck by her manner. Tilly, a self-appointed connoisseur of female flesh, was far more enthusiastic about Marie-Antoinette's grace and regal bearing than her physical attractions:

> I have heard many people speak of the beauty of this princess. I must confess I have never entirely shared this opinion. . . . She had eyes that were not beautiful but could reveal the whole range of feeling; kindness or aversion could be depicted in her looks more markedly than I have met elsewhere. I am not sure that her

nose rightly belonged to her type of face. Her mouth was decidedly unpleasant. . . . Her skin was admirable, her shoulders and neck matched it; her bosom was rather too full, and her waist might have been more elegant, but I have never met since with arms and hands more beautiful. . . . No one has ever curtsied with so much grace, greeting ten people with a single inclination, and, by look and the pose of the head, giving each one his due.[34]

The Marquis de Bombelles is in agreement: 'never have princes or princesses possessed the grace of the Queen when she wants to treat someone well.'[35] It was this very attractive, engaging manner which was to lead the young Queen into such deep water with the wily cynics who stalked the corridors of Versailles, and saw her as the means to achieve their ends. Sociable and impressionable, she was always far more easy to approach than the King, although when she failed to deliver favours (political or personal), the same courtiers were quick to discover 'Austrian pride' in her features. For those with no ulterior motive, this hauteur was never apparent. Madame Campan found the Queen 'kind and patient to excess in her relations with her household', and Tilly (one of her pages) declared that 'she was worshipped by her household'.[36]

The adoration of her servants, and the approbation of the Parisians, who 'did not cease, during the first years of the reign, to give proofs of joy whenever the Queen appeared at any of the plays of the capital', did not prevent the young Marie-Antoinette from falling foul of the one thing she should have most respected – Court etiquette.[37] Coming from the relative informality of the Hofburg Palace in Vienna, she was swiftly subjected to all the petty rules and restrictions of Versailles by her chief *dame d'honneur*, the stiff and severe Comtesse de Noailles. Marie-Antoinette, 'perpetually tormented by the remonstrances' of the comtesse, nicknamed her 'Madame l'Etiquette', and antagonized many austere old dowagers at Court by abolishing 'a multitude of established customs'.[38] These customs were 'insupportable' to her because often they invaded her right to privacy as a woman (the French had little delicacy indeed in

these matters), and in order to avoid the tiresome constraints of an etiquette which seemed absurd, the Queen 'attached herself to younger people, whose taste was more suited to her own. This was never forgiven by the old nobility, and her most innocent actions were represented in a bad light.' One source of slander was thus released, which, when added to the flow from other quarters, was to become a positive torrent of malicious rumour and innuendo.

Court etiquette was necessary, in Tilly's opinion, to preserve the sanctity of monarchy. In attempting to win a small degree of freedom from constant public inspection and ritual, the Queen only aroused suspicion.

> Her dislike of the restraint and strict observance of formalities pertaining to her station was mistaken for contempt and forgetfulness of her duties. Although no woman knew better than she did how to perform her part of queen when she so wished, the independence of her ways was interpreted as moral looseness, her dislikes were looked upon as fits of wanton temper, and her kindness as a sign of guilty lapses.[39]

On ne badine pas avec la Cour. Mrs Thrale did not think Marie-Antoinette very successful anyway in achieving the privacy she desired, and was astonished to find that

> The Queen . . . has only two Rooms in any of her Houses – a Bed Chamber & a Drawing Room – in the first she sleeps, dresses, prays, chats, sees her Sisters or any other Person who is admitted to Intimacy, & lives by what I can understand in a Bustle hardly to be supported all the Morning long. She has no second Room to run to for Solitude, nor even a Closet to put her Close Stool in, which always stands by the Bedside.[40]

This incessant bustle might explain Marie-Antoinette's frivolity, for in addition to her distaste for serious study, she had very little time in which to improve her mind. According to Madame Campan (a well-educated woman who after the Revolution set up a successful school near Paris), the Queen's

education 'was certainly very much neglected'. Groomed from an early age to adorn a throne, she had superficial accomplishments but no solid learning. Her Italian was fluent; but although she spoke French 'with the greatest fluency . . . she did not write French correctly', and her native German was almost forgotten. The Queen's poor written French, however, was probably no worse than that of many of her courtiers! She made 'rapid progress' in English under Madame Campan, but gave it up for her greatest love – music. Although not gifted as a player or singer, she was 'able to read at sight like a first-rate professor', and it is largely owing to her patronage that the operas of Gluck and Grétry received such a well-deserved welcome in Paris.[41] The Marquis de Bombelles found that his credit with the Queen soared when she discovered his talents as a pianist, and he played for her twice in Madame de Polignac's salon, once accompanying her in arias from popular operas.

In matters which demanded serious reflection, the Queen relied on her French reader, the Abbé de Vermond. He had been sent to Vienna to perfect her French in readiness for her marriage to the Dauphin, and Marie-Antoinette remained attached to him for life, notwithstanding the efforts of many of her 'friends' to have him dismissed. Even today, the extent of his influence has not been fully analysed. Marie-Antoinette also received much maternal advice and scolding from the Empress Maria-Theresa until the latter's death in 1780. Their letters and those between the Empress and the Austrian ambassador to France, Comte Florimond de Mercy-Argenteau (who kept her informed of the minutest details of the Queen's life), are highly revealing.

The Empress never flattered her daughter. She roundly dismissed Marie-Antoinette's claims to learning and talent ('you know they do not even exist') and was equally dismissive of her beauty. 'Do not give way to your taste for ridiculing others,' she also warned – one feels that 'Madame l'Etiquette' would have agreed.[42] The Queen's extravagant clothes and coiffure, late nights, heavy gambling, unwise choice of favourites, and her debts (which the King made light of, and always paid), occa-

sioned rebuke after rebuke from Maria-Theresa. 'I must avow my dissipation and laziness where serious things are concerned,' wrote the nineteen-year-old Marie-Antoinette after a particularly severe put-down from Vienna, adding hopefully, 'I want and hope to correct myself little by little.'[43]

She was ripe material for the courtiers who hoped to profit from the King's youth and inexperience. Boudoir politics were quickly learned at Versailles. Marie-Antoinette became the centre of intrigue between supporters of the disgraced Duc de Choiseul (who had negotiated the Franco-Austrian alliance cemented by her marriage to the Dauphin), and an anti-Austrian faction who sought every opportunity of undermining the Queen and keeping Choiseul's protégés out of office. Amongst the anti-Austrians Madame Campan ranked the Duc d'Aiguillon, Maurepas, and the Foreign Minister Vergennes, who 'kept up the intrigues carried on at Court and in Paris against the Queen'.[44]

It was a powerful lobby to contend with, but the Queen did not take the attacks without retaliating. She persuaded the King to dismiss d'Aiguillon, and even engineered a meeting with Choiseul ('I believe I used my right as a woman properly in this instance'), but earned herself a severe reprimand from Vienna.[45] Her mother compared her to a Pompadour or a Du Barry. 'Why do you interfere, my dear sister?' wrote her brother, Joseph II.

Have you ever asked yourself by what right you thus intervene in the affairs of the French government and monarchy? You, a charming young girl, thinking only of frivolity, your toilette, and your amusements all the day long . . . who, I am sure, neither reflect nor meditate nor try to weigh the consequences of what you do or say![46]

The Queen's position was made worse by the flood of conflicting advice which overwhelmed her every time a courier arrived from Vienna. On the one hand, she was urged not to interfere in state affairs, to maintain a strict neutrality and to devote herself to being a successful (and submissive) wife; on the

other, she was instructed to confide in the Comte de Mercy and follow his advice without question, and this usually involved putting the Austrian case to the King in important foreign policy matters. Maria-Theresa wanted to have her cake and eat it; it was her insistence on her daughter's acceptance of the pre-eminence of Austrian concerns which led many at Versailles to believe that Marie-Antoinette had a baleful influence on French politics.

In addition to the complications which arose from this unhappy division of loyalties, the young Queen had to fight for survival on another front. She had not yet provided an heir to the French throne, and her husband seemed unmoved by her charms. So she used to go to opera balls in Paris, to dance all night; she was perhaps a little too willing to be amused by personable young men, for she loved to laugh; and she gathered around her a group of friends (most notable among them the Princesse de Lamballe and the Comtesse de Polignac) to help while away the tedium of Court life. Her enemies could not have wished for more potent ammunition. As Tilly explained, 'to be bored is more useful in the long run than to please', and in France it was to prove 'an unforgivable crime to laugh when one is Queen'.[47]

Marie-Antoinette's quite innocent, though frivolous and silly pleasures became orgies indulged in at public expense. Her enemies 'exerted themselves in every way to render her unpopular. Their aim was, beyond all doubt, to have her sent back to Germany.'[48] Her 'friends' were equally industrious in trying to keep the Queen in France in order to run the government through her, rather than the King. And of course, the very nature of eighteenth-century French politics dictated that the whole issue was to be decided by sex.

Had Louis XVI and his Queen succeeded in solving the difficulties they experienced in the marriage-bed at an early stage, Marie-Antoinette might not have become the subject of so much slanderous gossip (eventually to prove fatal to the monarchy), as she tried to hide her frustration in a constant whirl of amusement. The frustration was far more than purely sexual; it

was absolutely essential for both her marriage and the Franco-Austrian alliance that she had children, but for seven long years it seemed that Louis XVI would never be able to give her any. His early indifference to her was attributed to youth and shyness, but as he grew older, and particularly after he became King, the lack of progeny became a subject for unfavourable rumour. The Queen's search for distraction elsewhere fuelled salacious gossip, and gave several men at Court ideas above their station. One of the less scabrous songs which could be heard in Paris illustrates the state of affairs in the mid-1770s.

> *La Reine dit imprudemment*
> *A Besenval son confident:*
> *'Mon mari est un pauvre sire.'*
> *L'autre répond d'un ton léger:*
> *'Chacun le pense, sans le dire,*
> *Vous le dîtes sans y penser.'*[49]

> The Queen says imprudently
> To Besenval, her confidant:
> 'My husband is a sorry sire.'
> He replies in a frivolous tone:
> 'Everyone thinks it, but says it not,
> You say it and think not a jot.'

The Swiss Baron de Besenval was a member of the circle of courtiers who gathered around the Queen's greatest friend, Madame de Polignac. In a letter to the Viennese Count von Rosenberg in 1774, Marie-Antoinette wrote glowingly of Besenval (whom she had only just met), speaking of the 'great confidence' she had in him. Doubtless she also felt that his fifty-two years precluded any implications of gallantry; but the baron had a reputation as a seducer, an eye to the main chance, and an indiscreet tongue. She could not have chosen worse. In his self-glorifying memoirs, Besenval claims victory for the dismissal of the Duc d'Aiguillon, saying he persuaded the Queen to act against the minister to benefit his own friends. This conflicts with the Queen's boast that the duke's departure 'was entirely

my own work'. Besenval had obviously been poisoning her mind against d'Aiguillon, whom she believed to be spying on her and spreading slanderous rumours.[50] Such were the politics of Versailles.

Besenval describes Marie-Antoinette as having 'a great desire for pleasure, much coquetry and frivolity, little natural gaiety', but it was 'her tender and benevolent heart' which most attracted him.[51] Could he but conquer it, lucrative political office might well be his reward. His spectacular fall from favour during 1775, when the Queen's smiles turned to glacial disdain, evidently caused him some puzzlement. In his memoirs, he attributes it to her fickleness. There was, however, another reason. Marie-Antoinette told Madame Campan that Besenval had taken advantage of a private audience, being so bold as 'to address her with so much gallantry that she was thrown into the utmost astonishment, and that he was mad enough to fall upon his knees, and make her a declaration in form'.[52] From that moment on, though he was still welcome in Madame de Polignac's salon, the Queen seldom spoke to him.

More dangerous was the Duc de Lauzun, who possessed attractions which Besenval lacked – youth, beauty, an illustrious pedigree, wit, and outstanding style. Vanity and pride were also noticeable characteristics of this gallant duke, and Marie-Antoinette was to discover to her cost how vindictive he could be when piqued. Lauzun was a protégé of the Duc de Choiseul, who remained exiled from Court at his country estate at Chanteloup, so his cultivation of the Queen was far from disinterested. As Besenval's star fell, Lauzun's was in the ascendant. Two months' assiduous charm in 1775 made him, in his own words, 'a kind of favourite'.[53] He believed that the Queen had 'a particular inclination' for him, and was not slow to try to interest her in his political schemes (which involved a treaty with Russia), about which Louis XVI remained in blissful ignorance.

I was sincerely attached to the Queen, whose acts of kindness and trust touched me. I wanted to make her govern a great empire, to

make her play at the age of twenty the most brilliant role, which would give her everlasting renown. . . . The Queen did not listen to me without astonishment. . . . She asked me for time to reflect, and I saw that all was lost.[54]

Undaunted, Lauzun describes a sentimental tête-à-tête in which he succeeded in embracing the Queen, though not in kissing her. She politely asked him to leave her apartments to allay suspicion.[55] Here again, Madame Campan has a very different version of events.

I was in the room adjoining that in which he [Lauzun] was received; a few minutes after his arrival the Queen re-opened the door and said aloud, and in an angry tone of voice, 'Go, sir.' M. de Lauzun bowed low, and withdrew. The Queen was very much agitated. She said to me: 'That man shall never again come within my doors.'[56]

According to legend, Lauzun attempted to win back the Queen's esteem by dressing as a footman and helping her to alight from her coach, but he makes no mention of this episode. This is not surprising in view of his assertion that a year after the scene described above, 'the Queen loved me more than ever' but was afraid to show it because her friends disliked him! Not until 1777 does Lauzun finally admit in his memoirs that he was entirely out of favour, yet during the American War he boasts of having refused a request from Marie-Antoinette to give up a risky expedition to capture British trading posts in Senegal. 'My vanity was satisfied; I refused the Queen with pride. I showed her that I wanted nothing from her and that I could play a great role without her.'[57]

Lauzun liked playing roles – too well, perhaps. A close friend of the Duc d'Orléans, he thought the Revolution offered the perfect stage for the exhibition of his talents, and became a bitter enemy of the Court. Did the Queen ever regret her refusal to yield to his embrace, or did he, as the 'Citizen General' Biron, wonder why his subsequent hatred of her failed to save him from the guillotine?[58]

There were always other aspirants to the permanently vacant position of lover to Queen Marie-Antoinette. She was too desirable, and the King too ineffectual, for it to be otherwise. The cool, sophisticated Prince de Ligne was amazed to find himself falling under her spell.

> Who could see the unfortunate Queen every day without adoring her? I had not however realized it until one day when she said to me: 'My mother thinks it ill that you should spend so much time at Versailles. Go and pass a few days at your post . . . and return.' This kindness, this delicacy and even more, the idea of spending a fortnight without seeing her, drew tears from me, which her delightful thoughtlessness of those days (which kept her a hundred leagues from gallantry) prevented her from noticing.[59]

Ligne managed to quell his passion ('because it could never have been requited'), and as a wise older friend from her mother's court in Vienna, he became the recipient of Marie-Antoinette's thoughts about the intrigue at Versailles. While they were out riding together, the Queen would tell the prince 'a thousand interesting anecdotes which concerned her and all the snares that had been laid to give her lovers. Now it was the house of Noailles which wanted her to take the vicomte, now the Choiseul cabal who proposed Biron [Lauzun] for her.'[60]

Very unwisely, she thwarted their political schemes by remaining chaste. If the Queen could not be persuaded into bed with a man chosen by one of the factions at Court, she might as well be sent back to Austria. It was easy enough to blacken her character; she loved dancing, and at the opera balls in Paris it was remarked that she nearly always spoke to young foreigners (in order not to be recognized). 'Hence a thousand stories and a thousand lovers: Englishmen, Russians, Swedes and Poles.' Ligne found Marie-Antoinette's recital of her exceedingly banal conversations with these foreigners 'insupportable' – his own stories were 'far more spicy than her so-called adventures'.[61] But as Madame Campan remarked, 'these accusations of gallantry once set afloat, there were no longer any bounds to the calumnies which circulated at Paris' about the Queen.[62]

Something had to be done. The King's sexual problem had been diagnosed as phimosis, a partially closed foreskin which not only made ejaculation very rare, but also completely dulled his interest in sex. The fact that he always went to bed at eleven whilst the Queen seldom retired before two in the morning did nothing to bring them closer together, although it is remarkable that from the day they married they were good friends. Despite her mockery of his passion for hunting and mechanics, Marie-Antoinette had done much to cure her husband of his shyness, and he treated her as an ally and confidante. Their discussions about their sexual difficulties, however, duly reported by either the Queen herself or Mercy to the Empress Maria-Theresa, reveal that Marie-Antoinette was as ignorant of the subject as Louis XVI.

The Court physician Lassonne cannot have been the soul of discretion either. It was soon known that the only cure for the King's condition (shared by his brother Monsieur) was circumcision, and he was extremely reluctant to undergo surgery. After five and a half years of marriage, the Queen had grown *blasée* about the whole business, writing to her mother in December 1775 that a wave of satirical songs had appeared; in some she was credited with lovers of both sexes, while the King's operation formed the theme of others. Her flippant dismissal of these libels, which eventually proved so harmful to her image, masked deep inner unhappiness. When the Comtesse d'Artois became pregnant in 1774, Mercy reported to Maria-Theresa that he saw 'with extreme chagrin that Her Majesty is inwardly affected by it in a very grievous manner'.[63]

The Empress was far from pleased with the situation. Monsieur posed no threat to the succession (his wife was even more unhappy than the Queen), but he was deceitful, politically active, and a purveyor of gossip and rumour concerning the regal couple. Louis XVI's youngest brother, the Comte d'Artois, was a greater problem. He was handsome, virile, and had already produced children. The archetypal dandy, he seemed more interested in pleasure than politics, but his close connection with the Queen's friends in the 'Committee Polignac' (as Gouverneur

Morris dubbed it) hinted at more than a passing interest in political intrigue. He was also widely deemed to be the Queen's lover, though no shred of evidence supported this assumption. The Queen, with her characteristic shrewdness in summing up others, was well aware of the traps set for her by both her brothers-in-law. She assured her mother that when Artois became too familiar she knew how to mortify him and bring him to his senses, and of Monsieur she wrote:

> We continue on a footing of friendship and cordiality; to tell the truth, I see it is no more sincere on his part than on mine; I am all the more convinced that if I had to choose a husband among the three, I would still prefer the one which Heaven has given me: his character is true, and although he is awkward, he shows me every possible attention and kindness.[64]

Converting this 'attention and kindness' into love and children was the difficulty; in 1777, the Empress decided to give the French a jolt, and sent her whimsical, sarcastic, worldly son Joseph II to Versailles to see what he could do. He did not exactly wreak havoc, but his manifest scorn for the rituals of the French monarchy, his travels incognito in Paris, and his visit to Madame Du Barry at Louveciennes caused more than Madame Campan to shudder. Joseph II was described by the Prince de Ligne as 'tormented' by his sexual appetite, and although he tried to impart to Louis XVI some of his ideas on enlightened despotism, it was his sexual expertise which was to be of most use to his sister and brother-in-law.

Joseph was pleasantly surprised to be able to refute all the slander about Marie-Antoinette which had raised eyebrows in Vienna.

> She is a good and lovable woman, a little young and thoughtless, but she has a depth of virtue, which, considering her position, is worthy of the utmost respect. With it all she unites an intelligence and a soundness of perception which have often surprised me. Her first impulse is always correct. . . . Her desire for pleasure is

very strong . . . people take advantage of this weakness, and those who provide her with the most amusement find both hearing and favour.[65]

The twenty-two-year-old Queen was lectured about her failings and scolded for not treating her husband with proper respect. She loved her brother greatly, and (for a while at least) heeded all his advice. Joseph had longer lasting success with Louis XVI. Their frank discussions on the King's inability to perform satisfactorily in the marriage-bed brought a solution to the problem, although it is not clear that Louis did in fact undergo an operation. On 30 August 1777, after her brother's return to Vienna, Marie-Antoinette penned a joyful note to the Empress Maria-Theresa, for once pre-empting Mercy, whose spies apparently did not have access to the royal bedroom. 'I am in the happy state most essential for my whole life,' she wrote. 'It has already been more than eight days since my marriage was perfectly consummated.'[66]

Madame Campan relates that when the Queen became pregnant during 1778, 'the King was in ecstasies. Never was there a more united or happier couple.'[67] Their very unity was, however, a barrier to the hopes of those *frondeurs* at Court whose main aim was to sow marital discord between the King and Queen. During her pregnancy, the Queen found her apartments too hot and stuffy, and used to walk in the evening along the terrace with her ladies, occasionally speaking (unrecognized) to visitors to the palace. This gave rise to 'the most scandalous libels', and 'odious couplets were circulated in Paris' in which the Queen was treated 'in a most insulting manner'. Madame Campan lays the blame squarely on friends of the Comte d'Artois, 'the only prince who for several years had appeared likely to give heirs to the crown'.[68]

They were probably delighted that the child born on 19 December 1778 amidst a crowd of shoving and curious onlookers was merely a girl. Under Salic law she could not succeed to the throne. The Dauphin born in October 1781, however, severely dashed their hopes, and when the Duc de Normandie

followed in 1785, the succession seemed assured. The gap after the birth of Madame Royale nevertheless worried her grandmother, the Empress Maria-Theresa, who was not best pleased to learn from Mercy in 1779 that the King often preferred to sleep alone because the Queen was still gambling or dancing into the early hours.

Marie-Antoinette, contrary to all expectation, proved to be an admirable mother – and in adversity, a devoted and courageous one. Parenthood also suited Louis XVI, who was an attentive and loving father; the Marquis de Bombelles, himself a tender *père de famille*, described with pleasure how the royal children rushed into the King's arms on his return from a trip to Normandy in 1786. It was quite unusual for the French monarchy to display such domestic harmony, threatening Court cabals which thrived on the careful manipulation of royal sex lives. A favour in bed used to be repaid by prestige, wealth and influence; but no longer. Once known to be virile, the King found no lack of ladies anxious to please him, but he refused them all, saying to his equerry, M. de Coigny: 'People would very much like me to take a mistress. I shall do nothing of the kind. I do not wish to renew the scenes of preceding reigns.'[69]

The Queen's feelings for her husband remained ambiguous. According to Tilly, though she did not love Louis XVI, she was 'absolutely devoted' to him, and Madame Campan describes Marie-Antoinette's sentiments for him as mingled 'respect and admiration for the goodness of his disposition'.[70] The King's love for the Queen made him 'a slave' to all her wishes; he indulged her every whim, and unwisely neither King nor Queen paid heed to the gossip and slander which resulted. When Marie-Antoinette was called to account for her extravagance, her interrogators forgot that it was the King who doubled her allowance unasked, who gave her the Petit Trianon and paid for the *jardin anglais* she had created there, and who granted pensions and high office to her friends.

They had no need to follow the hard road which lay ahead of most people who sought Court favour. It usually required constant attendance in ministerial antechambers, importunate

letters, imploring letters, often the granting of sexual favours, blackmail, bribes, and sometimes even arranged marriages with the children of ministers or Court officials. Nearly every method could be employed, though eventual success was far from assured. During the reign of Louis XV the best way to bypass this tedious process was to insinuate oneself into the good graces of the King's mistress, and though mortally hated by much of the Court nobility, both Madame de Pompadour and Madame Du Barry were fawned on in order to obtain a hearing from the King. Du Barry was not perhaps so successful in this department as her predecessor; the Prince de Ligne once told her that as she was so scatterbrained where important business was concerned, the only way to get it into her head was by writing it on her curl-papers – to which she agreed with hearty laughter!

Louis XVI's refusal to take a mistress, however, closed this well-worn route to royal favour. The Queen's marital fidelity raised a similar difficulty, but she left open one avenue of attack which was the more successful in that it was based on an ideal highly prized in the eighteenth century – friendship. Not until it was too late did Marie-Antoinette realize that not all her friends shared her sentimental view of the sacred ties of friendship. Her early attempts to attach herself to her sisters-in-law met with little encouragement, and she found her ladies-in-waiting both repressive and hostile. But she 'wanted to enjoy and to relish the charm of friendship and the sweetness of private life', unsurprising in view of the unhappy state of affairs which for a long time existed between her and Louis XVI.[71]

It seemed she found the friend she needed in the young, widowed Princesse de Lamballe, whose appointment as Superintendant of the Queen's Household in 1774 on a salary of 150,000 *livres* a year caused an outcry both at Court and in Paris. The Queen herself received only 250,000 *livres* per annum, although in any analysis of the cost of her 'favourites' it ought to be remembered that during the reign of Louis XIV some positions at Court carried salaries of 300,000 *livres* per *month*.[72] The Queen's affections were known to fluctuate.

Madame de Lamballe remained a devoted and loyal friend, for which she was to pay a terrible price during the Revolution, but her place in the Queen's heart was imperceptibly taken by an unsuspected rival – Yolande de Polignac.

Gentle, placid, beautiful, and outwardly as sentimental as Marie-Antoinette, the Comtesse Jules de Polignac might well have been obliged to pass her life on a distant provincial estate had she not been given a post at Court, for her husband, though of ancient lineage, was far from rich. She was to become as detested by the populace as the Queen, the pair of them characterized as avaricious, meddling lesbians, draining the Treasury to fund their debauchery and political intrigues. All who knew 'the Comtesse Jules', however, testify to her disinterested affection for Marie-Antoinette. According to the Comte de Ségur, 'the honours which she shunned came to seek her. It was necessary to compel her to receive any favours. A sincere friend, it was not the Queen, it was Marie-Antoinette, whom she loved.'[73] Indeed, the Queen used to say that only with Madame de Polignac was she truly herself. Required to receive and entertain all the Queen's visitors, Madame de Polignac found her role as favourite tiring, for her health was never robust. 'She detested the Court,' wrote the Prince de Ligne, 'and remained there only out of affection and gratitude.'[74] When the post of governess to the royal children fell vacant in 1782, the King himself had to plead with her to accept it; her elevation to the rank of duchess made her several more legions of enemies, and the Marquis de Bombelles, quite prepared to dislike this favourite because of the influence she was supposed to wield in affairs of state, was agreeably surprised when he met her. 'It is impossible to hate her. Her gentleness, her modesty, her courtesy are innate qualities which can never be gainsaid.'[75]

Devoted and disinterested Madame de Polignac may have been, but her relatives and associates were not. Her husband became equerry to the Queen and was created a duke in 1780; his sister, the *intrigante* Comtesse Diane de Polignac was appointed lady-in-waiting to Madame Elisabeth, and Madame de Polignac's lover, the wealthy Comte de Vaudreuil (a parvenu

in Bombelles's snobbish opinion) was placed in the household of the Comte d'Artois. In fact, the clique surrounding Madame de Polignac were all close allies or friends of the King's youngest brother, a situation Marie-Antoinette eventually realized was far from satisfactory. She detested Vaudreuil, 'whose imperious and exacting disposition had extremely displeased her', and by 1785 she would not visit Madame de Polignac without first ascertaining from a footman the names of those she might expect to meet in her salon.[76] The Polignac coterie profited very handsomely indeed from their positions at Court (to the tune of some 500,000 *livres* per annum), but they were not above circulating malicious tales about the Queen to whom they owed so much. Their flight into exile with the Comte d'Artois two days after the fall of the Bastille surely indicated where their loyalties really lay.

A healthy dose of cynicism might have enabled the Queen to avert the damage caused by these fairweather friends. According to Tilly, Madame de Polignac 'exerted some considerable influence over matters of state by causing the rise or fall of ministers', and it was generally accepted that the quickest path to success at Court lay through her salon door.[77] It is questionable that she had any great influence over important policy issues, but she, in conjunction with the rest of the 'committee', certainly pushed the Queen into meddling with the appointment of ministers and the granting of offices. From the mid-1780s, however, Marie-Antoinette began to have serious differences of political opinion with her friends, and Madame de Polignac confided to Bombelles that she often found it very hard to smile and keep a serene countenance when she suffered real distress as a result of her position. This disloyal tittle-tattle must surely have angered the Queen (Bombelles records numerous critical comments overheard *chez* Polignac, though only occasionally from the duchess herself), and by 1787 it was clear to most courtiers that the Polignacs had lost her esteem.

They cannot always have exerted their influence in state affairs through the Queen. In 1785 Bombelles wrote that it was Louis XVI who most liked Madame de Polignac, and this indicates the

strings pulled for the appointment of Calonne (a Polignac man) to the post of Controller-General, for he was heartily disliked by the Queen. The whole question of political influence and Marie-Antoinette's favourites remains unclear.

Bombelles, a protégé of the Baron de Breteuil (Minister of the King's Household), had a good record in the diplomatic service and connections at Versailles. Both his wife and his mother-in-law held Court posts, and he used every possible means to capitalize on this advantage to obtain another posting after being recalled from his German embassy. His wife wrote memoirs of his case for Madame Elisabeth, her close friend, to give to the King and Queen, while Bombelles himself haunted the corridors of Versailles in an effort to catch the regal eye. He also spent hours chatting with both Madame de Polignac and the Comtesse Diane de Polignac, and often spoke to the Queen, who always treated him kindly. Yet he was constantly refused office, and eventually discovered that the man blocking his appointment was the Foreign Minister, Vergennes. To what avail, then, the smiles of Court favourites or even the good opinion of the royal family? Only when Vergennes relented did Bombelles get his appointment, and it was the minister who fixed his salary and arranged all the details of his embassy.

It seems highly improbable that political control of the government rested entirely in the hands of Marie-Antoinette and her friends. Disgusting rumours about the Queen, who was commonly supposed to spend most of her time in orgies at the Petit Trianon, nevertheless continued unabated. The disastrous Diamond Necklace Trial of 1786, in which her reputation was dragged through the mire to absolve some extremely clever jewel thieves, irreparably damaged the French monarchy.[78] More and more libels followed, and by 1789 Marie-Antoinette was nothing more than 'the modern Messalina' in public opinion.

She had a faithful and kind husband, her children, two or three devoted women friends, loyal servants; but was there any truth in all the lurid stories about her private life? Insiders at Court declare her morals to have been unimpeachable, and not only because she believed in the sanctity of marriage. Tilly

points out a very practical barrier to the Queen indulging in amours, even had she felt so inclined – she was hardly ever left alone! He does, however, credit her with two loves – the Duc de Coigny ('an attachment . . . without, so I believe, any motive of passion'), and the Swedish Count Axel von Fersen.[79]

The Duc de Coigny was First Equerry to Louis XVI, and well liked by the King; this naturally made him many enemies. What better way to cause his downfall than by suggesting a liaison with the Queen? Bombelles was once offered a ride back to Versailles from Paris in the duke's carriage, and concluded that few peers had 'such noble manners as his, or his easy politeness, amiable and obliging towards everyone'.[80] M. de Coigny was acknowledged to be the best dancer at Court, which probably attracted Marie-Antoinette, but it is highly unlikely that he was anything more than her friend.

Fersen was different. 'He was one of the handsomest men I ever saw,' wrote Tilly, 'though with an icy countenance, which women do not disdain if they can hope to give it animation.'[81] Marie-Antoinette could animate this icy countenance, but their love ('a long and tender constancy') was doomed, and Tilly and others are unsure whether it was ever consummated. Fersen purposely left Versailles to fight in the American War in order to avoid the Queen, and returned to the French Court only at intervals thereafter. During the Revolution, however, he came into his own. He was a true friend who risked everything to try to save her, and planned the royal family's ill-fated escape from Paris in 1791 which ended so ignominiously at Varennes. On her return to the capital, the Queen wrote to tell Fersen she was safe. 'I can tell you that I love you and I haven't even time for that. . . . Farewell, most loved and loving of men. I embrace you with my whole heart.'[82]

For years historians have disputed the implications of Fersen's mutilated diary entries for 1792 (when he was a frequent visitor to the captive royal family in the Tuileries), but why linger on such banal details? He most certainly did love Marie-Antoinette, and it is perhaps right that he should write her epitaph. After her execution in October 1793 his anguish was almost palpable.

The only object of my interest no longer exists. She alone meant everything to me and it is at present that I feel how truly I was attached to her. I think of it all the time, her image follows me and will follow me ceaselessly, and everywhere I only want to talk of her and recall the happy moments of my life.[83]

Fersen's image of the dead Queen had little in common with the portrait of her left by her enemies: 'what gentleness, what tenderness, what kindness, what solicitude,' he enthused, 'what a delicate, loving and tender heart!'[84] So, perhaps giddy, thoughtless Marie-Antoinette was honoured at last.

For Louis XVI, however, life became unbearable on the day there ceased to be a Court of Versailles. October 6th, 1789: the mob had marched from Paris to bring the royal family to the capital. Their revenge for the snubs and humiliation inflicted by Louis XIV was complete. As he climbed into the carriage which was to drag him to Paris, the King turned to the Comte de Gouvernet with these words: 'You remain the master here. Try to save my poor Versailles for me.'[85]

3

Le Beau Monde

Despite its glitter and luxury, Versailles could not charm fashionable society to the extent it had in the days of the *roi soleil*, and during the reign of Louis XVI anyone aspiring to social success would undoubtedly have chosen Paris before the Court. The century-old battle between *la cour et la ville* was finally swinging in favour of Paris, and even young scions of well-established Court families found the capital far more enticing than Versailles. The Comte de Tilly noted that 'there was almost as marked a difference between the style and language of the Court and those of the town as between Paris compared with the provinces', and he was not alone in preferring social life in the capital.[1]

Even after long years of exile, followed in many cases by equally long years of obscurity under Napoleonic rule, members of pre-revolutionary Parisian high society retained happy memories of a world which the events of 1789 were to sweep away. Women recalled how they had reigned supreme; politics had not yet succeeded in displacing the arts as the main topic of conversation, and ladies were always to be admired and adored. Supper parties for a small number of guests were considered by virtually all memoir writers as the acme of good living. 'All the costumes, all the elegance, everything that the beautiful and good society of Paris could offer in refinement and fascination was to be found at these suppers,' wrote a nostalgic Marquise de

La Tour du Pin. Elegance, wit, good humour, gaiety were what the *beau monde* most prized during the reign of Louis XVI, and Parisian suppers, in the words of the Baron de Frénilly, achieved 'the perfection of the social spirit'.[2]

For Tilly, Paris in the 1780s was 'a whirlpool of dissipation, pleasure, and indulgence', where life was marked only by the progression from the theatre to supper, the gaming table to a ball, or the salon to a concert.[3] Good-looking, titled, and in possession of an independent fortune, he was born to join the social élite; but though far removed from the *bas peuple*, high society before the Revolution was nevertheless subject to its own stratification, as rigid in its way as the Court hierarchy. There was 'good society' and 'good company' (not entirely the same thing), and even a well-born member of the *beau monde* was not necessarily a leader of *bon ton*.

Sharp divisions always existed between the *haute noblesse* and the *haute bourgeoisie* (the latter more commonly known in Paris as *haute finance*, since the wealthiest bourgeois were in fact financiers). The salons of the nobility and the bourgeoisie rivalled each other in talent and brilliance; wits, men of letters and scientists were welcome everywhere regardless of birth, but without an intellectual passport, barriers remained. On the rare occasions they were overcome, a strict order of precedence among guests was observed. An impartial observer might well have been baffled to discover one count being given decidedly preferential treatment over another. The favoured aristocrat, having inherited his title from an old noble family, would be treated as 'a man of quality'. The other, perhaps the son of an important magistrate or *fermier-général*, probably a great deal cleverer and just as stylish as his fellow count, remained merely 'a man of rank'. He would be seated lower down the table, where his witticisms earned less applause. Surely this was very galling for the 'man of rank', who could either comfort himself with the thought that he was considerably richer than the 'man of quality', get himself married to a poor but respectably noble bride in order to advance his children in society, or overturn the hierarchy completely by setting himself up as a leader of *bon ton*.

Bon ton was the eighteenth-century equivalent of modern BCBG (*bon chic, bon genre*). Style and aristocratic birth were usual requirements for membership of the *ton*, but money always supplied the key providing one possessed the necessary panache. According to the Baron de Besenval in his *Réflexions sur le Ton*, courtesy was the quintessential feature of *bon ton*; more superficially, the *ton* had idiosyncratic mannerisms of speech and its own jargon. Humour could never descend to distasteful subjects, and most important of all, 'gallantry with women' was obligatory.[4] This gallantry manifested itself publicly in deference and attentiveness to women, and privately in the vigorous pursuit of sexual pleasure. Membership of the *ton* was therefore potentially a very risky undertaking for women, particularly for those who valued their reputations! The social status enjoyed by leaders of the *ton*, however, was on the whole considered a worthy prize. Their clothes and carriages were admired and imitated, their witty utterances repeated in countless salons; if they possessed literary talent, they could amuse themselves (and try to amuse their friends) by producing books of verse and epigrams. But not everyone fawned on leaders of the *ton*, nor was there universal support for their claim to be the arbiters of public taste and opinion on subjects which could be as diverse as female dress, horse-flesh, literature and music. Gouverneur Morris was very sceptical about the value of opinions expressed in Paris, where 'they know a Wit by his Snuff Box, a Man of Taste by his Bow, and a Statesman by the Cut of his Coat'.[5] The criteria chosen hardly inspired him with confidence in fashionable pronouncements on more serious topics!

'Frivolous' and 'superficial' are epithets often applied to high society in any era, and the Parisian *beau monde* during the reign of Louis XVI probably fully deserved both adjectives. Yet it was a frivolity and superficiality pursued with deadly seriousness, and not only by young dandies and their mistresses. High society embraced the nobility, financiers, the upper echelons of the church and the law, as well as the arts; hence a wide spectrum of personalities and age groups engaged in the constant battle to gain attention, and most importantly, to shine. Before

one entered the lists it was advisable to be armed with all the necessary social graces, for one false step or misplaced word could lead rapidly to oblivion, as the Comtesse de Boigne explains in a cautionary tale about the events at a Court ball in the 1770s.

> M. de Chabannes, of high birth, handsome, young, rich, and almost the man of the hour, in making his first appearance was so clumsy as to fall down while dancing, and was so tactless as to cry 'Jésus Maria!' as he fell. It was a fall from which he never rose again. . . . He volunteered for the American Wars, and distinguished himself in action, but he came back 'Jésus Maria' as he went out. Thus the Duc de Coigny observed to his daughters on the day they were presented at Court: 'Remember that in this country vice is immaterial, but ridicule is fatal.'[6]

Carried to extremes, ridicule indeed proved fatal. Madame de Boigne tells the sad story of another young man, turned away from a Court ball because he had not been presented (though a dashing officer, he was bourgeois), who returned to Paris and shot himself 'in despair at the ridicule to which he was exposed in an age when ridicule was the worst of calamities'.[7]

Perhaps it paid to have the supreme unconcern of that celebrated woman of letters, Madame de Staël. She too had bourgeois origins, but her father's ministerial rank and her marriage to a Swedish aristocrat entitled her to a Court presentation, and therefore gave her the right to disgrace herself at one of the Queen's balls, to which invitations were always eagerly sought. Madame de Staël's youthful antics at one of these balls in 1786 attracted a large crowd of spectators. Bombelles records that her dancing was so energetic (despite crippling three-inch high heels) that she fell down, and her elaborate coiffure tumbled down simultaneously. Undismayed, she got up to dance again until the Duchesse de Guiche (Madame de Polignac's daughter) tactfully drew her away from the suppressed mirth of fellow guests and did her best to repair the damage to Madame de Staël's appearance. With superb aplomb and a few

dangling curls which had defied her rescuer's rudimentary hair-dressing skills, she returned to the ballroom and astounded everyone as she demonstrated her highly idiosyncratic inter-pretation of a *contredanse* yet again.

Since Madame de Staël was widely admired for her intellectual capabilities, which fortunately also seem to have blinded her to the gravity of her *faux pas* in the eyes of lesser mortals, she had to be pardoned for making herself look ridiculous. Who, after all, would dare to mention the fact to her face when a well-written, cogently argued and witty essay on their own folly might confront them in a newspaper as a riposte? For those without such weapons of self-defence, however, it was infinitely preferable to avoid any hint of ridicule from the outset, and a watertight social persona had to be developed from an early age.

Dancing, of course, was obligatory for both sexes, and for those with children, giving balls was 'a kind of social duty'.[8] Boys and girls in France were dressed as adults as soon as they could walk, and it must have been quite gruelling for the future *jeunesse dorée* to manage skirts, coiffure, hat and sword as well as mastering the intricacies of a gavotte or minuet. Grand society balls were often preceded by *bals d'enfants*, and at Versailles during the carnival, the greatest childhood honour was to be asked to dance with the Dauphin or Madame Royale. The ability to dance well was considered of supreme importance because it entailed the acquisition of a graceful deportment in an age when elegance was all. Even the most trivial details of human motion were studied and refined so that the body never made an un-gainly movement. As the Baron de Frénilly remarks, he was taught to glide rather than walk by his dancing master – the acid test being a walk through rain and mud without soiling his silver-buckled shoes and white silk stockings. A feat indeed. He had to be able to execute his most elegant bow to his hostess without blushing, after all. Although a high instep was desirable for much of the eighteenth century (high heels were worn by men as well as women), by 1786 dancing masters had to alter their lessons to accommodate a change in fashion, as Frénilly explains.

I have not forgotten the hours of toil inflicted on me by the illustrious Petit, my dancing master, who three times a week made me take four or five turns around my mother's salon with the first phalange of my toes turned inwards, in order to lower my instep perfectly; for, alas! at that period (I was eighteen or twenty years old), heels had already fallen by half an inch, flat heels triumphed everywhere, and the Revolution was approaching.[9]

Revolution or not, no self-respecting man-about-town would be foiled by flat heels! Similarly, he could take lessons in how to wear a sword or the most graceful way to carry a hat. He was unlikely to be invited anywhere until he had mastered these essentials of deportment, for 'making one's entrance into society' was not perhaps so easy as it sounds.

It was no ordinary science to know how to enter with grace and assurance a salon where thirty men and women were seated in a circle around the fire, to penetrate this circle while bowing slightly to everyone, to advance straight to the mistress of the house, and to retire with honour, without clumsily disarranging one's fine clothes, lace ruffles, head-dress of thirty-six curls powdered like rime, hat beneath one's arm, sword whose point touched one's heels, and finally, an enormous muff, the smallest of which were two and a half feet long and nearly as great in girth.[10]

His entrance gracefully accomplished, the much-encumbered guest was not allowed to rest on his laurels. He had to make interesting conversation, and if he wished to shine in salon society, the ability to read aloud was also essential. Frénilly was initiated into the latter art by his formal grandmother, who listened to him mumble through two pages when he was seventeen before abruptly taking his book away with the words: 'Grandson, you read like a pig!'[11] She certainly altered his ideas on the matter!

It was quite possible to make a little humour and conversation go a long way, but true social success demanded much more than simply the right clothes, accent and manners. One of the

generally acknowledged and admired leaders of the *ton* was the Maréchal de Biron, who died in 1788 at the age of eighty-eight. Madame de La Tour du Pin called him 'the last great lord of Louis XIV's day', and she was not the only young woman to be fascinated by his charm.[12] He was a model for young noblemen, but few could match the grandness and grace of his manners, or equal the magnificent way he kept open-house at the Hôtel de Biron (now the Musée Rodin). His hospitality was not merely perfunctory. The portrait-painter Elisabeth Vigée-Lebrun expressed a desire to see the gardens of the Hôtel de Biron, famous for hothouses containing rare plants, and was astonished on her arrival to be greeted by the eighty-four year old Maréchal in person, who insisted on guiding her round the garden and explaining its merits. He also handed her into her carriage when her visit was over. The Maréchal, she declared, was charm itself.[13]

One would not expect, however, to satisfy the critical Parisians merely by sporting one's charm, elegant manners, learning, and witty conversation. It is perhaps worth noting that before Dr Johnson visited Paris with the Thrales in 1775 he defied one of his own maxims (to beware of any enterprise which requires new clothes) and spent thirty pounds on a new suit and wig – rather necessary, it must be admitted, in view of his general indifference to all matters sartorial. That he felt obliged to go to such expense for Paris, when in London his careless attire still gained him entry to the best drawing rooms, surely indicates the greater importance attached to dress on the other side of the Channel. The very pinnacle of *bon ton*, in fact, could only be reached by those who also had impeccable dress sense. A subtle trap therefore awaited the unwary; how to avoid becoming a fashion victim (for nothing could be more ridiculous), yet avert the storm of sneers likely to occur if one wore anything even slightly *démodé*? Fashion was not quite so important commercially in eighteenth-century Paris as it is today, but certain boutiques resembled the modern discount shops where designer clothes are sold without their labels. In these, a lackey would have been able to buy the very suit his fashionable young master

had worn the day before – and promptly discarded because he had seen someone else in the same cloth. Merely keeping abreast of fashion was an extremely expensive business, but if one seriously aspired to be a leader of the *ton* one had to cultivate an individual style, and this could be ruinous.

During the reign of Louis XVI, French style, previously imitated across the entire Continent, was subjected to a sustained assault by the English, and a revolution in costume was almost complete before 1789. Many saw this 'democratic' influence, added to the 'republicanism' brought back from the American War, as a warning of the political revolution to follow. But for much of the 1770s, French trends were unchallenged. Women wore very high heels and hooped skirts, with their hair piled up in massive superstructures on top of their heads. The great Léonard, hairdresser to the Queen, constructed such mountainous coiffures that a Frenchwoman in a hat was a rare sight indeed. Wigs were well on their way to the props cupboard, but powder and pomade were liberally used by both sexes. Mercier's frequent references to hairdressing in his *Tableau de Paris* lead one to the conclusion that it was a subject of deep concern to most Parisians. Male vanity was flattered by an elegant coiffure (curls were vital), and a richly embroidered coat and lace ruffles, although some men did not disdain rouge and beauty patches, even if they were not so highly painted as women. Swords were obligatory for gentlemen, who were also expected to use them with skill, but hats fared no better with men than with women. The size of wigs, followed by extravagant hairstyles, made a tricorne little more than an ornament, always carried beneath the arm.

The formality of French dress reinforced a formality of manner which extended through all layers of society. In the *beau monde*, it helped to maintain the distance between the nobility, the church, and the law. During the 1780s, however, a change took place which was seen by contemporary observers as indicative of a deeper shift in both manners and morals.

According to Frénilly, by 1787 *abbés* and prelates had abandoned priestly robes for suits of brown or violet cloth,

magistrates had forsaken their customary black clothes and heavy wigs for frock coats and powdered hair, and women of all ranks were flaunting their charms as never before. 'Women were wearing flat shoes, tight skirts, and appeared *en pierrot* in loose white gowns. . . . It was a revolution. . . . In a hoop, the most flighty coquette had the air of a matron; *en pierrot*, the severest matron had the air of a scatterbrain.'[14]

Men were not exempt from the rage for new fashions. They adopted the English waistcoat, and as the possibilities for change were limited in other respects, wore tighter breeches.

> To be fashionable, breeches even had to be so tight that help was required in putting them on; both skill and prudence were necessary for walking and even more so for dancing, talent was essential for sitting down and bowing, and the merest thoughtless movement exposed them to a catastrophe.[15]

The style was still considered French while silk stockings and buckled shoes were worn, though after the Anglo-French Commercial Treaty of 1786 gold and jewel coat buttons were replaced by steel buttons from England – not considered magnificent unless they cost twenty-five *louis*! Some bold souls transformed themselves entirely into Englishmen, carrying a cane and wearing an English frock coat, waistcoat, cravat, gloves and a round hat, though short and unpowdered hair (favoured by English dandies) was still too outrageous. As Frénilly reports, 'the first head that dared to appear *à la Titus* . . . was the subject of a general scandal'.[16] Yet the revolution in dress seemed unstoppable, and 'when a boot had passed the threshold of a salon, victory was complete. . . . It was the height of impertinence and the quintessence of *bon ton*'.[17] The less pleasant facets of this alteration in national costume manifested themselves in a fundamental transformation of *bon ton* itself. It had been based on chivalric notions of courtesy and style, but as the Revolution approached, *bon ton* was characterized by 'a lack of respect towards men and of gallantry towards women'.[18] French social life would never be the same again.

The need to show one's wealth on one's back did not disappear with the demise of hoops, high heels and tricornes. It was quite pointless being rich in Paris if no one knew, and the word modesty does not appear to have been in the Parisians' lexicon. Many of the functions attended by the *beau monde* were little more than excuses for the guests to parade their finery in an orgy of mutual admiration and envy. But there was one particular occasion, and one particular place, where this display was carried to an extreme.

The time was Holy Week, and the place was the Abbaye de Sainte-Claire at Longchamp. In the 1760s it had been the custom to hear the Easter service sung by famous opera singers at Longchamp, and so great was the crowd, many Parisians merely drove to the abbey and back to the capital without being able to attend a service. When the Archbishop of Paris tried to stop the indecent behaviour of the congregation by allowing only nuns to sing, the incentive to visit the abbey was gone, but the '*promenade de Longchamp*' during Holy Week, on Wednesday, Thursday and Good Friday, had become such a feature of the social calendar that it continued. After all, with the theatres in Paris closed, high society had nothing better to do. No hint of the incongruity of the occasion with the way it was celebrated appears in descriptions of this magnificent fashion parade; although it was revived in the nineteenth century (by which time the abbey had long been destroyed) all commentators seem agreed that pre-revolutionary Longchamp was unrivalled for luxury and splendour. It was certainly a pilgrimage with a difference! Frénilly, ever-conscientious society columnist, reveals what was necessary to create a stir.

I have seen Longchamp in its greatest brilliance. Two rows of carriages departed from the front of the Place Louis XV, two more returned likewise from the extremity of the Bois de Boulogne. . . . A *fiacre* was not to be seen; a hired coach would have been whistled at, and there was some disdain for a coach and four, which revealed the lower ranks of the law or finance, by the vanity of having more than two horses and the impossibility of

having six. At Longchamp, the height of *bon ton*, in effect, was to
have two horses or six, and only on the Wednesday and the
Friday, for the importance of being either first or last is one of
those caprices of fashion that can be well explained by vanity . . .
horses, harnesses, carriages, liveries, clothes, all had to be new if
one wished to be noticed. Courtesans above all had the particular
privilege of displaying themselves, on each of these three days, in
new equipages, for they had neither venerable coats of arms nor
ancient liveries to maintain.[19]

One such courtesan, Adéline from the Comédie-Italienne,
who was the mistress of the *fermier-général* Vémeranges,
exerted her privilege in full – appearing in a brand new coach
and six, in completely new and modish clothes, on three con-
secutive days. Small wonder *les filles* were so detested by married women whose husbands squandered millions of *livres* on
them, or that the populace who came to stare, catcall or applaud
hated the tax-collectors who could afford to be so lavish.

A claim to be noticed having been made at Longchamp, social
climbers would hope soon to be in receipt of invitations to all
the best mansions in Paris, and since 'one had no other business
but pleasure', life could be passed in a hedonistic whirl.[20] *Bon
ton* naturally precluded early rising, and dinner time was also
governed by fashion. Only provincials dined at noon. In Paris,
the favoured hour was between two and three in the afternoon;
by then gentlemen were in full dress, though ladies often still in
déshabille. Conversation followed before the ladies retired to
dress for the strenuous evening and night to come. Plays and
operas were performed between 5 p.m. and 9 p.m.; supper came
next at about 10 p.m., which was the truly important hour
socially. Suppers could last well into the early hours, prolonged
by cards, conversation, music, and 'more tender pursuits' as
Tilly so elegantly puts it. Balls lasted even longer – often until
five or six in the morning, and considerable stamina was required by those with several invitations to dance each week.

There even existed a snobbery in theatre-going which had to
be observed by anyone who aspired to belong to the social élite,

for 'each theatre had its good days, the days when the best actors performed and the most fashionable people came'.[21] According to this rule, the Opéra was to be attended on Tuesdays and Fridays, the Comédie-Française on Wednesdays and Saturdays, and the Comédie-Italienne on Mondays and Thursdays. Sunday usually saw all theatres full. If a newcomer to Paris happened to visit one of the theatres on the 'wrong' day, he could always restore his battered image by declaring in a surprised tone that it had been empty – 'empty' being the term employed in the *beau monde* to denote that the house was packed to the gods with the bourgeoisie! There was a similar law governing opera premières. The 'best society' never attended a first night; they went to the third performance, after the lawyers and financiers. One wonders how they would have reacted if confronted with modern previews!

The theatres themselves were nearly all new in the 1780s. The Opéra was rebuilt after burning down in 1781, the new Comédie-Italienne opened in 1783 as part of a private speculation by the heavily indebted Duc de Choiseul, and the new Théâtre Français (home of the Comédie-Française) opened in an isolated setting on the Left Bank in 1782, where the Odéon currently stands. It boasted the very first paved street in Paris as an added attraction to its 'magnificent portico'. Arthur Young, generally scornful of French architecture, was forced to admire Parisian theatres, and having visited all three leading houses in 1787, wrote despairingly, 'after the circular theatres of France how can one relish our ill-contrived oblong holes of London?'[22] He also found himself obliged to admit French superiority in the performing arts. England, apart from one or two 'brilliants' like Garrick and Siddons, had nothing which could compare with French plays, ballets and operas, nor with the actors, singers, costumes and scenery. Mrs Thrale had made the same mortifying discovery in 1775, writing less generously than Young: 'I am sorry to see the French beat us so in powers of Performance on a Stage. I think however it is the *only* thing they excel us in & that must be my Comfort.'[23]

Doubtless many French would dispute the last sentence, but

it seems fair to say that under Louis XVI the performing arts truly flourished – and not just in the public theatres. Amateur theatricals were all the rage among the nobility and *haute bourgeoisie*, and even the royal family staged plays in the Queen's theatre at the Petit Trianon to amuse the Court. Bombelles considered the family of the Comte de Caraman the most talented society actors and singers of his acquaintance, and it was a privilege to be invited to watch them at their home at Roissy.

Amateur plays, however, were often staged with the assistance and participation of professionals. The respectability of some of these plays is by no means unquestionable; although many were performed purely for innocent amusement, and drew large audiences of admiring elderly relatives, some private theatricals were decidedly more ambiguous. Those staged by the Prince d'Hénin and his mistress, the actress Sophie Arnould, were reported to be highly erotic, but this does not appear to have deterred well-known society figures from taking part! Cardinal de Rohan, again according to gossip, was supposed to enjoy private performances of Aretino's plays with a cast of opera dancers and noble amateurs. One doubts that the very correct Baron de Frénilly would have considered this a part of *bon ton*, but the Cardinal was nevertheless an extremely fashionable man.

Theatricals aside, there were numerous other opportunities for the display of culture and talent, for as Tilly remarked, 'one could not then go to theatres and salons without having to occupy oneself also with literature, epigrams, and songs'.[24] Admission to all the best salons was vital for those who desired social success; literary and musical talent, wit, and good conversation always guaranteed a full engagement diary.

The very notion of salon society is inseparable from the Parisian *beau monde*, both before and after the Revolution. A 'salon' was far more than a drawing room where visitors exchanged polite chat with their hosts. It was the venue for a gathering of like-minded individuals (preferably intelligent and witty) who were expected to obey the one great maxim which

governed *ancien régime* high society: they had to be amusing. The more serious function of salon society was its shaping of taste in literature and art, although Tilly was rather sceptical about the extravagant claims made in this area. 'Each salon's members looked upon themselves as the born dispensers of good taste, the leaders of public opinion, and anyone outside their circle as an inferior and a reprobate – this notwithstanding the fact that some hundred other salons were putting forth the same pretensions.'[25]

Some salons were nevertheless far more important than others. One of the most influential was hosted by Madame Necker (mother of the irrepressible Madame de Staël), although according to the Marquise de La Tour du Pin, her cook had a great deal to do with her ability to attract Parisian wits and intellectuals to the Necker household.[26] As the wife of Jacques Necker, a leading Swiss banker and Director of Finances to Louis XVI, Madame Necker had a high reputation to maintain. Nonetheless many thought her pretentious and pedantic, and her niece by marriage, Albertine de Saussure, was not very impressed by her hostess when she visited the Necker salon during the winter of 1786–87.

> One dares not speak. Madame Necker intimidates even the most intrepid. Supper finished, the guests arrange themselves with a constrained air around the fireplace. Madame Necker tried to start some fine topic for discussion. One could say that she has imposed upon herself a great role from which she never departs. She speaks of virtue, of decency, of sentiment, not with the warmth of her own heart, but with the ideas she has conceived of what it ought to be. I believe that her own character is perfectly unknown to her, and that she has never had a moment of abandon, even with her husband.[27]

As Monsieur Necker, in the opinion of Gouverneur Morris, had 'the Look and Manner of the Counting House', his wife's restraint may be partially excused![28] Morris found Madame Necker 'to be a Woman of Sense', rather masculine in her

outlook, but with 'the Appearance of a Chambermaid'.[29] He was never very tolerant of others' failings, but further acquaintance with the Necker salon, particularly when it was enlivened by Madame de Staël and her friends, swiftly drove him back to the less daunting intellectual atmosphere of the salons hosted by Madame de Tessé and the Duchesse d'Orléans. The wit and brilliance *chez* Necker when everyone was on form was simply too much for a man who only wanted to unwind after working hard all day.

The success or failure of a salon was largely dependent on the character and personality of the hostess. Frénilly, whose grandmother hosted 'an evening for wits on Saturdays, a dinner on Sundays and a supper on Wednesdays', pays tribute to the skills required by a busy hostess. She had to know how to:

> captivate her audience, to direct, prolong, revive or abridge a conversation, to have a look and a word for everyone; to introduce by a glance or a single word a third party into the chat of others . . . to make him known without either naming him or presenting him: what a charming and delicate art![30]

Politeness, of course, was the key. So much so, that in the eyes of some it destroyed any meaningful exchange of views, since disagreements were not permitted. Arthur Young went so far as to declare that 'all vigour of thought seems so excluded from expression that characters of ability and of inanity meet nearly on a par' – which does make one rather wonder what they actually managed to talk about![31]

The Comte de Ségur, who used to frequent the salons of Madame de Tessé, Madame de Luxembourg, Madame de Montesson and the Princesse de Beauveau, explains how 'the utmost good temper' governed salon conversations, so that 'disputes very seldom occurred; and as a delicate sense of propriety had carried the art of pleasing to perfection, all tediousness was discarded by carefully avoiding too much insistence upon any subject'.[32] Conversational butterflies, the guests flitted from topic to topic; in a single evening, discussion could turn upon:

the *Esprit des Lois* and the tales of Voltaire, the philosophy of Helvétius and the operas of Sedaine or Marmontel, the tragedies of La Harpe and the licentious tales of the Abbé de Voisenon, the discoveries in India by the Abbé Raynal and the songs of Collé, the politics of Mably and the delightful poetry of Saint Lambert or Abbé Delille.[33]

Even for the well-read, it was an extensive conversational agenda. Many young officers used to spend the four months a year they were obliged to pass in provincial garrisons reading in preparation for a successful return to Paris, which might have been one reason for the royal army's inefficiency.

Of course, French commentators who speak of the 'art' of holding a salon and generally take the whole matter very seriously indeed, were perhaps too blinded by the importance conferred on them by membership of salon society to perceive its pretentiousness. The last word on the subject ought to go to Gouverneur Morris, whose pervasive irony is such a refreshing feature of his diary. As an American, he was bound to be popular in pre-revolutionary Parisian society, which saw him as a champion of liberty and freedom of speech; and as a personable bachelor with a gift for repartee, he was a welcome guest in royal, noble and bourgeois salons alike. He had not been very long in Paris, therefore, before he received an invitation to dinner from the Comtesse Fanny de Beauharnais. She dabbled in literature, and according to Tilly, 'held what was wrongly called an academy of wits, but where one met good society, both men of the world and men of letters, though the worth of the latter was very uneven'.[34] Just how uneven Morris was quick to discover, although he made the indigestible error of arriving for dinner at 3.15 p.m. only to find that it did not start for nearly another two hours!

Towards four o'Clock the Guests begin to assemble and I begin to suspect that as Madame is a Poetess I shall have the Honor to dine with that exalted Part of the Species who devote themselves to the Muses. In Effect, the Gentlemen begin to compliment their

respective Works and as regular Hours cannot be expected in a House where the Mistress is occupied more with the intellectual than the material World, I have a delightful Prospect of a Continuance of the Scene. Towards five Madame steps in to announce Dinner and the hungry Poets advance to the Charge. . . . If the Repast is not abundant we have at least the Consolation that there is no Lack of Conversation. . . . They tell me, to my great Surprize, that the Public now condemn theatrical Compositions before they have heard the first Recital, and to remove my Doubts the Countess is so kind as to assure me that this rash Decision has been made on one of her own Pieces.[35]

Though invited for both future Tuesdays and Thursdays, Morris left after coffee, promising himself not to return. Poetry was not for the man with a healthy appetite; besides, as a wit he was in demand elsewhere.

Wit, indeed, could open any door. 'The supreme talent', in Mercier's opinion, was 'to be amusing'.[36] Madame de Staël told King Gustav III of Sweden that in Paris 'the most dreadful of accusations' was 'to be suspected of being a bore', and the Comtesse de Boigne goes even further: 'every extravagance, every vice, and every cowardice was sure to meet with indulgence, provided it was admitted and recognised with some show of humour.'[37]

It was always wise to have some amusing stories in one's repertoire, but a quick-witted reply was better, even if it proved to be less than brilliant in retrospect. Talleyrand relates how he extricated himself from potential embarrassment at a supper given by Madame de Boufflers at Auteuil. It was his first invitation to the house, and he was placed at the very end of the table, barely talking to his neighbour. The Duchesse de Gramont (sister of the princely Duc de Choiseul) suddenly attacked him from across the table.

Madame de Gramont, in a loud and harsh voice, called me by my name, and asked me what had so struck me as I followed her into the room that I said: *Ah! ah!* . . . 'Madame la duchesse', I replied, 'did not hear me correctly. It was not *Ah! ah!* that I said, but: *Oh! oh!*'

As Talleyrand himself admitted, it was 'a miserable reply', but it nevertheless raised a laugh and brought him invitations 'from the people I most desired to meet'.[38]

Wit could also be used as a subtle way of making one's disapproval known. A young Gascon, kept waiting too long in M. de Bissy's antechamber, drew his sword and began some fencing exercises. When Bissy finally emerged and asked him what he was doing, the pointed reply was: 'Monsieur, I'm killing time while I wait for you.'[39] An excellent riposte in every sense which did not infringe the rules of *bon ton*. Wit had to be refined to be deemed really clever, although this did not prevent it from being wounding. The Maréchal de Noailles, despite his high rank, was known to be far from brave as a soldier. When the King asked his son, the Duc d'Ayen, if the Maréchal would join them hunting one very wet day, the answer was short and cruel: 'Oh no, Sire: my father fears water as much as he does fire.'[40]

Wit did not always have to be rehearsed. The Duc de Laval was on the contrary known for his malapropisms ('he had received an anonymous letter signed by all the officers in his regiment'), and his great friend, the Duc de Lauzun, traded in 'Laval stories'.[41] When Laval took exception to being made to seem a fool, Lauzun told him he would fare worse in society if he insisted on being treated like a man of sense! But witticisms could sometimes prove costly. The Comte de Maurepas was dismissed from office by Louis XV and spent twenty-five years in the political wilderness because of a lampoon he had written on Madame de Pompadour. It did not make him mend his ways, however, and when reappointed by Louis XVI, he continued to amuse both himself and the Court. En route to fight in the American War, the Comte de Ségur was shown a letter by Maurepas to the Duc de Lauzun, which consisted of a mere two sentences. 'I have not been able', the prime minister wrote to the duke, 'to do anything in the affair you mentioned to me. You had only the King and myself in your favour on this occasion; such are the consequences of keeping low company.'[42]

The consequences of an epigram written by Louis-Edmond

de Champcenetz in 1781 were dire indeed. He wanted to be admitted to the salon of Sophie Arnould, and her lover, the Prince d'Hénin, arranged for an invitation. Champcenetz showed his gratitude by writing an insulting song about the little prince (the refrain was: 'you are not the prince of dwarfs, but the dwarf of princes'), who expressed his outrage so strongly that Champcenetz's father had him locked up in a country château and removed him as *survivancier* to the governor of the Tuileries. Tilly, who knew the mocking young marquis well, says that Champcenetz actually borrowed much of his wit from others, and was so convinced of his own brilliance that no amount of argument could persuade him that many of his sallies were not original! Another victim of his pen was Madame de Staël, who took her revenge during a masked ball in 1789. When 'in a string of biting pleasantries' Champcenetz told her he had been poisoned, she replied: 'You must have bitten your own tongue.'[43] Yet one has to admire the man. Condemned to death by the Revolutionary Tribunal in 1794, Champcenetz still possessed enough humour to enquire: 'It isn't like the National Guard then, where one can pay for a substitute?'

Despite the high value placed on wit, it was not always appreciated, as Gouverneur Morris once found when visiting the Duchesse d'Orléans at the Palais Royal. One of her ladies-in-waiting hobbled into the salon.

> She had something on her Toe which she in extracting had cut to the Quick. I tell her: '*Madame, quand on est touché au vif on s'en ressent longtemps*' – An old devout Lady who is present, taking the Thing with great Simplicity in the literal Sense, adds in the true Matron Tone: '*Et surtout au Pied.*'[44]

Pious elderly ladies were a force to be reckoned with in more formal households, where they often did far more to guide the morals of the young than those whose profession was supposed to fit them for the task. The outward trappings of religion were in fact highly visible in Paris during the reign of Louis XVI, as befitted the most important Catholic country in the world, but

the church rested on very unstable foundations. On her visit in 1775, Mrs Thrale remarked on the large number of crucifixes placed by the roadside, but was shocked by the lack of spirituality she observed when attending High Mass at a church in Rouen. Worshippers were anything but pious. 'Some were counting their Money, some arguing with the Beggars who interrupt you without ceasing, some receiving Messages and dispatching Answers, some beating Time to the Musick, but scarce any one praying except for one Moment when the Priest elevates the Host.'[45]

This was a far from uncommon scene, and the more fashionable the church, the more likely it was to occur. Morris attended a Mass at the Duc d'Orléans's seat at Raincy where 'immoderate laughter' was drawn from both high-ranking clerical and lay members of the congregation when practical jokes were played during the service by the Vicomte de Ségur and the Marquis de Cubières. As Morris ironically remarked, it must have been 'very edifying to the Domestics who are opposite to us and the Villagers who worship below'.[46] The divisions within pre-revolutionary French society could not be better illustrated than by the church. At the bottom: poor, badly housed parish priests and a populace who, whilst exhibiting a 'general Spirit of Infidelity & Scepticism', still turned to religion for solace in their misery.[47] At the top: aristocratic prelates who lived in princely fashion and shared all the vices and pleasures of the *beau monde*.

If the Church of England was 'the Tory party at prayer', Catholicism in eighteenth-century Paris might be said to have been the nobility at play. Younger sons of the aristocracy were pushed into ecclesiastical careers whether or not they had a religious vocation (the eldest son went into the army), though daughters might fare even worse, being obliged to take the veil because their parents could not afford the dowry required to marry them well. There were also thousands of *abbés*, found everywhere in good society, who survived on the hospitality of the nobility and bourgeoisie, generally as tutors, and not infrequently as men of letters. Known as 'commendatory abbots', they were given a tonsure as boys, endowed with a living, and

neither received (nor gave) any further religious instruction. Given this highly unpromising clerical material, it is hardly surprising that there was 'an utter Prostration of Morals' in Louis XVI's France.[48]

Many of the highest ranking clergy were indeed princes of the church; one thinks immediately of Cardinal de Rohan and Talleyrand (Bishop of Autun), both princes by birth as well as prelates. Noble clerics studied at the fashionable Parisian seminaries of Saint-Sulpice, Saint-Magloire, Vertus or the Oratory, found promotion to important sees assured, and left the capital only when they were required to be present at episcopal gatherings. The rest of the year they lived as *grands seigneurs* in Paris, and in the grandest manner. A bishop was very likely to be a leader of the *ton*, keeping an excellent table, hosting parties, hunting, gambling and womanizing.

The Marquise de La Tour du Pin was brought up in the house of her great-great uncle, the Archbishop of Narbonne, who enjoyed an income of 450,000 *livres* a year, yet still left behind debts of 1,800,000 *livres* when he emigrated in 1790.[49] If the Marquis de Bombelles is to be believed, the Archbishop was in fact Madame de La Tour du Pin's grandfather – a reasonable assumption in view of her grandmother's unwavering devotion to him. The immoral atmosphere which prevailed in his household also lends weight to the idea. 'From the age of ten,' wrote Madame de La Tour du Pin, 'I was witness to the most liberal conversations and heard the most impious principles expressed.'[50] Her religious education was entirely neglected, and she claims to have imbibed her piety from her maid Marguerite, a shrewd and honest country girl who was not afraid to pass judgement on the modish visitors to the house.

As well as entertaining lavishly in Paris, the Archbishop had a country residence, Hautefontaine, about sixty miles from the capital between Soissons and Villers-Cotterets. It was a favourite resort of the *beau monde* where, according to the Comtesse de Boigne, language 'was free to the point of licentiousness', and racy novels were to be found instead of prayer books in the chapel.[51] The hunt at Hautefontaine, jointly

funded by the Archbishop, the Duc de Lauzun and the Prince de Guéméné, drew many fine young horsemen from Paris and greatly excited the envy of Louis XVI.

Possibly the most revealing comment about life in a noble religious household is to be found on a very sad page of Madame de La Tour du Pin's memoirs. In September 1782 her mother, still beautiful and only thirty-one, lay dying of consumption in Paris, where 'she received every care'. The Queen visited her and sent a messenger daily from Versailles for a bulletin on her condition, while her lover, the Prince de Guéméné (who lived in the same house), wept for her openly. But 'no one spoke of the Sacraments or of making her see a priest. . . . There was no chaplain in that Archbishop's house.'[52] She died unshriven.

Perhaps the Archbishop could not afford to maintain a chaplain when he had to meet more pleasurable expenses. The *beau monde* always lived on credit ('without it a tradesman would sell nothing'), and debt was accepted as an inevitable accompaniment to high living.[53] Only financiers were rich in cash; the nobility relied on income from land or salaried appointments, which often failed to meet their extravagant expectations. Magnificent houses, horses, and entertainments could really be afforded by very few, but a limited income was no bar to a luxurious lifestyle – provided one always kept one step ahead of one's creditors!

Many noblemen replenished their depleted coffers by marrying rich bourgeois wives, though the stigma of such a *mésalliance* did not promise domestic harmony. Those who disdained such a step might attempt to work financial miracles by gambling, but they nearly always lost. The Duc de Laval was surely an exceptional case; according to Madame de Boigne, he counted with total assurance on an annual income of 100,000 *livres* by gambling, despite being famed for his fair play! Others were not so lucky. Madame de Staël writes of the excessive gaming that took place at Court (the Queen was unfortunately addicted to Faro and Tric-trac), where in March 1786 a raw young M. de Castellane lost his entire fortune in a single evening.[54] Bombelles's brother-in-law, M. de Travenet, regularly lost

sums as high as 5,000 *louis* in a night's play at Versailles. The King greatly disapproved of Court gamblers, and in an effort to mend her ways, the Queen eventually forbade high stakes and banished notorious gamesters from her apartments. It was far too late for some. In 1782, a self-styled marquis, M. de Chalabre, had plucked 1,800,000 *livres* from the purses of gaming courtiers in a mere four hours. He was the banker![55]

The spectacular bankruptcies which occurred during the 1780s might therefore have been expected. It was in any case an age of high inflation. Bombelles found that in 1785 people complained of poverty if they had an income of less than 100,000 *livres* a year, whereas in the 1750s a quarter of the sum would have paid for a very comfortable existence. But 100,000 *livres* was nothing to a committed spendthrift. The disarray in the financial affairs of some of the most illustrious figures in pre-revolutionary France was of a greater magnitude altogether.

The Duc de Lauzun was quite casual about his debts of 1,500,000 *livres* in 1776, since his income was four million, though much of his fortune came from his shamefully neglected wife. When they separated in 1777, he was left with a greatly reduced income of 80,000 *livres*.[56] This did nothing to cure him of extravagance, however; by 1779 he owed two million *livres*, and still possessed enough cheek to ask the Queen to try to persuade the King to pay his debts! This manoeuvre, which met with complete failure, possibly fuelled his later aversion to the Court.

Lauzun's tangled finances were insignificant when compared with the bankruptcy of the Prince de Guéméné in October 1782, which sent shock waves throughout France and marked the first stage in the decline of the noble house of Rohan as a powerful political force. Guéméné had lived at a ruinously expensive pace, and his steward was alleged to have kept him in ignorance of the true state of his financial affairs. Parisians, however, were sceptical about the prince's protestations of innocence, for many had invested money with him in good faith, and stood to lose it all. 'One cannot move a step in the capital', wrote the Marquis de Bombelles, 'without hearing the name of M. de Guéméné

uttered with blame and anger.' Some people even wanted the prince hanged as 'a fraudulent bankrupt', for taking money he knew he could not repay.[57] But Guéméné was a Rohan, far too important to be sacrificed to the vengeance of the people. He and his wife lost their Court positions, but the King rescued them from utter shame. The prince's debts, originally estimated at 26,800,000 *livres* finally totalled thirty-three million, while his assets were only 26,900,000.[58] Louis XVI was obliged to buy Guéméné's assets to enable him to meet his creditors' demands, a charitable gesture which added another burden to the royal treasury, already depleted as a result of the American War.

The Duc de Chartres found a more subtle way out of his financial embarrassment at the time of the Guéméné scandal. His treasurer, afraid that Chartres would discover the disorder in his accounts, borrowed a large sum from the banker Kornmann for twenty-four hours to conceal a deficit. Chartres inspected his books, dismissed the treasurer, and took the money as his own! Kornmann could not get his loan repaid, and went bankrupt.

Well might Bombelles write that 'the luxury and confusion of our *seigneurs* are at their height'.[59] Of course, everything could still be dismissed with a joke, and the laws of *bon ton* really dictated that sang-froid and humour were the best weapons against any unfortunate pecuniary situation. When the Prince de Ligne heard of the disaster facing the Prince de Guéméné, he wrote him a letter from his magnificent estate of Beloeil near Brussels. 'My dear friend, in your unhappy position there is nothing better you can do than to come to Beloeil . . . I have taken a fancy to English gardens, and I could not erect a more handsome ruin in mine than my dear friend Guéméné.'[60]

Wit, as usual, conquered all.

4

Trysts and Tragedies

Louis XVI's subjects in Paris were not notable for either discretion or modesty, and vanity or malice often led them to make scandalous revelations about themselves and others in their memoirs. Yet one somehow suspects that even the most *blasé* and cynical members of the *beau monde* would have been at least mildly displeased to learn of the existence of one of the Parisian police force's best kept secrets – an entire department devoted solely to the task of compiling weekly reports on sexual activity in the capital for the edification of the Lieutenant of Police.[1] Or perhaps it was merely for his amusement. It is difficult to perceive the practical value of much of the information so laboriously collated by the 'department of gallantry and prostitution': how Monsieur de ＿＿＿ caught a disease from Mademoiselle X from the Comédie-Italienne, how a wealthy financier failed to perform satisfactorily *chez* Madame Y, how the Prince de ＿＿＿ ended his liaison with Madame de ＿＿＿ and was now keeping a mistress on the Chaussée d'Antin.

No matter how trivial the detail, the Lieutenant of Police was kept informed. What use he made of this *chronique scandaleuse* (of interest, conceivably, only to aggrieved spouses) is unclear. What is certain is that 'gallantry' was the principal recreational activity of Parisian high society, and the police deemed it sufficiently important to know who was indulging in this favourite pastime, and with whom, that they employed a veritable army of

spies to feed them information. One priest who complained to the authorities that his parish was 'infested with immoral women' received the following cool reply from a magistrate: 'Monsieur le curé, I want three thousand more.'[2] Perhaps that was why *les filles*, as Mrs Thrale was horrified to observe, were in the habit of wearing crucifixes as they patrolled the streets in search of customers!

The criminal activity associated with prostitution rightly interested the police, but why they also took such pains to acquire details of private liaisons is less clear. Possibly the practice originated with Louis XV, an extremely inquisitive man, who used to have personal letters sent through the Parisian *petite poste* opened and gossipy ones copied for his own entertainment. A greater mystery is how prostitution survived in a society where the purchase of sexual pleasures seemed so unnecessary. After a perusal of eighteenth-century French memoirs it is hard to disagree with the Comte de Ségur's assertion that France was the home of gallantry – bearing in mind that in France at that period, 'gallantry' was not something that earned soldiers rows of medals.

Galanterie is a word open to many interpretations, not all of them strictly translatable as 'gallantry' in its most frequently accepted sense in modern English. While *galanterie* still retained its medieval meaning of courtesy or chivalry, in the eighteenth century it usually described a love affair, with an emphasis on the physical rather than the emotional. Similarly, though *un galant homme* might possibly be brave and courteous, he was most definitely a ladies' man.

The prevalence of gallantry in Parisian high society during the eighteenth century is not simply attributable to the French love of romance, intrigue and seduction, although this should not be underestimated. What truly caused gallantry to flourish was neither romantic nor seductive, and involved intrigue of an altogether less tender kind: matrimony. For the upper classes, the marriage market was mercenary in the extreme. It was not at all rare for a marriage to take place between children, who usually remained with their parents until the union could be

consummated (occasionally they might be widowed before this happened!). Naturally, this allowed no personal choice of marriage partner, and often led to the yoking together of people of vastly differing tastes and interests. The drafting of aristocratic marriage contracts entailed months of negotiation and haggling over money, and when the lawyers had finished their work, the solemn articles were presented to the principals as a *fait accompli*. Wealth and prestige were the chief considerations of noble and bourgeois parents anxious to do well for their offspring. Marital harmony, so popular in sentimental fiction and plays, resulted only for a lucky few. Most survived without it, although they always resented the way they had been forced into unhappy matrimony.

The Duc de Lauzun complained of being married as a youth to 'a woman who neither loved me nor suited me', while the Prince de Ligne, as a slightly more mature twenty year old, was taken to Vienna by his father, introduced to his fourteen year old bride, and married the following day.[3] He remained faithful to her for a fortnight. Lauzun's wife was 'an angel of goodness' according to Madame de La Tour du Pin, who was a regular visitor to Madame de Lauzun's *hôtel* on the rue de Bourbon; her library was famous for its Rousseau manuscripts, which she had inherited from her grandmother, the Maréchale de Luxembourg. She nevertheless failed to hold the affections of the philandering Lauzun, and they parted after a few empty years. Madame de Ligne, who seems to have accepted her situation with good humour, bore her husband several children and turned a blind eye to his many infidelities. Good breeding always ensured that nothing so undignified as a quarrel ever took place between them.

Paris virtually overflowed with well-born men and women who endured similar loveless marriages, although the problem was not confined to the *beau monde*. In *Les Nuits de Paris*, Rétif de la Bretonne describes his rescue of a young woman from the Faubourg Saint-Antoine who had tried to frustrate the matrimonial schemes of her *petit bourgeois* father. He planned to marry her off to one of his middle-aged friends, so the unwilling

girl hastily got herself pregnant by the young man she loved, hoping this would change her father's mind. On the contrary, he locked her up, determined to hand the child to the Foundling Hospital as soon as it was born so that his daughter could still become the wife of a man she detested.[4] Fortunately Rétif intervened and she was at last happily united with her lover, albeit by adopting a strategy simply unavailable to daughters of the nobility and *haute bourgeoisie*, who were often summoned from convents to be married the same week. In fact, given the choice between an arranged marriage (which promised freedom if not happiness), and life as a reluctant nun, most girls would probably have opted for a husband. Even though he was likely to be totally incompatible, if he came from the same background he was aware of the rules of the game and would usually allow his wife to do as she pleased. There was no divorce in *ancien régime* France, so compromises had to be found; if couples stayed together, they often led separate lives.

The impossibility of divorce and the frequency of separation among ill-matched couples led to a great deal of concubinage. Mercier estimated that a third of the female population in Paris lived as concubines of noblemen, clerics, merchants and 'even workmen'.[5] So blurred was the distinction between married and unmarried women that 'Madame' served as a universal form of address. *Demoiselles* and *grisettes* added to the confusion in nomenclature. Generally, *demoiselles* were from good families, unmarried, and permitted to venture into society alone. *Grisettes*, so named from the grey cloaks formerly worn by Parisian shopgirls, came from poor families: 'they leave their poverty-stricken parents at the age of eighteen years and take rooms for themselves and live in their own way.'[6] Though most earned a frugal living working with their hands, particularly in dressmaking, they not unnaturally proved attractive to Parisian men. Many *grisettes* thus found themselves 'protectors', and the institution of marriage suffered another blow.

It is refreshing to discover that some people did not share the general dissatisfaction with matrimony, although if they valued the good opinion of fashionable society, they voiced their

happiness only in private. The Marquise d'Osmond was advised
by a well-meaning friend to conceal her affection for her husband whilst staying at Hautefontaine, where conjugal love was
the object of scorn and ridicule.[7] A lonely Marquis de Bombelles, engaged in a tedious embassy in Germany, was angry to hear
that rumours circulating at Versailles had it that he had sent for
his wife to join him because he suspected her of coquetry in his
absence. In reality he adored her, and was unusual too for a man
of his class in being an admirable father in an age when, as the
Prince de Ligne commented, 'it was not fashionable to be either
a good father or a good husband'.[8]

One remarkably unfashionable lady was the Marquise de La
Tour du Pin (until 1794 known as the Comtesse de Gouvernet),
who did not meet her husband until the articles of their marriage
contract were agreed in 1787. He was a twenty-eight year old
army officer, she a pretty seventeen year old blonde with
romantic expectations. She was not disappointed. Their love was
to endure the Revolution, the vicissitudes of exile and family
tragedies, but in the giddy early days of their marriage most of
their acquaintances found their happiness inexplicable. Madame
de Staël was not the only woman to urge the young Comtesse de
Gouvernet to capitalize on her good looks and take a lover. Had
she been blessed with such attractions, she declared, 'she would
have wanted to turn the world upside down'. When the happy
wife explained that she was perfectly content with her husband,
Madame de Staël's mystification was complete. 'Evidently,' she
concluded, 'you love him as your lover.'[9]

Although there might be some merit in remaining faithful to a
lover, fidelity to a husband was absurd. Madame de Staël herself
was not a woman to ignore the dictates of fashion. If the laws of
bon ton required that she submit to the embraces of men other
than her husband, she was far from unwilling to be *à la mode*,
despite her lack of beauty. Indeed, Madame de La Tour du Pin
thought it was her very plainness which drove Madame de Staël
'to yield without a struggle to the first man who showed himself
more aware of the beauty of her arms than the charms of her
mind'. Her marriage was one of convenience. Her husband,

seventeen years her senior, had been attracted initially by her wealth, but failed to maintain sufficient calm when faced with his bride's indifference. The handsome Baron de Staël, Swedish ambassador to France, actually committed the unpardonable error of falling in love with his own wife. It was to make him a very unhappy man.

Gouverneur Morris attended a dinner at the Neckers', at which both Madame de Staël and her husband were present. She flirted outrageously throughout the meal with Morris, who was sitting next to her, speaking in broken English so that M. de Staël could not understand. Morris, however, remained wary, very conscious of the baron's distress at his wife's behaviour. 'I tell her that he loves her distractedly, which she says she knows and that it renders her miserable.' After dinner, Morris talked to M. de Staël to set his mind at ease, and was regaled with a long tale of woe. 'He inveighs bitterly against the Manners of this Country and the Cruelty of alienating a Wife's Affections. He says the Women here are greater Whores with their Hearts and Minds than with their Persons.'[10] Poor M. de Staël. Love alone could have blinded him to his wife's many liaisons; the list of her lovers provokes admiration for her energy and unflagging romanticism. Her husband, as Frénilly rightly observed, 'earned from her the reputation of a fool', although 'he was truly a man of very good sense, great style, very good hearted, well-educated, a lover of literature, magnificent without ostentation, and cut a very noble figure as an ambassador'.[11] It was not enough to captivate the demanding Madame de Staël. The baron eventually realized the futility of trying to control her wandering affections, allowed her to give his name to the children she had by other men, and found comfort elsewhere.

The laws governing gallantry had to be scrupulously obeyed if it was to be fulfilling, for though affairs were generally conducted in a carefree manner, they were not completely spontaneous. Some could even be described in tactical and strategic terms, as the pursuit of love became a game which none of the players cared to lose. The Vicomte de Ségur, a fashionable young seducer with all the required attributes – looks, wit,

charm and, it has to be said, a bad character – told Gouverneur
Morris that 'the Pursuit of a Woman is like a Game of Chess,
where in Consequence of a certain set of Moves the Success is
certain'.[12]

Ladies too played by their own set of rules, for as Tilly
explained, 'in France women were chiefly occupied with repell-
ing advances or anticipating them'. Consequently they 'engaged
in a combat where they feigned to be conquered by skill', and
'surrendered with some difficulty in order that they might not
be abandoned on the following day; even coquetry was foreseeing enough never to be in a hurry.'[13] Thus men deluded
themselves that they had perfected the most effective battle plan,
whilst women (nursing different self-delusions) yielded on their
own terms. It was checkmate by consent.

General agreement also prevailed in the selection of players.
All men were eligible, provided they were of the same rank as
the ladies they hoped to conquer, though success naturally
depended on the individual; but not all women were pursued,
even by inveterate gallants. Only the most hardened rake would
attempt to seduce unmarried girls. It was not only dishonourable, but exceptionally difficult, as they were invariably guarded
by fearsome chaperones or locked in convents until marriage.
Similarly, women known for their virtue were avoided, since no
man cared to risk his reputation by failure.[14] Given the vast
army of women who were only too eager to escape irksome
matrimonial ties and devote themselves to amorous dalliance,
there was little prospect of anything but success.

Social life was itself conducive to gallantry. Married couples
seldom paid visits together; they had separate friends, and
usually also separate rooms. It was customary for ladies to
receive visitors while they dressed; Morris was very surprised to
find himself chatting to a female acquaintance while she performed her toilette – 'we have the whole undressing and dressing
except the Shift, and among other Things, washing the Arm Pitts
with Hungary Water'.[15] He was not the sort of man to allow
such intimacy to affect him, although Mercier claimed that
pretty women made their toilette twice every morning: once 'in

complete privacy', while the second toilette, to which visitors were admitted, was 'merely a game played out of coquetry'.[16] More daring coquettes also received callers when they were in the bath. If one thinks of Marat and Charlotte Corday, this French practice does not have much to recommend it!

The rituals accompanying gallantry did not always produce the correct response in the uninitiated. Morris's phlegmatic demeanour when surrounded by feminine beauty apparently displeased the Vicomte de Ségur, and, hoping to shock the American at a dinner party, the vicomte succeeded in locking himself and their attractive young hostess in an adjacent *cabinet* – leaving no doubt in the minds of fellow guests as to what he intended to do. When the smiling couple emerged a few minutes later, arms entwined, to explain that it was simply a joke, Morris was (for once) completely baffled.

Ségur, the reputed son of the Baron de Besenval, and 'as remarkable for Seduction as his Father', seems to have relished teasing Morris. When informed that no such thing as gallantry existed in America, he was 'incredulous' but 'positive that it could easily be introduced'. He 'next enquires of my Amours here', recorded Morris, who was forced to admit that he had none, because 'I dare not hazard offending a virtuous Woman'.[17] The vicomte's hearty laughter at this lame excuse altered Morris's perception of Parisian woman, and soon he was paying much more attention to tender glances in his direction. At a restaurant in the Palais Royal he had 'a good deal of light trivial conversation' with a Madame de Boursac and a Madame d'Espinchal, 'in which these Ladies intimate to me that their nuptial Bands do not at all straighten their Conduct, and it would seem that either would be content to form an Intrigue'.[18] However, nothing came of their encouragement, and an even greater amorous fiasco occurred when Morris, having received two passionate *billets doux* from an anonymous lady, failed to spot her at a rendezvous in the theatre and returned home exasperated: 'from the whole I collect that the Lady has infinite Address and that I am abominably stupid.'[19]

The Vicomte de Ségur ought perhaps to have given his

American protégé more intensive lessons in the rules of gallantry. Morris gradually learned them on his own, and his eventual conquest was not to be disdained. Adèle de Flahaut was twenty-eight, beautiful, well-educated, and the hostess of a salon of wits, literary figures and politicians in her grace-and-favour apartments in the Louvre. Her aristocratic mother had been obliged to make a hasty marriage to bourgeois Charles-François Filleul after a liaison with Louis XV which led to the birth of Adèle's elder sister, Julie. As the Marquise de Marigny, Julie was to become notorious for accompanying her lover, the flamboyant Cardinal de Rohan, on jaunts around Paris, thinly disguised as a priest. Adèle herself, married to the fifty-three year old Comte de Flahaut in 1779, when she was a mere eighteen, was 'not a sworn Enemy to Intrigue' as Morris correctly surmised at their first encounter in Madame de Tessé's salon at Versailles.[20] But in addition to her elegant manners, coquettish ways, and considerable sexual appetite (which as Morris was to discover, sometimes sought gratification at perilously inopportune moments), she had a penetrating and shrewd mind, and was later to earn a reputation as a novelist. Adèle's political flair was also exercised in the management of her love life, for she somehow succeeded in reconciling the rival claims of Talleyrand (then the Bishop of Autun, and father of her son Charles), Morris, and her husband, who was not perhaps so docile as he should have been.

The ingredients of a French farce are clearly visible in the love quadrangle that resulted. Morris arriving for a tête-à-tête only to find Talleyrand already ensconced in an armchair in Adèle's salon and determined to outstay him; M. de Flahaut coming home unexpectedly and forcing the postponement of an afternoon's love-making; even all three men maintaining a perfect sang-froid as they mistimed their visits and arrived at the loved one's door within minutes of each other.

The life of a *femme galante* was busy indeed, particularly if she also demanded that her lovers made intelligent conversation, wrote and translated poetry, and gave inside information or sensible opinions on the eventful political news of the day.

Morris passed each test successfully, though when he tried to claim his reward, Adèle, as a true coquette, created difficulties. She had, she said, made a 'Marriage of the Heart' with Talleyrand; how could she be unfaithful to him? After all, he was the father of her son.[21] By now fully conversant with the rules of gallantry, Morris issued an ultimatum and found that a short absence made Adèle's heart distinctly fonder.

Once admitted to all the privileges enjoyed by a lover, Morris was rapidly initiated into the duties they imposed. His horses and carriage were frequently called for to convey Adèle and her friends around Paris, his political knowledge was tapped for the preparation of essays on the constitution, and countless little favours were demanded – and granted, for Adèle's *savoir-faire* and her influential friends were also at Morris's disposal. In France a lover was always known as a 'friend', and lifelong friendship often resulted from affairs of gallantry. Women used liaisons as a means of gaining influence in many spheres of life, and their success in manipulating political decisions was far from negligible. It always paid to be on good terms with a minister's mistress. Of course, she might fall from favour, which made it all the more essential that she remained friends with her lover, or else found another who was more powerful. Few, however, could equal the record set by the Marquise de Monconseil (b.1708), described by Bombelles as 'mistress to five successive ministers in the same department', who in 1785 was still enjoying the influence conferred by her liaison with the Foreign Minister Vergennes over twenty years previously. She kept him informed daily of all the news in Paris, and her recovery from a severe illness in February 1785 occasioned public rejoicing.

During the dangerous and uncertain days before the final collapse of the French monarchy in 1792, Adèle de Flahaut had enough foresight to try to exact promises of marriage from both Morris and a young English peer she had ensnared, even though she was still legally bound to her husband. She should have known it was the swiftest way to end a love-affair. As the Vicomte de Ségur remarked when reminded of his long-standing attachment to Madame d'Oudenarde, whom he was preparing

to drop for the actress Madame Dugazon: 'There is no question of that now . . . *we are married.*'[22] Marriage, or an affair which continued for long enough to resemble it, was the end. Some liaisons did last for decades, achieving respectability as a result, but for most people, as Tilly noted, 'the spirit of gallantry and the manner of life' were such 'that one seldom had the inclination to continue the same union forever'.[23] Inevitably, therefore, Morris and his attractive countess drifted apart, but at least they retained fond memories of each other.

It would be wrong to assume that everyone who indulged in gallantry was equally fortunate. The stakes could be very high, and losing was sometimes fatal. Although a woman took the most risks in a love affair, damage to her reputation was the least of her problems. According to Madame de La Tour du Pin, no trouble was taken to conceal liaisons and 'women of high society were remarkable for the boldness with which they flaunted their amours'. Marital fidelity being held in such contempt, the only reputation worth preserving was that of a desirable woman; a lover thus became a badge of honour. Some ladies were known for their virtue, but they were 'ridiculed and dismissed as rustics'.[24] A good reputation was not an asset in the Parisian *beau monde*.

Madame de Matignon, the daughter of Bombelles's patron, the Baron de Breteuil, became a laughing-stock in 1782 when she resisted the advances of a friend of the Vicomte de Noailles. Piqued that he could not supplant the vicomte in her good graces, the rejected suitor penned an epigram 'which entertained the whole of Paris'.

> *Matignon me défend de paraître à sa vue.*
> *Je la perds; je ne peux la voir ni lui parler.*
> *Je la perds; mais je crois qu'il faut m'en consoler*
> *Car ce n'est, après tout, qu'une femme perdue.*[25]

Matignon banishes me from her sight.
I am losing her; I can neither see her nor speak to her.
I am losing her; but I believe I should console myself,
For, after all, she is only a lost woman.

Bombelles attributed the cutting last line to jealousy inspired by the elegant young Madame de Matignon's advantages in being 'a widow, fresh, pretty, rich and independent'. Such vengeful verses were exceedingly common, although not all ladies found them cruel. The elderly Maréchale de Luxembourg (formerly Duchesse de Boufflers) gloried in her reputation as a *femme galante*, and long after she had ceased to enslave the courtiers of Louis XV would sing with gusto the following tribute to her charms.

> *Quand Boufflers parut à la Cour*
> *On crut voir la mère d'Amour;*
> *Chacun s'empressait à lui plaire*
> *Et chacun l'avait à son tour.*

> When Boufflers appeared at Court
> One seemed to see the mother of Love.
> Every man made haste to please her,
> And each one had her in his turn.

In the reign of Louis XVI, it was a mark of distinction to be received by Madame de Luxembourg. But even with such blatant disregard for reputation, certain forms still had to be observed. At Hautefontaine, for example, though conversation was often licentious, a gentleman could not even rest his arm on a lady's chair, let alone sit with her on the same sofa.[26] Such behaviour not unnaturally created confusion for gossip-mongers: 'a man is given a mistress who is not his, another is denied the favours of a lady whom he had enjoyed longer than was his wish.'[27] For a woman, the secret was not to make her husband look a fool. If he had affairs of his own, he was likely to countenance his wife's amours without resentment. Madame de La Tour du Pin's assertion about acknowledged liaisons, how-ever, probably applied to only a small number of high society women, who were merely continuing the tradition of open gallantry established during the reign of Louis XV.

Many ladies in slightly less elevated circles, or those burdened with jealous husbands, certainly did take the trouble to maintain

a respectable reputation – but the price of hypocrisy could be impossibly high. The greatest risk incurred by a woman in affairs of gallantry was, of course, pregnancy. If she were lucky, her lover's child could be passed off as her husband's. If she were not, the alternatives were decidedly grim. The Founding Hospital in Paris took in 6,000 abandoned infants every year. Many did not survive the rudimentary nursing which was available; those that lived were sent to the country and brought up very democratically indeed, for the same hard life awaited the unwanted offspring of noblewoman and servant girl alike. A 'lady of quality' who wanted to give her child a better chance of survival might have preferred another well-known arrangement: a trip under an assumed name to a distant province, where the baby would be born and placed with a respectable family who would never connect it to its mother in the glittering social whirl of Paris.

Even these far from satisfactory solutions required a degree of tolerance from a cuckolded husband, who had to consent to the subterfuge necessary for a successful smokescreen. Not all men were so obliging, and terror of their husbands' wrath forced some women into desperate remedies. Adèle de Flahaut told Gouverneur Morris how an acquaintance, Madame de Villeblanche, 'died a Martyr to Gallantry'.

> She admitted the Embraces of all who offered, only requiring Secrecy. She was with Child when her Husbd. returned, and in taking violent Medicines to procure Abortion, broke a Vessel in her Stomach. All this is known since her Decease, but previous thereto she had preserved a Reputation tolerably fair.[28]

Such deaths from abortion-inducing drugs were not as rare as might be supposed. The Comte de Tilly's liaison with a young Madame de Broc in his native city of Le Mans ended tragically in 1785 when she took 'a drug which a surgeon had assured her offered no danger' in order 'to avoid giving birth to a being not yet formed'.[29] Three weeks later she died of haemorrhages, though her demise was so sudden and unexpected that many

people believed Tilly himself had poisoned her. The truth, however, could not be told, for she had enjoyed the esteem of the whole city, and provincial morals were not nearly so vitiated as those of Paris.

Tilly was to escape with nothing worse than a grieving heart, perhaps pierced a little by his lover's deathbed confession of how she had killed both their child and herself; one is dismayed to report that it had only a temporary effect on his rakish behaviour. Had her husband known the truth, he could have challenged Tilly to a duel, although this was not a discreet method of revenge, since it exposed the origin of the quarrel in a way hardly likely to enhance a woman's reputation.

Tilly relates the chilling tale of two girls who attracted the attention of a dishonourable nobleman while they were at a convent school in Arras. Against all the laws of gallantry and decency, and in defiance of monastic walls and vigilance, the roué succeeded in seducing them both. Shortly afterwards, one girl asked to leave. A week after her return home she told her brother she was pregnant and gave him the name of her seducer, before also admitting that she had taken poison. Medical attention came too late to save her, but her death could not be avenged. Her heartbroken brother (Tilly's close friend) was forbidden by his father to challenge the roué to a duel because his sister's honour demanded that the whole affair be shrouded in silence.[30]

Duels nevertheless arose from the flimsiest pretexts, and many were fatal. 'France is the country of duels', noted Tilly, who denounced the practice of settling every quarrel by cold steel.[31] No insult, slur or insinuation could pass unavenged, and death could result from the most trivial remark. That duelling was not regarded in law as a crime only encouraged this bloody method of arbitration. Whereas in England a man who killed another in a duel usually had to flee the country to avoid being hanged as a murderer, a Frenchman 'often went to the Opéra the day after having killed a man in the Bois de Boulogne'.[32] The Maréchal de Richelieu, a notorius roué who died at the age of ninety-two in 1788, was not at all exceptional for the century in

having killed two men in duels and wounded countless others. His only punishment was a brief spell in the Bastille for calling out a royal duke. His 'affairs of honour' were usually related to women, but the Comte de Ségur actually fought a fellow army officer over a hat! Both were garrisoned at the time in Lille, and their quarrel arose at the theatre.

> Monsieur de Villeneuve, a lieutenant in the regiment of infantry of the Dauphin, took his seat by my side, and said to me: 'Sir, you have thrown down my hat which was upon that chair.' I had, in fact, done so quite unintentionally on sitting down. I made him a polite apology, but he replied with unaccountable ill-humour, that such an act of impertinence could not be redressed by a bad excuse.[33]

Ségur therefore promptly challenged Villeneuve, and they left during the interval to settle the affair. The result was a wounded Villeneuve, who refused Ségur's offers of assistance, telling him to return to the theatre to catch the end of the performance. Afterwards, Ségur sought out his opponent at his lodgings, saw that he received the attentions of a doctor, and actually became his friend. Yet their pointless dispute could so easily have proved fatal.

Duelling was one facet of French life that did not disappear as a result of the Revolution, and was in fact common for much of the nineteenth century. Madame de La Tour du Pin's eldest son was killed by a fellow staff officer after he refused all apologies made for some sneering remarks about his uniform, and Madame de Staël lost her second son to the murderous skill of a Russian with whom he had quarrelled at the gaming table. Perhaps the inappropriate glamour which surrounded duelling gave rise to the difficulty of its abolition. Ségur's combat in Lille, as he was pleased to discover, 'far from drawing down any disgrace upon me, brought me into greater vogue and contributed to increase my success both at Court and in town'.[34]

Duelling was naturally an occupational hazard for roués, for whom gallantry was not simply a pastime, but almost a *raison*

d'être. Although the word *roué* originally described a criminal (i.e., a man executed by being broken on the wheel), by the 1780s its more familiar modern usage was fashionable. 'People say of a man of rank who is licentious, he is a great *roué*,' wrote Mercier, 'his effrontery and audacity justify his vices.'[35] Noble birth and wealth also helped to palliate the sins for which a lesser man would have been condemned, and good looks and charm were even greater assets. Though a roué and a gallant pursued the same ends, certain subtle differences distinguished one from the other. The roué's quest was less likely to be for love, his liasons often conducted purely for the pleasure of chalking up yet another tribute to his virility. He also wanted the world to know he was a sexual dynamo, and many a woman's reputation was to be lost as the ink dried on the vainglorious memoirs of an old roué.

It is interesting to note that life for two roués who were highly active in Paris during the reign of Louis XVI started in a similar fashion. The Duc de Lauzun and the Comte de Tilly also both left memoirs, but as social and literary documents, Tilly's are far superior to Lauzun's self-absorbed tale. The mothers of both men died giving birth to them, and their fathers were not the most attentive of parents. 'The difficulty of finding a good tutor for me made my father entrust the task to a lackey of my late mother, who knew how to read and could write tolerably well,' confesses Lauzun, whose father seemed a very shadowy figure in his life.[36] He was fortunate in that his lackey-cum-tutor had the good sense to engage 'the most fashionable teachers of all kinds' to conduct the real business of his education. Tilly, similarly 'entrusted to valets and some sort of tutor', did not receive much learning until he entered the household of Queen Marie-Antoinette at the age of fourteen, and was swiftly initiated into the curriculum followed by royal pages at their school in Versailles.[37]

Court life played a large part in the upbringing of many roués. Perhaps the presence of so many attractive and amorous women was the key to future developments, although Tilly claims he first felt the stirrings of sexual desire at the tender age of nine. The object of his passion was his father's housekeeper, who

encouraged his precocious advances for the sole purpose of handing him over to his enraged parent for chastisement.[38] Full satisfaction was not to come until later, and then in an inglorious way. An outing to Paris with a fellow page at the age of fifteen led to a night with a prostitute and venereal disease. Tilly responded well to treatment and recovered quickly, but his friend was ill for much longer, and it was on his account that Tilly's reputation at Court suffered.[39] The Prince de Ligne recounts an equally tawdry first seduction, again at the age of fifteen. He was returning home from Vienna, where he had just been appointed a Court chamberlain, and to celebrate this honour, succumbed to the charms of a chambermaid at the Black Bear Inn at Munich, 'in a little corner of the house which is not at all fit to be named'.[40]

By these standards, Lauzun was a king. He had not been long at Versailles before he noticed that his handsome face earned him enticing smiles from ladies at Court, but at the age of fourteen, and brought up with little knowledge of women, he was not sufficiently aware of their significance. A tête-à-tête with Madame d'Esparbès (cousin of Madame de Pompadour) led to nothing but an embarrassing conversation which left him in no doubt that he was considered a complete boor. Something had to be done. Lauzun betook himself to Paris, and after a fortnight's 'lessons' from a dancer at the Opéra, Mademoiselle Desmarques, was ready to do battle. He reported with no show of false modesty that his teacher was so impressed she refused all offers of payment for her tuition. His next encounter with the disdainful Madame d'Esparbès had a much more passionate outcome, and Lauzun's reputation for gallantry was established. He rapidly adopted the philosophy and jargon of a roué.

> Madame d'Esparbès's person pleased me a great deal, and my vanity was infinitely flattered to have a woman. I was honourable enough not to speak of it; but it gave me inexpressible pleasure if people guessed it, and in this regard she gave me every satisfaction, for she treated me in such a manner as to show the truth to the whole world.[41]

A roué seldom loved a woman; what really mattered was whether he *had* her, 'according to the noble and chaste jargon of the Court', as Chateaubriand sarcastically remarked in his condemnation of Lauzun.[42] Two, however, could play at that game. The teenage duke was dropped by Madame d'Esparbès for the Prince de Condé after only a few weeks. Lauzun became a member of the Choiseul set, and dallied briefly with the young Comtesse de Choiseul-Stainville, whose mad passion for the actor Clairval led to her incarceration in a convent at Nancy under a *lettre de cachet* obtained by her ugly and jealous older husband. Her name was often mentioned as a warning of the fate which awaited the unlucky.

Lauzun, of course, was never at a loss for female company, though any woman who fell into his arms was liable to suffer as a result. Like all roués, his vanity was insufferable, and could only be truly gratified by the knowledge that his love affairs were public property. Eighteenth-century gallantry was very different from medieval courtly love, in which discretion was essential. On the contrary, roués made a point of recording their conquests, and even compared notes, as Morris discovered when he asked Adèle de Flahaut about a mutual acquaintance.

> Enquiring of her [Adèle] who Madame de Fersensac is she tells me that it is the Wife of a Relation of Montesquiou. That Narbonne had her as appeared from her Letters which he shewed to the bishop d'Autun [Talleyrand], for this it seems is a Practice with these Gentlemen.[43]

This very ungentlemanly practice could lead to what one might term vengeful liaisons. The Comte de Narbonne, another fashionable roué, principally remembered as Madame de Staël's lover (he was the father of her two sons), proposed 'a pleasant Vengeance' with Adèle de Flahaut after discovering that Talleyrand, her lover, had taken advantage of his friendship to seduce Madame de Staël. Morris, another closely interested party, actually sat through the whole proposition with perfect composure![44]

Two or three concurrent affairs appear to have been favoured by roués. The Prince de Ligne once loved three women at the same time, which he seemed surprised to discover 'cost me much embarrassment and many reproaches'.[45] But he claims his feelings for all three were genuine, and that giving up any one would have hurt him! Tilly, too, vows that all his conquests were motivated by love rather than lust. One has serious doubts after reading the dizzying tale of his exploits, especially how, as a mere youth, he had an affair with an older Madame de M___, then seduced her ward, Mademoiselle de Lorville, after a sham marriage at Versailles. When the girl became pregnant, Madame de M___ (who Tilly claimed still loved him) buried the whole affair in oblivion by whisking Mademoiselle de Lorville off to the country and renewed respectability. Like so many of his fellows, Tilly had a complete and callous disregard for the fruits of his liaisons; the Prince de Ligne was unusual in providing for his illegitimate offspring (though none survived childhood), and adopted his eldest son's illegitimate daughter, who became the darling of his old age.

However dishonourable their own behaviour, roués observed double standards and still expected women to treat them with decency and respect. Lauzun was furious when he learned from a servant that 'M. le Comte d'Artois had Lady Barrymore at the same time as I did', and a melodramatic scene with the unrepentant Englishwoman soon brought that particular affair to a close.[46] Angrier still was the Prince de Ligne when asked to pay for his pleasures; such an unprecedented demand was an insult to his virility.

> I was too foppish, and dare I say it, too handsome and too much in demand besides, to pay. The purchase of pleasures seemed odious to me. However, one day I allowed myself to succumb to that stupidity . . . Mlle Grandi told me that I was the only man in the entire supper party who had not had her, and she said her fee was a hundred *louis*. I gave her sixty. She accepted them and refused me.[47]

Ligne, enraged, found another forty *louis*, but the experience that resulted was far more painful than pleasurable. His wounded self-esteem took some while to recover.

Hurt pride of a different kind led the Vicomte de Ségur to exact a vile revenge in which his sexuality was the main weapon. A cool, tactical pursuit of a woman had horrible consequences, and it was all because her lover had had the temerity to criticize Ségur's literary ability. In fact, the bold M. de Thiard called Ségur's poems worthless. Instead of laughing off the remark, or challenging him to a duel, the vicomte decided on a roué's revenge. He travelled to Normandy, where Thiard's mistress lived, and seduced her after an assiduous courtship. Having made sure of victory by ascertaining she was pregnant, he told her he despised her and returned to Paris to boast of his success. The lady died giving birth to Ségur's daughter, and her widower, unwilling to have his wife's name further besmirched, brought the child up as his own.[48]

The story is worthy of Laclos. Equally resembling a novel, though less tragic, was Tilly's encounter at Versailles with a *femme galante* who might well be termed a *rouée*. While walking back to his lodgings one evening, Tilly was accosted outside the inn *Au Juste* by a veiled woman who asked him to accompany her home. She led him to a house in the rue de l'Orangerie, and when she removed her veil, confounded his expectations by proving to be young, beautiful, and refined. Having mistaken her for a prostitute, he apologized profusely and prepared to leave; but the lady made it clear that she wanted him to stay. She went on to seduce him, and a baffled Tilly left the house much later without even knowing her name.

He learned it some days later at a dinner given by the Prince de Montbarey, Minister of War, to which his mystery lover had also been invited. Despite his confusion, she treated him as a perfect stranger, but by a carefully orchestrated conversation with their hostess, let it be known that she was married and newly arrived at Versailles to take up a post at Court. She also succeeded in making another assignation with Tilly, who arrived promptly at their rendezvous. Further love-making followed

before the lady chided him for nearly betraying her at the dinner by his surprise and embarrassment. Curious, and possibly hoping for a compliment, Tilly enquired if she had been expressly looking for him outside the inn.

'I was looking for pleasure.'
'Whom were you after?'
'The first man I should take a fancy to.'

Hypocritical to the core, Tilly was absolutely horrified by her candour. But the lady was shameless and cynical. After all, she told him, 'it is merely appearances that deserve to be taken seriously'.[49] Her unconventional approach to gallantry would ensure that her amours remained secret, and she would keep her good name.

Her philosophy is not unlike that of the scheming Madame de Merteuil in Laclos's *Les Liaisons Dangereuses*, a novel that created a scandal when it was first published in March 1782. Like many works liable to inflame the censors, the book purported to be printed in Amsterdam, but it was available from the Parisian bookseller Durand in the rue Galande, and became an instant success. Its author, Choderlos de Laclos, a forty-one year old Lieutenant-Colonel in the artillery known for his military skill and the probity of his conduct, was not to remain anonymous for long. His work brought him an *entrée* into the very society so mercilessly exposed in his novel; it was surely rather gratifying, not to mention deeply ironic, that the libertine Vicomte de Ségur should have been responsible for placing Laclos in the household of the even more licentious Duc d'Orléans.

In Bombelles's opinion, *Les Liaisons Dangereuses* ought to have been banned immediately, although he thought it 'the most wittily written novel which has yet appeared'. Laclos's portrait of high society was only too convincing, and Bombelles made the common error of identifying him with the anti-hero, Valmont; but 'a work written to lose him his reputation makes him fashionable, because all we want is wit'.[50] Tilly's opinion of the novel is both self-revealing and highly amusing.

It is a book for which its author has not feared to claim a moral purpose, though it is an outrage to the morals of the whole nation; it is a book that every woman admits having read, though it should have been condemned by all men as deserving to be burnt by the hand of the public executioner.[51]

Strong stuff indeed from such a paragon of virtue as the gallant Comte de Tilly! In fact, Laclos's irony seems to have entirely escaped some readers who could not see that his characters condemn themselves through their own words. Perhaps readers identified too readily with the protagonists. The Marquise de Coigny, 'a witty woman, immoral to excess, and at one time worse than a courtesan', a great love of the Duc de Lauzun and grudgingly acknowledged by Marie-Antoinette to be 'the Queen of Paris', had her doors closed to Laclos when *Les Liaisons Dangereuses* came out, apparently believing he had used her as the model for Madame de Merteuil.[52]

Many people saw the book as a *roman-à-clef*, with the Maréchal de Richelieu widely supposed to have been the original of Valmont; but according to Tilly, Laclos's sources lay elsewhere. When both men were in London in 1789, Tilly took the opportunity to tackle the normally reserved, even saturnine author about his celebrated novel. Laclos described how, bored with garrison life on the Île de Ré, he resolved to write a book 'which would make a sensation *and echo over the world after I had left it.*' Valmont's adventures were based on those of a friend 'who bears a name celebrated in the sciences', whilst Madame de Merteuil was but 'a feeble copy' of a 'Marquise de L.T.D.P.M.' he had known when stationed in Grenoble, 'of whom the whole town used to tell stories worthy of the days of the most insatiable Roman empresses.' The Prévan story 'had happened a long time before to M. de Rochech', an officer in the musketeers. Laclos also set down 'several little affairs of my youth which were rather spicy', and invented the rest, particularly the virtuous Madame de Tourvel.[53]

Fact or fiction, his book was to have a profound, even revolutionary impact, for it not only exposed debauchery in high

places, but also the hypocritical way it was concealed. It also whetted the public's appetite for more lurid revelations, largely satisfied by the libellous publications about the Queen which began to appear. Surely it was no coincidence that many of these emanated from the Palais Royal, where Laclos rapidly established an ascendancy over the Duc d'Orléans. He was to become a model republican, and according to Orléans's former mistress Grace Elliott, during the Revolution 'that monster Laclos' was 'the cause of all the crimes which the Orléanist faction has been supposed to commit'.[54] Perhaps one should therefore take note of Tilly's final judgement that *Les Liaisons Dangereuses* was 'one of those disastrous meteors which appeared in a blazing sky at the end of the eighteenth century'.[55] It certainly more than lived up to its author's sensational expectations.

Laclos's implicit warning of social collapse brought on by moral degeneracy went unheeded, and scenes like those described in his novel were replicated throughout high society. For those who had neither time nor inclination to master the rules and rituals of gallantry, less elaborate means of sexual gratification were always to be found in Louis XVI's Paris – especially at the Palais Royal. Morris soon discovered the real business of this aptly named 'pleasure garden' on a visit in June 1789, when he fell into conversation with 'a Saxon Girl, just landed from the Diligence to supply the flesh Market of this Capital'. His tidy mind duly recorded that 'she works on Shares with the Matron to whose Hospitality and Protection she is now indebted'.[56]

Prostitution was in fact tightly controlled by 'matrons' or bawds, who aimed to please their customers by offering a variety of *filles*. As Mercier explained, 'you may call for plump or slender, ardent or sulky, pale or passionate, or even for a charmer with a limp', and each girl had a nickname which indicated her type.[57] The only rule governing this 'flesh market' was a ban on virgins, in order to prevent the deflowering of innocent young girls. Otherwise, the police merely kept an ear to all the latest gossip retailed by the prostitutes they recruited as spies, and never tried to curb their spies' excesses. As a consequence, disease was rife. Both Mercier and Rétif de la

Bretonne called for reforms of prostitution in order to stamp out venereal disease, but their arguments were ignored.

Morris, uncharacteristically foolish, once accepted an invitation from 'a Lady' at her window in the Palais Royal to 'pay a Visit', but tried to beat a hasty retreat when he could see she was diseased. She denied she was ill, and promptly locked Morris in her room in order to prevent his departure. When he threatened her with the police, she merely laughed and said she was already well known to them. Morris decided to sit it out, and was released from his imprisonment only when she realized she would gain nothing from him. He was escorted downstairs by 'a Profusion of Expressions whose Excellence consists more in Energy than Elegance'.[58]

Life for many such women was far from pleasant or profitable, though some managed to elevate themselves to the rank of 'courtesans', very superior creatures indeed, who consumed many a noble fortune and were the envy and despair of gallant ladies. It was hard for amateurs to compete with such consummate professionals. One such courtesan, not yet at the zenith of her career, is described in an anecdote recorded by Madame de Staël in 1786 for the amusement of King Gustav III of Sweden.

The Maréchal de Duras, First Lord of the Bedchamber and in charge of the department of the Comédie-Française, a few days ago received a visit from a young lady who wanted to make her début.

'Well, Mademoiselle,' he said to her, 'which roles do you wish to undertake?'

'Monsieur, it's all one to me; I can recite comic or tragic verse, whatever is wanted.'

'And who taught you to recite?'

'Ah, Monsieur, it was an abbé who took an interest in me. I may say that he taught me with extreme care, but nevertheless it is not he who has been most useful to me.'

'Who then, Mademoiselle?'

'An important vicar, with whom I spent some time, and who, I may say, truly loved me, and greatly helped to school my talent.'

'*Parbleu!*' said the Maréchal, 'we go up by rank. Is that all,

Mademoiselle?'

'No, Monsieur,' she replied, 'the man who is the most sincerely interested in me, and who still gives me lessons, is a bishop – who will recommend me, if you wish.'[59]

A story which lends a decidedly French slant to the proverbial tale of the bishop and the actress! The two *abbés* involved were the poet Jacques Delille and the Abbé d'Espagnac (who made a fortune speculating in the Compagnie des Indes), while the bishop was coadjutor to the Bishop of Orléans, M. de Jarente. The decadent moral climate which allowed gallantry to flourish unchallenged could not be more succinctly illustrated.

The Revolution dealt gallantry a heavy blow, which women in particular felt severely. During the reign of Louis XVI, women were supreme; in Tilly's words, they 'embellished every assembly and every moment'.[60] Revolution toppled them from their pedestal, and gallantry, though it survived Robespierre's asexual idealism and Napoleon's bogus bourgeois morality, nevertheless lost much of its charm. The elegance, wit and attention to women disappeared as politics, rather than feminine beauty, became the chief focus of interest for men. This was a serious loss indeed, for with a written constitution and a clearly defined political structure from which women were entirely excluded, what role remained for all those ladies who used to settle affairs of state in seductive boudoirs?

Quite a number of them wrote their memoirs or semi-autobiographical novels, which evoked the gaiety and grace of the past. One can hear the rustling skirts, smell the powder and pomade, even catch the whispers and the sighs. But nostalgia is seldom a completely reliable historian. How does one distinguish a heartfelt protestation of love from the cynical ploys of a callous roué, or reconcile romance with libertinism, passion with death from abortion? Gallantry would seem to have been a multi-faceted delusion. Though its glamour was never better captured than by Fragonard, its cruel and sordid underbelly would have taxed even the talents of Hogarth.

5

Age of Miracles?

The facile labels which characterize the eighteenth century as the 'Age of Enlightenment' or the 'Age of Reason' can be very misleading. Though the century saw a rapid evolution in political philosophy, important geographical and scientific discoveries, and the birth of heavy industry, it was an 'enlightenment' which nonetheless left many in the dark. Reason also appeared to be wanting in an age that glorified the emotions at the expense of the intellect, made 'sensibility' a virtue, yet at the same time failed to redress those ills of society which evoked attractive tears of sympathy and compassion. One might more justly call the eighteenth century, in European terms, an age of contradictions. Fabulous wealth lived side-by-side with desperate poverty, cynical logic cloaked itself in sentimental jargon, great technical progress coexisted with archaic political structures, and atheism was but one of many alternatives to established religion.

Louis XVI's France was no stranger to these contradictions; in fact, as a leading power, she probably exemplified them more than many other European countries. Politically France remained locked in feudalism right up to the Revolution. In agriculture, both structure and method were medieval, and the detrimental effect this had on productivity was ultimately disastrous for a nation with a large and ever increasing population. But although industrial growth was slighted for the fine arts (a result, according to Morris, of 'a Government oppressive to

117

Industry but favourable to Genius'), France was highly advanced in both science and engineering.[1]

Amongst other things, the reign of Louis XVI saw great improvements in transport. New roads were built to a high standard, although the detested *corvée* system still demanded the forced labour of peasants in their construction, and the commercial potential of canals was also beginning to be realized. A growing awareness of the causes of disease led to large scale works to improve water supplies and sewerage, while advances in medicine finally began to stem the ravages of smallpox. The royal family took the lead in encouraging inoculation: Louis XVI and his brothers were all inoculated at Marly in June 1774, shortly after his accession, their decision probably hastened by Louis XV's death from smallpox, which struck down many Bourbons during the eighteenth century.

As a technically minded man, Louis XVI also took a keen and active interest in the modernization of the French armed forces. Prestige buildings, such as those erected by Louis XIV to celebrate his own glory were not really Louis XVI's style; but no expense was spared for works deemed to have a sound practical value. The fortification of Cherbourg against attack by the British Navy even drew the King from splendid isolation at Versailles to view the new harbour in 1786. He was equally anxious to modernize the French fleet, and the costs incurred in building new ships, as well as in re-equipping the army (which could boast the best artillery in Europe), added greatly to the national debt. It is ironic that Louis XVI was to be plunged into the horrors of the Revolution because of his inability to control this debt, bequeathing to the revolutionaries the impressive arsenal he had amassed. They were to employ it to devastating effect as republican armies spread across the Continent.

Innovative and audacious they undoubtedly were, yet republican generals failed to exploit an important invention which captured the imagination of the French public during the early 1780s – the hot-air balloon. Often called a *montgolfière* after its inventors, Joseph and Etienne Montgolfier, paper manufacturers from Annonay in the Haut Vivarais, the *ballon aérostatique*

opened up vast new vistas to a France eager for change and novelty. The Comte de Ségur was probably not alone in seeing the military potential of the balloon (what better way to launch a surprise assault on England?), or in wishing to make a trans-atlantic crossing in a *montgolfière*, which became the talk of Paris after its maiden flight on 5 June 1783. The ascent took place at Annonay before a crowd of local dignitaries, who watched the wood-and-paper structure float to a height of 6,000 feet in a matter of minutes before it fell to the ground.

Paris could hardly wait to see this wonderful machine, and the first ascent in the capital took place from the Tuileries on 27 August 1783. The balloon this time had been built by the Montgolfiers' collaborator Jacques Charles with the Robert brothers, who substituted hydrogen for the hot air employed in the *montgolfière*. It nevertheless fell to Etienne Montgolfier himself to give a demonstration of his flying machine at Versailles on 19 September, in the presence of the entire royal family and thousands of enthralled spectators. The azure *montgolfière*, shaped like an inverted pear, sixty feet high and forty feet in diameter, was released from its moorings at 1.10 p.m. after being filled with a 'gas' produced by burning straw and wool, and took a sheep, a duck, a cockerel, and a barometer on a short westward journey of one and a half miles. Bombelles reported that Louis XVI expressed 'great satisfaction' at the success of the flight; the only victim was the cockerel, which broke its foot. Among uses of the balloon suggested by the King's physicist, Le Roy, was the lifting of heavy objects on building sites, the salvage of ships which ran aground, the dispatch of messages from besieged towns, and the rescuing the prisoners from hostile fortresses![2]

Animals had been entrusted to the mercy of the winds; it now remained for a human to test the balloon's capability as a means of aerial transport. The Duc de Chartres, quick to recognize the *montgolfière*'s mass appeal, sponsored the first manned flight from the gardens of his château at La Muette on 21 November 1783. It was an overcast autumn day, but hordes of Parisians turned out to cheer on the two daring aeronauts, the young

Pilâtre de Rozier (whose honorary Court post enabled him to indulge his passion for physics and chemistry), and the Marquis d'Arlandes, an infantry officer. At a quarter past noon, the *montgolfière* floated up and away towards Passy, its sky-blue paper casing decorated in gold with the King's monogram, fleurs-de-lis, and the signs of the zodiac – a somewhat eclectic array of symbolism. Pilâtre de Rozier was the undoubted hero of the flight, during which the balloon reached an altitude of 3,000 feet, landing twenty-five minutes after take-off on the Butte aux Cailles. Just over a week later, Jacques Charles and Nicolas Robert took to the skies from the gardens of the Tuileries in a hydrogen-inflated balloon; their safe landing at Nesle earned Charles a royal pension of 2,000 *livres*.

Further manned flights followed as the fame of this marvellous new invention spread across Europe. London witnessed a balloon ascent in 1784, and it was not long before a flight across the Channel was attempted. The intrepid Jean-Pierre Blanchard and his English companion, Dr Jefferies, crossed from Dover to Guines in two and three-quarter hours on 7 January 1785. Blanchard was also royally rewarded, though Jefferies, who had signed a legal document undertaking to throw himself into the sea should the balloon lose too much height, merely obtained a dinner at Versailles.

Spurred on by Blanchard's success, Pilâtre de Rozier and a Monsieur Romain attempted a crossing from Boulogne to England in a balloon which combined the methods of the Montgolfiers with those of Charles and Robert – fire and hydrogen. Both aeronauts fell to their deaths off the French coast on 15 June 1785 as the balloon caught fire and disintegrated. This horrible accident spelt the end of the *montgolfière* in much the same way as the crash of the R101 signalled the decline of the airship, although as Madame de Staël recorded in the very same month as the disaster, plans were afoot for even more ambitious balloon expeditions.

> . . . this cruel accident occupies Paris. It is said, however, that M. Meusnier, an engineer and a man of sense and learning, wants to

circle the globe in a balloon with an aerial frigate which could hold twenty people; but one hundred thousand *écus* are required for it to succeed. . . . There is talk of opening a subscription, but rich people, as always, do not have even a small *écu* in their pockets.[3]

Whether a lack of funds or the horror inspired by the accident was responsible, public enthusiasm for ballooning decreased noticeably, and the very real progress that had been made in aerial transport was gradually forgotten, superseded by new miracles. The reign of Louis XVI in fact witnessed a marked reaction against scientific and technical advances, and a strong upsurge of interest in the paranormal, occultism, and alternative medicine. The unremitting quest for amusement might explain the popularity of some of these decidedly unscientific and irrational fads, while the abysmal state of organized religion probably fuelled the growth of mysticism. Even before its death throes, the *ancien régime* was undergoing something of a 'new age' revival.

One highly popular diversion of the Parisian *beau monde* during the 1770s was Freemasonry, often cited as an important source of political dissent which contributed to the downfall of the monarchy. Yet the King was himself a Freemason, as were most members of the royal family, and the Masonic events recorded by memoir writers appear to have been harmless and apolitical. The active participation of women, including the Queen, constituted one salient difference from contemporary Freemasonry. High society flocked to join lodges, each of which had a different name, usually indicative of a moral virtue. The Prince de Ligne belonged to several lodges in Paris; one, 'La Persévérance' counted the Duc d'Orléans's mistress, Madame de Genlis, as a member. Meetings were attended in fancy costume (each lodge had its own), and generally consisted of the performance of silly penitences for peccadilloes which the lodge president deemed punishable.[4] Shades of the confessional thus appeared in this pseudo-religion, in which men were always called 'brothers' and women 'sisters'. But in all other respects,

Masonic lodges were little more than exclusive clubs, providing yet more occasions for high society to dress up and gossip. Initial interest in these meetings waned, although a resurgence of activity occurred in the 1780s.

The Marquis de Bombelles, however, found his lodge exceedingly boring, and only the insistence of a friend made him attend the fête given by 'La Candeur' to another lodge, 'La Fidelité' in March 1784. The members were 'of distinguished rank', and required all their good manners to sit through the initiation of two new 'sisters', during which the lodge president, the Marquis de Gouy, exercised his vocal chords in long and tedious speeches. The 'crowning' of Montgolfier and a young hero of the American War followed, before supper was served to the hundred guests. Afterwards the lodge was turned into a playhouse for the performance of a comedy by Riccobini given by the Comédie-Italienne, and proceedings ended with a ball. Bombelles, utterly exhausted, retired as the play commenced![5] It was hardly an evening devoted to plotting the overthrow of the government.

Perhaps the supposed Masonic involvement in the Revolution may be explained by the prominent role of Orléanists in Freemasonry. The Duc d'Orléans was French Grand Master, having been elected to succeed the Comte de Clermont in 1771, while his sister, the Duchesse de Bourbon, was 'Grand Mistress', and a fervent follower of the Illuminati.[6] The Duc de Lévis actually claimed that certain aristocrats found a French equivalent of the House of Lords in Masonic lodges, so one cannot rule out a function in the shaping of political thought.[7] The very mention of the House of Lords, however, points more to the influence of *anglomanie* than to any philosophy inherent in Freemasonry. What is of interest is the founding of the 'Neuf Soeurs' lodge in 1776, which boasted a brilliant membership, including Franklin, Voltaire and Helvétius – a combination that made political dynamite.

Franklin's involvement in Freemasonry drew in many French aristocrats who played a prominent part in securing American independence, most notably Lafayette, and it would be highly

improbable that their lodge nights were spent playing party games. But the question of the relationship between Freemasonry and the Revolution remains a vexed one; though Lafayette and the Duc d'Orléans were both Freemasons who opposed Louis XVI, they disliked and mistrusted each other, and their respective factions did not work together to bring down absolute monarchy. With such a wide and varied membership, Freemasonry was bound to be a diverse force, probably as divided in political opinion as the public at large. Its attractions for liberal aristocrats possibly lay only in the potential for the formation of secret societies, so that in fact two very different types of Freemasonry evolved. The first, open to all, was little more than a social club with rituals, while the second type used this innocuous cover to form political groups with a far more sinister purpose.

Declining interest in Freemasonry during the later 1770s was partially due to the appearance of a new craze – 'animal magnetism'. This alternative therapy was pioneered by the Austrian doctor Franz Anton Mesmer, who, chased out of Vienna for his pains, arrived in Paris in 1778. Given the high levels of real illness as well as hypochondria in the French capital, he found a ready clientèle for his unorthodox medical skills. Mesmer claimed to cure people by 'magnetizing' them. The theory behind his technique was that heavenly bodies acted on living creatures by the emission of a fluid which could penetrate all matter. If the path of this fluid was obstructed in any way, illness would follow; the cure lay in treatment by 'animal magnetism', an earthly substitute for the planetary fluid, and available (of course) only from Mesmer himself.

Parisian society was soon as divided about the merits of this new discovery as it had been over the musical talents of Gluck and Piccini. According to Madame Campan, magnetism was more than just a fashion, 'it was absolutely a rage', but she herself remained unconvinced.[8] Her husband, however, asked to be treated by Mesmer for a lung complaint. A cure was worked in Madame Campan's absence, which her husband attributed solely to magnetism, but which she put down to the conventional

blistering and bleeding Mesmer had also carried out. Madame Necker shared her opinion that Mesmer was a quack, and neither the entreaties of her family nor the assurances of M. de Suffren, *bailli* of the Knights of Malta and an ardent supporter of Mesmer, could persuade her that magnetism was worth trying for her poor health in 1785.[9]

At Court, the King and Queen ranked among the sceptics, although the Comte d'Artois was a champion of magnetism – not that Mesmer needed royal endorsement. He succeeded in winning the confidence of a large part of Parisian high society, and at the height of his success also had twenty-four provincial branches called *Sociétés d'harmonie*. In the capital he held seances where he 'magnetized' up to thirty people at a time, all attached by cords to a *baquet*, or trough. The resulting convulsions and trances in his patients, as well as the delicate matter of his 'hands on' approach (deemed scandalous where women were being treated), prompted a royal commission of enquiry. Benjamin Franklin was a member of the investigating team of doctors and scientists who eventually concluded that the strange effects produced in people after 'magnetism' were the consequences of nervous excitement and an 'overheated imagination', and that magnetic fluid did not even exist. What they failed to appreciate was that although Mesmer's theory lacked credibility, their outright dismissal of it did not explain how he induced the same trance-like state in such large numbers of people; surely not *all* were subject to nervous excitement and overheated imaginations?

Mesmer had in fact discovered the principles of hypnotism, but this was not understood until long after he had ceased to be the wonder of Louis XVI's Paris. One of his most ardent disciples was the Marquis de Puységur, who published a book on 'animal magnetism' and entertained *le Tout-Paris* during the winter of 1784–5 with seances at his home. Drawn by reports he had heard of the marvels performed at Puységur's seances, the sceptical Bombelles availed himself of his former friendship with the marquis and attended one in April 1785.

On his arrival he found Puységur busily attempting to cure a

sick girl, assisted by none other than the hero of the American War, the Marquis de Lafayette, who 'was rubbing his back against M. de Puységur's in order, he said, to reinforce the magnetic power'. Bombelles, nonplussed, awaited the entrance of fellow guests (among them Madame de Genlis, the Duc de La Châtre, and another haughty American War veteran, the Comte d'Estaing) before Puységur performed his *pièce de résistance*. This was the 'magnetizing' of a twenty year old servant girl, Magdeleine, who could then be ordered by the power of thought alone to perform various tasks by the assembled company. In order to 'send her to sleep', Puységur spent 'several minutes rubbing Magdeleine's breast and back with his hands, occasionally covering her face with his left hand while the right always rubbed her stomach'. Eventually she was judged to be asleep and, with eyes firmly closed, she faultlessly executed a number of commands transmitted to her by thought, moving objects about the room, and even untying one guest's cravat and attaching it to the collar of another! This had been wished for by M. de La Châtre (obviously a practical joker), and Bombelles was amazed that Magdeleine 'obeyed as if she had her eyes open and had heard aloud what M. de La Châtre only thought'.[10] He could not help but be impressed, although later he recanted, writing that he had been a fool and the whole seance was mere chicanery. It also remains very hard to perceive the medicinal benefits of Magdeleine's trance.

Perhaps the best illustration of the fanatical belief in animal magnetism held by some people is to be found in the Comte de Ségur's memoirs. Ségur himself was deeply interested in the subject, and witnessed many of Mesmer's experiments, but even he was greatly amused by the antics of a noble friend who claimed to have learned the secrets of magnetism, and insisted on trying out his skill in the most unpromising circumstances. One very wet evening, Ségur's friend was on his way to a Court ball when his attention was caught by a man being carried on a stretcher along the Versailles road. He immediately ordered his coachman to stop, as Ségur relates:

The rain fell in torrents, my friend was in his ball dress, and merely wore a light silk coat, but nothing could cool his zeal. He alighted, vainly interrogated the bearers as to the state of the patient, but astonishment had rendered them mute. He, however . . . bent over the body of the sufferer, and proceeded to magnetize him with the utmost fervour. Having repeated the trial without effect, he at length exclaimed: 'What is really the malady of this poor man?' The wondering bearers . . . replied: 'He is no longer sick, for he has been dead these three days.'[11]

A truly mesmerizing experience!

Mesmer's devotees nevertheless faced competition from other quarters, since several quasi-religious sects flourished during the 1780s, most of them claiming they possessed secret healing powers. The *breuillistes*, who had elevated a Dr Dubreuil of Saint-Germain to the status of a god after he had performed various successful cures, maintained their belief in his supernatural abilities even after his suicide; while *martinistes*, followers of Louis-Claude de Saint-Martin, who published *Des erreurs et de la vérité* in 1775, occasioned serious government disquiet because of their religious unorthodoxy.

Bombelles, who notes the multiplication of these sects with world-weary cynicism, was pained to report a woeful story he heard from the Vicomte d'Ermenonville in 1785. Eldest son of Rousseau's friend and patron the Marquis de Girardin, the vicomte and his sister found themselves virtually excluded from the parental home at Ermenonville, which had been taken over by 'a self-styled adept'. The Girardins and several other aristocrats lived under his despotic rule, believed him to be in direct communication with God, showered him with gifts, and closed their doors to any members of their families who refused to adopt his maxims.

Mesmer's greatest rival, however, dabbled not only in medicine, but also in alchemy, occultism and Freemasonry; his name was Cagliostro. The man himself remains a mystery, and although commonly supposed by historians to have been the charlatan Giuseppe Balsamo, a native of Palermo born in 1743,

he was never known as anything other than 'le Comte de Cagliostro' in France. When later tortured by the Inquisition in Rome, Cagliostro admitted he was Balsamo, but no witnesses corroborated his confession, which he then retracted. Like Baron von Münchausen, he often claimed to have been alive for several centuries – and many in the Parisian *beau monde* believed him. Although the Christian faith was under severe strain in France for much of the eighteenth century, interest in the occult and paranormal thrived. According to Madame de Boigne, the Princesse de Guémené 'was always surrounded by a multitude of dogs, to which she paid a kind of worship, asserting that by their means she was in communication with intermediary spirits'.[12] Paris was a natural destination for a man who preyed on the superstitions and credulity of others.

For once, however, the provinces had the honour of testing the miraculous powers of this psychic and healer before he reached the capital. It was at Strasbourg in 1780 that the 'Comte de Cagliostro' first established his credentials, and formed a friendship that was to have devastating repercussions for the French monarchy. But as with Mesmer, not everyone fell under his spell. Writing with the benefit of hindsight, the Prince de Ligne recounts how he tried Cagliostro's magic skills and found them merely mundane.

> I cannot conceive how, with the figure, dress, accent and long ponytail of an orvietan seller, Cagliostro made dupes. He was mine. I presented him with my then daughter-in-law, who was not at all ill. He gave her some of his meaningless yellow liqueur and, after having told me that he had cured the entire harem of the Emperor of Morocco, said that when he was not certain of his remedy for some desperate malady, he raised his eyes to heaven. . . . And God helped him. There were one hundred persons in his antechamber.[13]

Evidently not all of them shared Ligne's scepticism or his wry sense of humour. It was not long before Cagliostro made the acquaintance of Cardinal de Rohan (who was also Bishop of

Strasbourg), and became a welcome guest at the Cardinal's magnificent château at Saverne. The Baronne d'Oberkirch met Cagliostro here in December 1780, and found him a remarkable man indeed.

She thought his accent was either Italian or Piedmontese, despite his reputed Arabic origin, but most arresting were his piercing black eyes, which utterly transfixed her. What struck her most about his dress was the large quantity of magnificent diamonds he wore; Cagliostro claimed to make them himself, and Rohan was completely convinced of his alchemical genius. At a dinner party a month later he showed the baroness a huge diamond, worth at least 25,000 francs, which he said he had watched Cagliostro make. He also declared he had witnessed Cagliostro's transmutation of base metals into gold; the patronage of this 'genius' by the perennially indebted Rohan was hardly disinterested!

Madame d'Oberkirch felt just a little nervous, for Cagliostro barely took his eyes off her during their first encounter, and when he did, it was to demonstrate his clairvoyance. He delivered a brief resumé of her life, announced that she would have no more children (she didn't), and also predicted the imminent death of the Empress Maria-Theresa. Despite this, her phlegmatic husband was distinctly unmoved – and as a good Protestant, somewhat perplexed by the Cardinal's total credence in a man he considered a mountebank.[14]

Rohan ensured that his protégé was not molested by the authorities, and Cagliostro's fame increased. Passing through Strasbourg in 1781, the Marquis de Bombelles heard a great deal about the miracles wrought by Cagliostro, who claimed 'to cure illnesses whose malignity defeats the art of all known doctors'.[15] He could also foretell the future and would relate a person's life history merely by looking at their portrait. Expecting such a psychic to have an exotic air, Bombelles was not disappointed when he met him; Cagliostro's peculiar accent was mystery enough.

> The Comte de Cagliostro is a short, stocky man with quite an intelligent countenance. He might be forty years of age. Some

people believe him to be a Jew; he speaks French like an Italian who does not know our language well, but as he expresses himself no better in Italian it is supposed that his native country is Spain.[16]

According to a memoir issued before his trial in 1786, when he was implicated in the Diamond Necklace Affair, Cagliostro was brought up in Medina in Arabia under the name Acharat. He claimed to be the orphan of Christian noble parents, possibly Maltese, and that at the age of twelve he had set out on his travels with his tutor. They travelled to Mecca, then to Egypt, where he was initiated into the ancient mysteries from which he derived his alleged powers of healing and clairvoyance. After extensive travels through Africa and Asia, Cagliostro landed on Rhodes in 1766. Europe beckoned . . . and the rest is mystery.

It is probable that Cagliostro's diamonds were not made through alchemy, but bought with the money he raised through his own 'Egyptian' Masonic lodges, which attracted some of the richest names in France. He was later to be imprisoned by the Papacy for peddling Freemasonry in Italy, but in the early 1780s, no hint of future doom threatened. He lived in a grand style at Strasbourg, and then in Paris, almost a familiar of the gullible Rohan, who trusted him implicitly. Surely the Cardinal's confidence was shaken when Cagliostro's powers proved to be entirely ineffectual in foreseeing their combined imprisonment in the Bastille as a result of one of the most audacious robberies in history – a robbery so carefully planned and so smoothly executed that it almost seemed a miracle.

L'affaire du collier, or the Necklace Affair: a crime to puzzle even the sharpest sleuth, a mystery never satisfactorily solved. A large and diverse cast of characters was involved, and the entire affair had a revolutionary impact, deeply damaging to both the image and the very foundation of the monarchy. One thing is certain: a plot that implicated Cardinal de Rohan, Queen Marie-Antoinette, Cagliostro, and an adventuress who claimed descent from France's Valois kings, was never going to be boring.

Yet it all started innocently enough. Enter one opportunist

jeweller, finding that times were hard in the splendid courts of Europe. Charles-Auguste Boehmer and Paul Bassenge were official jewellers to the Court of Versailles, and in the early 1780s found themselves in possession of a magnificent diamond necklace (2,800 carats) which no one wanted to buy. Originally designed for Madame Du Barry, it seemed likely that after the death of Louis XV it would be purchased for the Queen, whose youthful passion for jewellery was well known. But she had plunged deeply into debt indulging her taste for diamonds, and as the King was trying to make economies in the royal household, she repeatedly refused to buy the necklace for the princely sum of 1,500,000 *livres*. Bombelles was shown this ruinous item at Court in February 1783, when Boehmer confidently expected the end of the American War to change the King's mind about acquiring it as a gift for the Queen. Madame de Polignac herself had promised to speak in his favour; any string that could be pulled was tugged hard by the anxious Boehmer and Bassenge, who had borrowed heavily to finance the purchase of the necklace's 647 flawless stones. Their creditors were pressing for payment, and no sovereign in Europe would relieve them by consenting to take the necklace off their hands.[17]

Enter a Cardinal. A man who boasted the motto: *Roy ne puis, prince ne daigne, Rohan je suis* had no right to be anything other than exceptional, and His Eminence the Cardinal Prince Louis de Rohan did not disappoint – although he was exceptional for all the wrong reasons.[18] According to the Baron de Frénilly, though 'universally despised for his bad morals, his scandalous conduct and his debts', he was nevertheless 'a handsome figure of a man, very lordly in his manners, very amiable, fashionable, and witty'.[19] In short, a dissolute spendthrift with enormous charm, who hunted both game and women furiously, entertained lavishly, and nursed an *amour propre* bitterly wounded by the enmity shown him by the Queen. When all the great ladies of Paris were falling at his feet (many also tumbled into his bed), it was hard that a handsome Cardinal with nearly 800,000 *livres* a year should have to endure the displeasure of a pretty Queen; a Queen, moreover, whom he had welcomed to France.

They had first met at Strasbourg in May 1770, when as bishop-coadjutor of the city, Rohan had greeted the fifteen year old Marie-Antoinette on the steps of the cathedral, and given her a blessing on her marriage to the Dauphin. As a member of the most powerful princely family in France, which enjoyed distinction and privilege at Court, he had to be respected. As a man, he was mistrusted. Marie-Antoinette's dislike of Rohan originated during his tenure of the French embassy in Vienna from 1771–1774, where he not only spoke ill of her, but scandalized her mother and many Viennese besides.

The Empress Maria-Theresa deplored his public amours, his arrogance, his immense debts, his blatant scorn for religion, and his lies: 'he denies what he says from one hour to the next.'[20] She actually enjoined her daughter to speak to Rohan's family at Versailles in order to work some improvement in his conduct, and when her son-in-law became King, ordered Marie-Antoinette to rid her of Rohan altogether. He was duly recalled from Austria, for Louis XVI was equally unhappy with his over-exuberant ambassador, but a Rohan could not be snubbed. The prince was given 50,000 francs to pay his debts, and did not have to wait long for further lucrative offices to fall into his prodigal hands. He manipulated himself into the post of Grand Almoner in 1777, the King being caught off guard by a posse of Rohans at Court who claimed the office for their favourite son on the strength of a half-promise made some years earlier, and Rohan's triumph seemed complete when he became a cardinal in 1778.

The Empress Maria-Theresa was aghast at the honours being heaped on his unworthy head, and wrote an angry and anxious letter warning Marie-Antoinette of his treacherous character. 'He is a cruel enemy, not only towards you but in his very principles, which are the most corrupt. Beneath an affable, easy, attractive exterior he has done much harm here, and yet I must see him at your side and the King's!'[21]

Small wonder, therefore, that the Queen was remarkably cool towards Rohan, even when he baptized the Dauphin in 1781. That a man who enjoyed enormous wealth, prestige, and the favour of Parisian high society should still consider his every

moment 'poisoned' by the Queen's hostility is almost ridiculous; but according to the Abbé Georgel, Rohan's secretary for over twenty years, this was the case. The Cardinal would give anything to win the Queen's esteem. Fate was about to show him how.

Enter 'Madame la Comtesse de La Motte', née Jeanne de Saint-Rémy de Valois, an attractive woman in her late twenties with a razor-sharp mind and an ambition as overweening as the Cardinal's. Her early life was hardly propitious to either fame or fortune. All she bore was an illustrious name, being descended from a bastard branch of the Valois who had done little to curry favour with the Bourbons. Her father lost what remained of the family's estates near Bar-sur-Aube in Champagne through his own stupidity, and her beautiful peasant mother abandoned her three small children to the cold comfort of Paris when a trip to the capital to try to improve their miserable existence went awry.

Young Jeanne, with a winsome charm, caught the eye of the philanthropic Marquise de Boulainvilliers; impressed by their Valois pedigree, the marquise took Jeanne, her brother Jacques and sister Marianne under her protection, paid for their modest education, and fired Jeanne's imagination with glories to come. Jacques joined the Navy, and it was the good impression he made on a fellow officer which led to his presentation at Court on 6 May 1775, the recognition of his title as Baron de Valois, and a pension of 800 francs. His sisters shared his honour, Jeanne being officially recognized as Mademoiselle de Valois, and Marianne as Mademoiselle de Saint-Rémy, though the 800 francs per annum which they each received failed miserably to satisfy Jeanne's noble expectations.

Her chief ambition was to reclaim the lost Valois lands in Champagne, a task made all the more difficult by her confinement in a convent for daughters of the nobility at Longchamp, where, it was doubtless hoped, the Valois girls could be persuaded to take the veil and thus ensure no future unwanted cousins popped up to trouble the Bourbons. Madame de Boulainvilliers and the Court had not reckoned with Jeanne's

ingenuity. She and Marianne fled to Bar-sur-Aube in 1779, where they lived on the hospitality of the local gentry and greatly enlivened provincial balls and soirées.

It was at Bar-sur-Aube in 1780 that Jeanne, aged twenty-four, married an impecunious cavalry officer, Nicolas de La Motte. According to La Motte's regimental companion, Louis Rétaux de Villette (who was to figure prominently in Jeanne's life), the ceremony was hastily arranged so that a father could be provided for the child she had conceived with the Bishop of Langres. She was not lacking in sexual energy. Villette himself 'loved her to distraction', and Jacques-Claude Beugnot, then a promising young lawyer and a native of Bar-sur-Aube, was also her devoted slave. He left an interesting description of her sought-after charms.

> Mme de La Motte was not what one would call a beauty; she was of average height, but slim and well made; she had blue eyes which were full of expression, beneath black, well-arched eyebrows; her face was a trifle long, the mouth large but well furnished with teeth; and what is right for such a type, her smile was enchanting. She had beautiful hands and tiny feet. Her complexion was of a remarkable whiteness. . . . She was devoid of all learning, but she had a great deal of quick, penetrating wit.[22]

Such assets could not be allowed to go to waste in Lunéville, where La Motte's regiment was garrisoned. The newly married couple quickly ennobled themselves and set off for the capital; the fact that a titled family of the same name existed meant that no one thought the 'Comte and Comtesse de La Motte' anything other than genuine. A title was absolutely essential to obtain the credit they needed in Paris while Jeanne pursued her ambitions at Court. Of course, she still relied on the goodwill of men, for La Motte was neither rich nor clever, and lovers came and went with regularity. Lusty Rétaux de Villette was one; Cardinal de Rohan was to become another.

Jeanne and Rohan were introduced to each other by Madame de Boulainvilliers at Saverne in 1783, when he deigned to take an

interest in her unfortunate plight as a dispossessed Valois. As the
Grand Almoner, he also gave her charity from the royal purse.
Why he should have deemed his intervention on Jeanne's behalf
necessary when she was often to be seen lurking about the
staircase leading to the Queen's apartments at Versailles, claiming to be on intimate terms with her, is another of the Necklace
Affair's unsolved questions. Had Jeanne really been so close to
Marie-Antoinette, the protection of Cardinal de Rohan (as even
he ought to have realized) would have done her case more harm
than good. But she was slowly weaving a web which was to
enmesh both Queen and Cardinal; the Queen was blissfully
ignorant of the whole business, and Rohan was either an accomplice, or chose to blind himself to the inconsistencies in
Jeanne's tales.

A man like Rohan was easily subjugated by sex anyway.
According to Villette, who was privy to every secret of Jeanne's
life, Rohan seduced her (after an audience to discuss her claims
to her birthright) in the magnificent Hôtel de Rohan in the
Marais, where his lovers were guaranteed discretion by a secret
spiral staircase leading from his bedroom to the garden.[23] Not
long after the commencement of this liaison, Beugnot found the
'Comtesse de La Motte', whom he had last seen in distressed
circumstances at a run-down Parisian inn, living in considerable
style, talking Court jargon, and entertaining 'the very best Parisian society' in her salon.[24] She had even taken to calling herself
'de La Motte-Valois' and boasted openly of her supposed intimacy with the Queen. The necklace plot was about to be
hatched.

The aim of the plot was clear enough: a diamond necklace
worth 1,500,000 *livres* was no mean prize, and Jeanne had even
received a visit from Boehmer, who offered her a generous
commission if she could only use her influence with the Queen
and sell it for him. It immediately occurred to her that Cardinal
de Rohan was the very man to help her to Boehmer's commission – as well as to the necklace itself. In addition to the sexual
hold she had over Rohan, Jeanne ensured the continued arrival
of desperately needed money from his coffers by promising to

win him the smiles of the Queen. Trading on her 'friendship' with Marie-Antoinette, she had encouraged Rohan to write letters to the Queen justifying his conduct, and returned answers which gave him every reason to expect that his former misdeeds would be forgiven. This correspondence was to prove invaluable in the execution of the breathtaking fraud which was to lead both of them to the Bastille.

Exactly what Rohan hoped for as he eagerly scanned the epistles from the Queen so artfully forged by Rétaux de Villette was not clarified during the Necklace Trial. In some, the Queen claimed she required money for private 'charitable purposes'; the grateful Cardinal twice borrowed 60,000 francs in the Queen's name from the Jewish moneylender, Cerf-Beer. These sums, entrusted to Her Majesty's 'intimate friend' Madame de La Motte, enabled Jeanne to live the high life, both in Paris and at Bar-sur-Aube, where she thoroughly enjoyed her chance to *épater le bourgeois*, especially young Beugnot. Surely Rohan guessed something was amiss? Or was he hoping for amorous favours from the Queen, his expectations boosted by his vanity, ambition, and the Queen's ill-deserved reputation for gallantry?

Jeanne de La Motte later claimed in her memoirs that in addition to Rohan's burning desire to become prime minister (a post from which he felt the Queen's enmity would forever bar him), his virility did him no disservice with Marie-Antoinette. That their 'correspondence' was of a gallant nature seems highly probable in the light of subsequent events. The 'Grove of Venus' scene, admirably staged by Jeanne to convince the Cardinal that his letters were producing the desired effect on the Queen, could have graced the pages of a romantic novel. Rohan was overjoyed to be granted a nocturnal rendezvous with the Queen in the gardens of Versailles, as a sign of her good faith; yet he had every opportunity to speak to her officially at Court. It would appear that he hoped she would utter words which no Queen of France could address in public to a Cardinal.

August 10th, 1784. The monarchy fell on the very same day eight years later, but on this warm, moonless summer night the actors in Jeanne's farce little foresaw how it would contribute to

that ultimate catastrophe. The Cardinal, doubtless pleased and excited, entered the secluded Grove of Venus, otherwise known as *la Bosquet de la Reine*, one of the Queen's favourite walks situated just below the Hundred Steps. It was a nice choice of location by impresario Jeanne. Rohan saw a female figure attired in a white muslin gown of the type made fashionable by the Queen. He hastened towards her, dropped to his knees, and reverently kissed her hand. She pressed a rose into his with the words 'You know what this means', and departed.

Was the Queen concealed somewhere in the bower, secretly laughing at Rohan's foolishness in making an obeisance to a mere *grisette*, one Nicole Le Guay, recruited by Jeanne in the garden of the Palais Royal especially for this role because of her resemblance to Marie-Antoinette? Historians have often thought so, despite the implication which then arises that the Queen *was* intimate with Jeanne de La Motte, probably knew every detail of her 'correspondence' with Rohan, and maybe even arranged the theft of a magnificent necklace. Could she really have witnessed the scene without personal knowledge of its ramifications? Or was the entire episode masterminded by someone who knew both the principals and the palace grounds – the Polignacs, or even the Duc d'Orléans?

Rohan was nevertheless utterly convinced of his good fortune. His letters to the Queen continued, and her answers were ever more reassuring. It was time to spring the trap. Jeanne made Villette express the Queen's interest in a splendid necklace which the Court jewellers had offered to her, but which the King resolutely refused to buy. She so much wanted to possess it, but of course, as Mgr. le Cardinal must realize, such a purchase might cause offence. Perhaps the Cardinal could negotiate privately on her behalf with Boehmer and Bassenge?

Rohan was only too anxious to serve his honoured sovereign in any capacity. His first visit to the Court jewellers' palatial premises on the rue Vendôme in Paris took place on 24 January 1785. He asked to see the necklace, and satisfied himself that it was truly fit to adorn the throat and bosom of a dazzling Queen. Boehmer and Bassenge were told that he was negotiating for a

mystery purchaser, and the price rose equally mysteriously to 1,600,000 francs. How delighted everybody was to oblige each other! The jewellers to oblige the Cardinal, the Cardinal to assist the Queen, Jeanne de La Motte to help both the Cardinal and Boehmer and Bassenge, whose gratitude to her for sending Rohan to them was boundless.

The business, so long in preparation, now moved ahead very swiftly. Within days Rohan received a contract for the purchase endorsed and signed by the Queen, and hurried with it to Boehmer and Bassenge, who were satisfied that it was genuine. Nobody noticed the glaring flaw in the signature, which was 'Marie-Antoinette de France'. Villette, the forger, declared that the entirely redundant 'de France' was appended at Rohan's suggestion, merely to fool the jewellers and exonerate the Queen (who always signed herself 'Marie-Antoinette') from any involvement in the robbery.[25] Rohan always vehemently denied any knowledge of a forgery, vowing that he was firmly convinced he was acting for the Queen.

Boehmer and Bassenge delivered 1,600,000 *livres'* worth of diamonds to Cardinal de Rohan on 1 February 1785, with the earnest wish that their gracious sovereign would be happy with her staggering purchase. The same day, at the appropriately named *Belle Image* inn at Versailles, the Cardinal hid in an alcove of Jeanne de La Motte's room as the necklace was handed to a footman wearing the Queen's livery. Jeanne must have been a consummate actress. The footman was none other than Rétaux de Villette. Rohan's gullibility almost defies belief.

The necklace was quickly broken up, and though Villette was picked up by the Parisian police the same month because of a large number of diamonds he had been attempting to sell, the theft was not discovered, and he was quickly released. Monsieur de La Motte now made himself useful as a courier and fence. He travelled to London, where on 20 May 1785 he received £6,900 cash and £4,000 in merchandise from the Bond Street jewellers Grey and Jeffreyes, for a large quantity of high quality diamonds.[26] But the necklace intact would have been worth almost £67,000; even allowing for the depreciation caused by breaking it up and

pay-offs to various people involved in its disposal, £10,900 was a paltry return. What therefore happened to the greater part of the 2,800 carats? Yet another question that was never solved. According to a memoir for Jeanne which appeared in December 1785, Rohan himself received 300,000 francs as his share of the necklace, while La Motte, who was to escape justice altogether, always claimed that the highly placed instigator of the robbery kept most of the stones. Who this personage was, he declined to say.

Meanwhile, Jeanne was enjoying her riches and Cardinal de Rohan waited vainly for some token of gratitude from the Queen. Jeanne again returned to her roots in Bar-sur-Aube, where she set herself up as a lady, lived in splendid style, gave generously to local charities, and once more entertained the young lawyer Beugnot, who was rather amazed at her metamorphosis. At Court, weeks passed, and the Queen neither appeared wearing the necklace nor treated the Cardinal with anything other than her habitual indifference. He began to worry.

So too did the jeweller Boehmer who, as the date for payment of the first instalment on the necklace drew near, slipped a note into the Queen's hand as she walked to Mass on 12 July, expressing the hope that he would soon see her wearing 'the most beautiful diamonds in the world'. Perplexed, but scatter-brained as usual, she told Madame Campan that Boehmer was mad and burned his mysterious note. The payment date of 1 August passed. Boehmer, exceedingly anxious, went to Versailles four days later, and in a meeting with Madame Campan demanded 400,000 *livres*.

The Queen was immediately informed, and the whole plot began to unravel, despite Jeanne's skilful warning to the jewellers that she now believed the contract was a forgery, and that they would have to fall back on Rohan's guarantees. She correctly assumed that Rohan would pay for the necklace; this, as he later admitted, he would have done, had Boehmer not panicked and gone to the Queen. The events which followed were calamitous for the throne of France.

Affronted and insulted, Marie-Antoinette was determined to make Rohan suffer for his impudence; she was convinced he had used her name to steal the necklace, for his debts, as ever, were enormous. Acting on the advice of the Abbé de Vermond and the Baron de Breteuil (a long-standing enemy of Rohan), the King inflicted the utmost humiliation on the Cardinal by ordering his arrest in public at Versailles as he was on his way to celebrate the Assumption on 15 August 1785. Rohan's attempts to explain the matter were far from satisfactory; all elucidation was to be totally defeated by his lightning reactions. Fury seems to have blinded the King and his ministers to sensible police practice, and the Cardinal had time to instruct his faithful secretary Georgel to burn all the letters he had received from Jeanne de La Motte as well as the Queen's forged correspondence before they could be seized by the law. Was it because, as he claimed, he believed the Queen's letters to be genuine and wanted to protect her reputation (in which case they must have been very compromising), or was it to conceal his own part in the robbery? Given Rohan's character, either explanation is likely. A third, more sensational possibility, was that the Queen or someone close to her was actually romantically involved with the Cardinal, and his destruction of the evidence was a genuine act of chivalry.

Jeanne had decamped to Bar-sur-Aube before the storm broke, and had three days in which to burn her own share of incriminating documents. She was assisted by Beugnot, who was surprised by her insistence on reading each letter before agreeing to commit it to the flames. He read some love letters from Rohan, so passionate and furious in tone, that they gave him a decidedly unfavourable impression of the state of the Cardinal's soul. Jeanne was duly arrested on 18 August, but her husband, who returned to Bar-sur-Aube after she had been taken to Paris for questioning, escaped to England.

The scandal was only now gathering momentum. When it became public, the monarchy was to suffer incalculable damage. Had he been the tyrant his enemies always affirmed he was, Louis XVI would have incarcerated all the principals in the affair

under *lettres de cachet*, conducted a private investigation, and kept the whole sorry tale quiet. But he had a naïve belief in fair play and justice, and in entrusting the trial of Rohan, Jeanne and her accomplices to the ever-rebellious Parlement de Paris, displayed exemplary rectitude but an appalling lack of political acumen. The trial was a godsend to the militant magistrates, who in their interrogation of the suspects (all admirably defended by the sharpest legal minds in France), did more to discredit the victim of the plot – the Queen – than to incriminate the robbers.

Rohan's arrest, in the words of the Baron de Frénilly, was like 'throwing a lighted fuse into a barrel of powder, and the barrel exploded with an appalling noise'.[27] He was imprisoned in the Bastille (albeit in luxury, for as a Cardinal and prince he was treated with great courtesy and received a constant stream of visitors), where he was soon joined by Jeanne de La Motte, Rétaux de Villette, Nicole Le Guay, as well as Cagliostro and his wife, who were implicated by Jeanne in her efforts to lay a trail of red herrings.

Parisian pamphleteers had a field day. As Madame de Staël wrote to Gustav III of Sweden, 'in this country, the victims of authority always have public opinion on their side'.[28] Detention of the chief suspects in the Necklace Affair in the Bastille, that notorious symbol of repressive royal power, was another serious mistake by the Court. House-arrest for Rohan at least would have been much more tactful; but the matter was soon out of the King's hands altogether. The defendants' lawyers seized every opportunity to promote their clients' version of events. No restrictions were placed on the publication of *mémoires*, and Paris was showered with pamphlets detailing many interesting features of the case. It was the Queen who suffered most; the Grove of Venus scene, a secret correspondence with Cardinal de Rohan. . . . Her reputation, already undermined by enemies at Court, was torn to shreds. 'Characteristics and words were attributed to her which made her descend from the role of queen to that of a desirable woman,' wrote Beugnot.[29] Her charm and gaiety proved fatal qualities in

a Queen. People began to believe she *had* met the Cardinal in the dead of night and written him intimate letters.

Many other juicy snippets of information were fed to the public, and Cagliostro provided a particularly fabulous store of anecdote and amusement.

> M. de Cagliostro, who sometimes pretends to be several centuries old, was being interrogated by the Lieutenant of Police.
>
> 'Do you reproach yourself with nothing in your whole life?' M. de Crosne asked him.
>
> 'Alas!' replied M. de Cagliostro, 'I have committed but a single crime, but one for which I shall never forgive myself: I killed Pompey.'
>
> 'Pompey!' said M. de Crosne. 'I have never heard of that particular murder. It must have happened in my predecessor's day.'[30]

With such inane interrogations, it is hardly surprising that the judges were presented with a web of conflicting (and occasionally ridiculous) evidence. Rohan denied all knowledge of the plot to steal the necklace, and presented himself throughout as the hapless dupe of Jeanne de La Motte. As one caustic commentator noted, he must have required all his considerable intelligence to make himself seem such a fool. He also denied all sexual involvement with Jeanne. Villette corroborated Rohan's story, later claiming that he had been threatened with torture by the Foreign Minister, Vergennes, if he failed to frame his evidence in a way favourable to the Cardinal.[31] Jeanne made claim and counter-claim, and audaciously persisted in declaring that the Queen was at the bottom of the whole affair.

By the time the verdicts were delivered at the end of May 1786, Marie-Antoinette stood condemned in the public mind as an avaricious, libidinous woman, ruthlessly pursuing a vendetta against a Cardinal who had fallen prey to a gang of thieves solely through his desire to serve her. He was, of course, acquitted. So too were Nicole Le Guay (elevated by Jeanne to the title 'Baronne d'Oliva') and Cagliostro. Rétaux de Villette was banished (in

order to keep him quiet?), while Monsieur de La Motte was condemned *in absentia* to flogging and the galleys. Jeanne de La Motte's pedigree did her no favours; she was found guilty and condemned to flogging, branding and life imprisonment.

The sentence, which was executed early in the morning of 21 June, was harsh indeed. The branding was carried out in the courtyard of the Palais de Justice, in front of an enormous crowd of Parisians, all eager to feast their eyes on the body of a woman who had acquired no small reputation as a *femme fatale*. Jeanne writhed so much to evade the punishment that the 'V' for *voleuse* was imprinted beneath her breast instead of on her shoulder.

The pain and humiliation she suffered both that day and during her confinement in the Saltpetrière, a prison notorious for the depravity of its female inmates, fuelled a burning hatred of the Queen, which was to explode in an entirely unexpected way. For, far from languishing for years in gaol, Jeanne de La Motte escaped from custody just under a year after being sentenced. She was helped by anonymous, highly placed people, who ensured that she was smuggled from under the very noses of the French authorities to the security of England. Did it have anything to do with the letter written by her husband to the London *Morning Chronicle* in December 1786, threatening to expose the real villain of the piece by publishing letters which would exculpate his wife? Did the trips made to London by the Duchesse de Polignac, the Princesse de Lamballe and even the Abbé de Vermond in the spring and summer of 1787 involve the purchase of these incriminating letters? If so, were they written by Marie-Antoinette?

Satisfactory answers to these tantalizing questions have never been found. If Jeanne's freedom was obtained by a promise of silence, the bargain was not kept. From the relative safety of London she launched diatribes against Marie-Antoinette which brought the Queen low indeed. Jeanne's memoirs, first published in 1789 and edited by another enemy of the Queen who was exiled in England, disgraced Controller-General Calonne, were entirely in tune with the public taste for salacious scandal.

She claimed that the Queen had seduced her and described torrid scenes of lesbian passion – then betrayal, persecution and imprisonment. No more was required to win her both a hearing and sympathy.

Marie-Antoinette's portrait as 'the modern Messalina' was thrown into high relief by the Necklace Trial and its repercussions. From 1786 onwards the monarchy was under constant attack, and as political dissent gathered strength, the unanswered questions arising from *l'affaire du collier* faded from view. But who really stole the necklace? According to Bombelles, Madame de Polignac was 'much more serious' when she returned from her visit to England, and courtiers were 'persuaded that the Queen is weary, exceedingly weary of the commitments she has made to her former favourite'.[32] Was the 'Committee Polignac', then, at the bottom of the necklace plot?

The final mystery is Jeanne's fall from the window of a London house on 12 June 1791, after she was supposedly frightened by bailiffs at the door. Did she really die as a result on 23 August, or was her death faked so that she could escape the continual harassment she was subjected to by French spies? Perhaps the omniscient Cagliostro, expelled from France after his acquittal, survived another two centuries and could tell the whole story. He traded in miracles, after all.

6

Towards the Precipice

On 27 April 1784, *le Tout-Paris*, somewhat forgetful of its manners, pushed and jostled its way into the Théâtre Français for the opening night of a play that Louis XVI had attempted to ban for years – Beaumarchais's *The Marriage of Figaro*. A lively comedy, it was a huge success, not at all surprising in view of high society's fevered quest for amusement and the play's reputation as forbidden fruit. Beaumarchais's frequent tussles with the censors only increased the public's interest in his daring new piece, which was to enjoy an extended run at that bastion of French classical drama, the Comédie-Française. When Mrs Thrale visited Paris in 1784, shortly after her second marriage, she soon noticed that Parisians could talk of nothing else.

They are all wild about a wretched Comedy called *Figaro* full of such Wit as we were fond of in Charles the Second's Reign; all Indecent Merriment, & gross Immorality mixed however with Satire. . . . The Author is Mr de Beaumarchais, & possesses so entirely the Favour of the Public, that the Women weare Fans with Verses on 'em out of his Comedy as they did by the Beggars Opera in London 40 Years ago.[1]

The nobility, the *haute bourgeoisie* and much of the Court flocked to applaud the play; they found Figaro's caustic tirades against his master Count Almaviva highly amusing, and admired

144

the valet's quick wit and enterprise. The satire, so obvious to Mrs Thrale, was apparently lost on a large part of the audience. Madame d'Oberkirch found it exceedingly difficult to get a seat to see the play, and when she did, wondered why so many aristocrats sat through it and laughed 'at their own caricature'. Though she could not help responding to its comic spirit, she was keenly aware of the work's underlying message, and noted its 'indecency' and 'immorality'.[2] But Beaumarchais's comedy was the height of *bon ton* nevertheless, as Frénilly noticed.

> *The Marriage of Figaro* had just forced the doors of the Comédie-Française in spite of the police, the Archbishop of Paris, and the King. Everyone declared the work to be scandalous, dangerous, and revolutionary: it was fashionable. Everyone rushed to see it: that was even more fashionable.[3]

Beaumarchais, born Pierre-Augustin Caron in Paris in 1732, shared certain personality traits with his hero Figaro. His father was a Protestant watchmaker, and Beaumarchais followed him into the profession before branching out into finance and literature. He bought himself a Court post as well as a title, and set his sights firmly on success. His first play, *Eugénie*, was staged by the Comédie-Française in 1767, followed by *The Barber of Seville* in 1775; but in addition to his literary and financial activities, which brought him enormous wealth, Beaumarchais dabbled in espionage and shipped arms to the American insurgents. He married three times, had a reputation for gallantry, and was no stranger to prison. One incarceration resulted from his brawl with the Duc de Chaulnes in 1773 over the favours of a Mademoiselle Mesnard. In Beaumarchais's opinion, authority was to be mocked and scorned. His fertile brain had a riposte for anyone who tried to put him down, and he was always quick to defend his rights. A nobleman at Court, hoping to humble the flamboyant playwright by reminding him of his bourgeois origins, asked him to examine a watch which he claimed did not work. The former watchmaker took the magnificent timepiece and let it drop to the floor, where it broke on impact. He also

shattered the aristocrat's arrogance with his profuse apologies: 'Excuse me, Monseigneur, it's been *such* a long time. . .!'[4]

Beaumarchais's relations with the Court were far from equable, and Louis XVI's opinion of him contributed to the difficulties he encountered. According to the Queen, as early as 1774 her husband considered Beaumarchais to be 'a madman, despite all his wit'.[5] Perhaps it was madness to challenge regal, ecclesiastical and legal authority when silence would have enabled him to enjoy his fortune without inconvenient *lettres de cachet* and prolonged lawsuits, but Beaumarchais, like Figaro, was unwilling to bow and scrape to people of inferior brains and talent merely because they could boast an ancient lineage.

The revolutionary thrust of *The Marriage of Figaro*, which was only gradually perceived by the nobility (though the King saw it from the outset), lay in its robust support for the underdog. In his preface to the play, and later in his *Court Mémoire* of 1787, Beaumarchais defended both the nobility and the monarchy; after all, he had traded on his Court connections and relied on noble patronage, and as a financier, was possibly more detestable in the eyes of the populace than either courtiers or aristocrats. The Revolution was unfavourable to Beaumarchais, and his backing for the Americans also caused him heavy financial losses. Perhaps he was too dazzled by his own pyrotechnic wit to appreciate the true impact of his play, although as a shrewd financial operator, the lucrative benefits of audacity in ridiculing the established order doubtless occurred to him as he wrote. It must have been doubly rewarding to have his pockets filled by the very people he mocked. As with *Les Liaisons Dangereuses*, Parisian society saw only wit and ignored the insults it cloaked.

Intentionally or not, Beaumarchais's work signalled the impending demise of the *ancien régime*. Though he cannot seriously be said to have argued the case for the utterly miserable *bas peuple*, his elevation of Figaro to the status of hero when the American War had already raised the issues of liberty and equality, constituted a public attack on the old order, where birth established a man for life. Mrs Thrale, herself married to an

English brewer, remarked that there was little point in a French-man trying to succeed in commerce, for 'a Frenchman who should make his Fortune tomorrow by Trade, would be no nearer Advancement in Society or Situation'.[6] Figaro challenged this dogma in a very uncompromising way. What had Count Almaviva done to deserve his privileges, except taking the trouble to be born? Possibly he merely wished to remind the count of *noblesse oblige*, a concept alien to many aristocrats in Louis XVI's France, who insisted on claiming their rights but frequently ignored their obligations. More alert members of the audience, however, saw Figaro as a champion of meritocracy, and his speeches as an overt condemnation of *les privilégiés*.

The Marriage of Figaro undermined the very basis of the monarchy through its questioning of the placing of birth above merit. If Figaro's arguments were accepted, what right had the King to rule? Birth alone had granted him the power of life or death over twenty-four million French citizens. Louis XVI was not the fool he was so often made to appear. Beaumarchais's revolutionary message was clear to him long before it penetrated the public consciousness, which is why he had taken all possible measures to prevent the play's performance. His eventual capitulation, after a great deal of persuasion from the less foresighted Queen (who played both Suzanne and the Countess in productions of *Figaro* at the Petit Trianon), highlighted his fatal flaw as a ruler, which was his complete inability to hold a firm line. He was too benevolent to be a successful autocrat, but too rigid and conservative to be a democratic monarch, and the vicissitudes of his reign are marked by the constant warring between his moderately liberal instincts and the constraints imposed by his belief in the divine right of kings.

The Marquis de Bombelles's only criticism of *The Marriage of Figaro* when he heard Beaumarchais read it in Madame de La Vaupalière's salon in 1783 was that it was too long. Otherwise he found it very entertaining, though he doubted that permission would ever be granted for its performance. By 1785, however, Bombelles's opinion had changed; he was convinced that the King ought to have exerted his powers of repression to

the full, and prevented this scandalous play from reaching a public theatre. When Louis XVI finally took action, sending Beaumarchais to prison for a week in March 1785 as punishment for a journalistic attack on the Archbishop of Paris, it was too late. Pandora's box was already open, although Bombelles was not without hope that the lid could be forced shut again.

> It is a stain on our century to have permitted the performance of *The Marriage of Figaro*; this condescension has already had the greatest consequences, and the multitude of printed follies, indecent pamphlets and scandalous songs which have since appeared, prove to sensible people how right it was to inflict punishment on the insolent Beaumarchais.[7]

Indeed, Beaumarchais's mortification at being locked up in Saint-Lazare, a house of correction 'for all the petty crooks of Paris', rather than in the Bastille (a worthier destination for subversive writers), chastened his ardent spirit not a little. *The Marriage of Figaro*, however, remained hugely popular, and with fresh scandal about to break in the form of *l'affaire du collier*, the monarchy was far from secure.

Yet for all their apparent novelty, the ideas in Beaumarchais's comedy were hardly new. As early as 1765, William Cole had been astounded by the virulence of the verbal onslaughts on the church and established authority, writing that 'the present Situation of France has much the Appearance of being soon the Theatre of a Civil War'.[8] Louis XV's *laissez-faire* approach to government gave rise to political dissent, the dissemination of liberal ideas, and the reading of books which were supposedly banned but nevertheless reached a wide and intelligent Parisian audience. The *philosophes* came into their own.

By the eighteenth century the word *philosophe*, as defined by the Académie Française, not only signified a philosopher in the classical sense, but also a man who rose above the obligations of civil life through his freedom of thought.[9] The *philosophes*' most important contribution to the French Enlightenment was undeniably their advocacy of *libre pensée* (free-thinking), rather

than the ideas they promulgated, many of which were borrowed. The revolutionary potential of *libre pensée* should not, however, be underestimated, for it led to a direct questioning of all established dogma. In a France still riven by religious controversy, the *philosophes* challenged both Jesuits and Jansenists, placed reason above all, and reserved the right to think without being hampered by faith or sentiment. The root of the 'general Spirit of Infidelity & Scepticism' observed by William Cole may be clearly traced to the influence of 'free-thinkers', although it leaves one unhappy with the term *philosophe*.

Any word that can be used to describe Voltaire, Montesquieu, Rousseau and Diderot has to be very elastic in meaning. If all championed free-thinking, they nevertheless expressed themselves in very different, even contradictory ways. The *philosophes* in fact fall into two groups; some appealed purely to the mind, their writings characterized by logic, satire and scepticism, and others spoke to the heart through sentimental and occasionally mystic works. All challenged established religion because it stifled independent thought, yet most felt God was needed – in Voltaire's famous dictum, 'if God did not exist it would be necessary to invent Him.' He viewed God as a restraining force, to prevent anarchy, but Rousseau thought religion was essential to console the poor for their misery. Robespierre strangely combined these diverse theories by abolishing God and the Church and enrolling patriotic citizens in worship of the Supreme Being.

Rousseau was remarkable among the *philosophes* for wrapping up his most influential ideas in sensual mysticism. His famous novel, *La Nouvelle Héloïse* (1761) fuelled the cult of sensibility, whose emphasis on tender feelings, sympathy for the oppressed, and the righting of social injustice had a great deal to do with the growth of revolutionary idealism. But Rousseau was no great innovator, despite his individual and daring style. Not only did he draw on the sentimental works of Marivaux and Prévost, he also borrowed heavily from the English novelist Samuel Richardson, and *La Nouvelle Héloïse* combined elements of both *Clarissa* and *Sir Charles Grandison*. Similarly,

Montesquieu's *De l'Esprit des lois* drew French attention to the advantages of the English constitution, and Voltaire also commented on British institutions in his *Lettres philosophiques*. One of the most potent sources of revolutionary ideology, which was fully tapped by the *philosophes*, lay in the domains of France's traditional enemy: England.

Even in the 1750s English influence on French ideas was strong enough to provoke retaliatory attacks against what was known as *anglomanie*. It was Locke (1632–1704) who had the most profound influence on French philosophers. His practical, empirical approach to philosophy and his anti-clericalism appealed to the French love of reason. Although Locke's *Essay concerning Human Understanding* (1690) was his most well-known work, his theories on kingship (set out in his *Two Treatises of Government*), which directly opposed Hobbes's views on the divine right of kings, could not fail to interest a country ruled by that most absolute of monarchs, Louis XIV.

It was not until 1748, however, that Montesquieu's *De l'Esprit des lois* brought the first proper analysis in French of British political structures, and awakened a desire to achieve English liberties in France. The effect of *De l'Esprit des lois* was long-lasting. The Comte de Ségur, born five years after the book was published, was still discussing Montesquieu in the salons of the 1780s, where between satirical songs and love poetry, 'the laws of England were studied and envied'.[10]

Anglophobes not unnaturally fulminated against this importation of ideas and culture from a nation so inimical to France, but despite their warnings, and in the very shadow of a humiliating defeat at the hands of the British in the Seven Years War, *anglomanie* increased in popularity. William Cole, visiting Paris in 1765, found the English language 'in no small Vogue and Reputation . . . as is every Thing that is English, even to Politics'. But he was not flattered by this French craze, accurately predicting that it 'bodes no great Prospect of their future Peace & Tranquillity'.[11] In the eighteenth century, however, when much of Europe was in thrall to despotism of greater or lesser severity, it is no wonder that English 'liberty' was so envied.

What is more surprising is the length of time it took for ideas to be translated into action. Well into the 1780s, Mercier railed against the iniquities of French law, blaming Cardinal Richelieu for the rise of state tyranny and the suppression of civil rights: 'where is our great Charter, the basis of the government of England and formerly the basis of ours? Where is our *Habeas Corpus*, of which the English are so justly proud?'[12]

The abuses which arose from *lettres de cachet*, by which innocent French citizens could be imprisoned on the whim of relatives or by the will of the state, with no recourse to the law, was a topic that exercised many minds under the *ancien régime*. Though Louis XVI was much less inclined to use *lettres de cachet* than his immediate predecessors, glaring injustices still continued. The Marquis de Bombelles accompanied the Baron de Breteuil on a ministerial inspection of the Bastille in 1783, and found that the strictest secrecy still surrounded the twenty to thirty prisoners housed in its gloomy towers, in cells 'armed with an immense quantity of iron'. Even the exact number of inmates and their identities were secret: 'they are at the Bastille under assumed names, and, if they do not tell the governor those they really bear, he does not know whom he has in his custody.'[13] It is not surprising, therefore, that the marquis and the minister were unable to satisfy their burning curiosity about the long-dead Man in the Iron Mask!

More fortunate than the pseudonymous occupants of the Bastille was an elderly and ill Comte de Sanois, who was able to publicize his plight through the merciful intervention of a gaoler. Madame de Staël records that a *mémoire* had appeared in his defence which brought him a great deal of sympathy. A *lettre de cachet* obtained by his family had led to his incarceration at Charenton, where he might have languished until his death without the public outcry that followed news of his unhappy situation. He was released from prison after nine months; whether he ever trusted his perfidious relatives again is another matter.[14]

Comparisons between English and French law and government, particularly those of an odious variety, were not altogether

without risk in a country where dissidents were treated as criminals. More widespread features of *anglomanie* therefore had a superficial character, not readily connected to politics. The French admired English style in such diverse areas as horticulture, fashion, literature, horses and carriages. Even so, there were two distinct sides to *anglomanie*: on the one hand, admiration led to imitation (the sincerest form of flattery?), on the other, knowledge of English culture merely sparked envy and a greater desire to vanquish England entirely. In some people, this mixture of admiration and envy is impossible to disentangle.

Under Louis XV, *anglomanie* was tolerated rather than encouraged. One of the leading anglomaniacs during his reign was the Duc de Lauraguais (eldest son of the Duc de Brancas), who took his passion to the point of aping English eccentricity. He frequently incurred the King's displeasure, and was the recipient of numerous *lettres de cachet* exiling him from Paris, which he called 'his Correspondence with the King' and habitually ignored![15] He also once began a lawsuit against a Prince ____, who was attempting to lure away his mistress, the actress Sophie Arnould. Lauraguais declared that the prince (possibly the Prince d'Hénin, who did enjoy a liaison with the actress), 'had formed the design of killing him, as well as Mademoiselle Arnould, with *ennui*', and before instituting proceedings, took advice from a doctor that death from *ennui* was possible, and ascertained from a lawyer that such a death would in fact constitute murder![16]

Leading anglomaniacs during the reign of Louis XVI were the Duc de Chartres ('Philippe Égalité'), the Duc de Lauzun, the Marquis de Conflans and the King's brother, the Comte d'Artois. Lauzun, Chartres and Artois, all avid followers of the turf, were largely responsible for the introduction of horse racing to France with imported English bloodstock. Races took place on the Plaine des Sablons near Neuilly, or at Vincennes, where according to Mercier (who had never set foot in England), one was reminded of Newmarket.[17]

It was not a comparison which struck Mrs Thrale when she attended a race meeting on her visit to Paris in 1775: 'such is the

ingenuity of French Horsemanship that they give the greatest
Weight to the slightest Horse – but they had the Sense to send
for Riders from England.' Queen Marie-Antoinette, who was
also present, thoroughly enjoyed racing, and impressed Mrs
Thrale by her enthusiasm. 'The Queen is still handsomer by Day
than by Night, tho' dressed with the greatest Simplicity. . . . She
& her Ladies clapped their Hands, & almost shouted when the
Winner came in.'[18] But the Thrales, and even short-sighted Dr.
Johnson, were absolutely flabbergasted by the appearance of the
jockeys, who were all 'habited in *one Colour*, and that Colour
was *Green*' – the worst possible choice, since it made them
indistinguishable not only from each other, but also from the
surrounding foliage!

The Duc de Lauzun and the Duc de Chartres paid frequent
visits to England to buy English horses. Lauzun often wore
English clothes, had stables at Newmarket (he was always hoping to win the Gold Cup), and like Chartres, also had a penchant
for Englishwomen. One of his more serious love affairs was
with Lady Sarah Bunbury (née Lennox), and he flirted with
several of her compatriots. Chartres, as a royal duke, was a
friend of the Prince of Wales (later George IV), and borrowed
one of the latter's mistresses, Grace Elliott. He also joined the
prince's London club. Even the Comte de Tilly, who scoffs at
anglomanie in his memoirs, was curious enough to cross the
Channel in the early 1780s to discover that there were 'perhaps
more beautiful women in England than elsewhere'.[19]

Lauzun and Chartres were highly active supporters of the
Revolution (to which both also fell victim), but whether this was
attributable to their *anglomanie* is doubtful. Marie-Antoinette
(certainly no revolutionary!) also liked English style, and was
always especially gracious to English visitors to Versailles. 'The
Queen paid them a marked attention,' wrote Madame Campan,
because 'of the esteem she felt for their noble nation'. Of course
this did her no favours at all with backbiters at Court. 'These
attentions were called infatuations. This was illiberal; and the
Queen justly complained of such absurd jealousy.'[20] Marie-
Antoinette's creation of a *jardin anglais* at the Petit Trianon, and

the royal taste for English books (all the most popular were translated immediately into French by an army of hacks, unrestrained by modern copyright laws) were, however, common features of *anglomanie*, and the Queen's interests were shared by many in Parisian high society.

English clothes in particular enjoyed a great vogue in the 1780s, and some years before 1789 a complete revolution had taken place in costume. French fashions were formal, impractical and decorative. English styles were comfortable and much less ornate, and men especially appreciated the freedom of movement they brought. 'Englishmen', pronounced Tilly, 'look best in morning dress. It is in this attire that we view them as masters of fashion in Europe.'[21] According to the Comte de Ségur, only 'boots and dress-coats after the English fashion' could 'suit the fancy of young men' in Paris, a fact which amused Mercier, who found that 'when you begin to discuss matters with the so-called Englishman, at the first word you recognise an ignorant Parisian'.[22] He firmly believed that Frenchmen should retain their national dress of tricorne, sword and embroidered coat, 'the costume for talking nonsense on all subjects', but his admonitions went unheeded.

Children, who in France had always been dressed as adults, were also fashion-conscious enough to want English clothes. The young Baron de Frénilly used to be taken for a daily walk in the gardens of the Tuileries, where he first saw the three sons of the anglophile Marquis de Girardin with cropped hair and dressed 'in English sailor suits, round hats, short jackets and trousers'. This strange attire earned them hisses and catcalls, but it was not long before other boys realized the advantages of such clothes. Frénilly pleaded his case with his father: 'I exalted the happiness of the Girardins in being exempt from curl papers, curling tongs, powder, and pomade.' Soon he found himself in the same fortunate position, to the great delight of his valet.[23] Even the Marquis de Bombelles, who considered *anglomanie* 'ridiculous', approved of English dress for children, since they could not give themselves airs if they did not wear adult clothes![24]

Tilly, however, considered the adoption of English costume both subversive and dangerous, since it encouraged the 'abolition of distinction in dress once so useful to influence unsteady imaginations', and placed 'all men on the same level'.[25] The liberal Comte de Ségur praised them for exactly the same reason! But the passion for 'the English look' was sometimes carried to extremes. Madame de La Tour du Pin recalls that by 1787 it was 'essential' for riding dress, including the hat, to come from London, and:

> Some young people, like Charles de Noailles and others, even affected an English accent when speaking French, and studied the awkward manners, the style of walking, all the outward signs of an Englishman, in order to use them. They envied me the happy ability to provoke frequently in public places the exclamation: 'There's an Englishwoman!'[26]

Blonde, with Irish and English ancestry, Madame de La Tour du Pin had a definite edge over most of her friends. Yet despite the vogue for English fashions, as well as the proliferation of English books (and even newspapers) in Paris, few anglomaniacs had 'ever seen England, neither do they understand one word of English'.[27]

That was a minor point, of course. In the Parisian *beau monde* glamorous appearances always counted for more than reality. Once transformed into the English leisured classes, anglomaniacs searched for other ways to improve their English credentials, and one of high society's more popular pastimes during the reign of Louis XVI was the attempted imitation of English country life. Some nobles adopted the English practice of spending summer and autumn on their country estates, most notably the Duc de La Rochefoucauld-Liancourt, who was also deeply interested in English agricultural methods. He was, however, more or less unique in seeking out the practical aspects of *anglomanie*.

For most anglomaniacs, a flirtation with the English countryside came only in the form of *jardins anglais*. The many 'English

gardens' which were laid out in the 1770s and 1780s were often decidedly idiosyncratic interpretations of landscape gardening as pioneered by 'Capability Brown'. One of the most famous was at Ermenonville, seat of the Marquis de Girardin, who was also Rousseau's friend and patron. Though supposedly 'natural' in the English style, the garden boasted a Doric temple and fake rustic buildings, its *pièce de résistance* being Rousseau's tomb on an island in the middle of the lake. By comparison, Marie-Antoinette's horticultural experiments at the Petit Trianon were rather restrained. The true spirit of an English garden nevertheless proved very elusive; the very rigidity and flatness of formal French gardens, which had to be removed before the *jardins anglais* could be laid out, contributed to failure, since Capability Brown's designs made great play of the natural undulations or 'capabilities' of the English landscape.

Arthur Young was mystified by the 'English garden' designed for Monsieur Le Pelletier de Morfontaine near Chantilly, which contained 'a profusion of temples, benches, grottos, columns, ruins, and I know not what: I hope the French who have not been in England do not consider this as the English taste.'[28] The garden was worthy of its owner, who was Prévôt des Marchands in Paris from 1784 to 1789; according to Elisabeth Vigée-Lebrun, Morfontaine wore rouge (even on his nose!), sported a huge full-bottomed wig, and made loud boasts about his virility despite, or perhaps because of, his perennial body odour.[29]

His notion of English gardening was, however, entirely fashionable. The Duc de Chartres's garden at Mousseaux (now better known as Parc Monceau in the 8th *arrondissement*) also had temples, ruins and grottoes; and although its designer Louis Carmontelle asserted that it was '*not at all an English garden*', most people persisted in calling it one because it was not recognizably French.[30] Its alternative name, *La Folie de Chartres*, was probably more appropriate.

The mania for English gardens grew steadily during the 1780s, and after the successful transformation of Ermenonville, tombs became very desirable garden accessories. Madame de Staël recounts how, in 1786, the Duc de Luxembourg was staying on

his estate at Châtillon when he was told by excited servants that
a treasure chest had been found in the castle's cellars. The chest
was duly brought up, cleaned, and marvelled at – but when
opened, was found to contain a lead coffin which bore the
inscription: 'Body of Admiral Coligny, massacred at St. Barth-
olomew'. The duke was not at all pleased to find himself in
possession of the remains of a Huguenot martyr rather than a
hoard of gold.

At a supper party that evening he spoke of his disappointment.
M. de Montesquieu, First Equerry to Monsieur, was present.
   'What!' he cried, 'you place no value on the bones of Admiral
Coligny?'
   'No, I vow,' replied M. de Luxembourg.
   'Would you be generous enough to give them to me?'
   'I shall gain little credit in doing so; they will be with you
tomorrow.'
   'Ah, what kindness!' cried M. de Montesquieu, and, the
happiest of men, he made the tomb of Admiral Coligny a feature
of his English garden at Maupertuis.[31]

One hopes the poor admiral was allowed to rest in peace.
Why he was unceremoniously interred in the cellar at Châtillon
and so entirely forgotten is unknown. Still, the French would
eventually have run short of suitable candidates for romantic
tombs in *jardins anglais*, for as with any whim of high society,
only the illustrious dead would do. It is quite probable that
peculiar French interpretations of English gardening resulted
from reading too many books on the 'picturesque', a fashionable
cult in England at the time. The 'English gardens' which were
created, though far from representative of true English taste,
were nevertheless so different from formal French gardens, such
as those laid out by Le Nôtre, that they passed as authentic.
   Many anglomaniacs doubtless enjoyed English clothes and
gardens without realizing that English life consisted of much
else besides; but those who delved beneath the surface of *anglomanie* soon perceived its political significance. Tilly had no
doubt that imported English culture was bad for France, having

produced a 'contempt for our ancient proprieties and our conse-
crated etiquettes' which inevitably hastened the collapse of the
old social hierarchy. Highly chauvinistic, he claimed superiority
for France in everything from warfare to literature, and berated
his fellow countrymen for being 'imbued with a fondness for
foreigners who never return the feeling'.[32]

Mercier (an anglophile, and in later life a raging anglophobe)
was also keenly aware of the political thrust of *anglomanie*, as
was the Comte de Ségur, who hankered after 'the dignity, the
independence, the comparatively useful and important life of an
English peer, or of a member of the House of Commons'.[33] For
him, the aping of English fashions merely masked a much deeper
desire for change in France, and was not intended as a compliment to those arrogant *anglais*.

> Our imitation of their dress and manners was not a triumph
> accorded to their taste, industry, or superiority in the arts, it was
> the expression of a very different sentiment . . . it was the desire
> to naturalize among ourselves their institutions and their liberty.
> These were the advantages of which we were jealous.[34]

Such covert insults reveal the uglier face of *anglomanie*. Jealousy
was an unfortunate by-product of the craze for all that was
English, and thence it was but a short step to anglophobia. Ségur
felt acutely the humiliation France suffered at the end of the
Seven Years War, and longed to even the score with the English.
'We were compelled, in 1763, to conclude a disastrous peace, by
which we lost great and rich colonies. The wounds inflicted by
these reverses upon our national pride were deep and severe.'[35]
The ideal opportunity for revenge came with the American
Declaration of Independence.

French interest in the American rebellion began with the
Boston Tea Party in 1773, when according to Ségur, the 'daring
courage' of the rebels 'electrified every mind, and excited universal admiration'. It also had the immediate effect of displacing
whist from the card table in favour of a new game called
'Boston'.[36] On her visit to France in 1775, Mrs Thrale rather

naïvely succumbed to the charm of an aristocratic abbess at the Benedictine priory of St Louis in Rouen, 'a mighty pleasing Woman indeed, and . . . very desirous of Information. She was particularly anxious to have me explain to her the Nature & Cause of the Rebellion in America.'[37] One has no doubt that a very interesting letter was despatched the next day to the abbess's important connections in Paris!

France was, however, initially hesitant in her reaction to the American Revolution. When the liberal Duc de La Rochefoucauld-d'Enville translated the Declaration of Independence in 1777, it was banned by the government, though circulated widely in the salons of the nobility. Some aristocrats enthused about liberty and drew parallels with their own unfranchised condition, but most saw only the chance to diminish the might of Great Britain. The time was ripe, as Bombelles put it, 'to bring down the British colossus always at work to crush our trade'.[38] Of course, on a diplomatic level matters were hardly so straightforward. The early stages of the rebellion saw no French involvement, overt or covert, but when Benjamin Franklin arrived in Paris in December 1776, ostensibly to oversee the education of his two grandsons, in reality as a representative of Congress, French participation in the war became a foregone conclusion.

As the unaccredited envoy of a nation that as yet had no officially recognized existence, Franklin wisely stayed just outside Paris in the splendid Hôtel de Valentinois at Passy, formerly the residence of the princes of Monaco. Here he was well situated on the route from Paris to Versailles, and made a rapid conquest of the *beau monde*. Everyone wanted to know Dr Franklin, and many important people, Beaumarchais included, were eager to furnish him with loans to buy arms for the American insurgents. In fact, his popularity was such that he was almost mobbed in the streets. A stream of Franklin souvenirs appeared: fans, snuff-boxes, and even a specially commissioned Sèvres chamber pot with his portrait on the base, a gift from the exasperated Louis XVI to one of Franklin's most ardent admirers at Court, the Comtesse Diane de Polignac!

In addition to guiding Franco-American relations throughout

the War of Independence, as a man of science Franklin participated in the French Académie des Sciences, and also tried to
interest the French in the nutritious qualities of the potato. A
grand potato dinner was staged in 1778, at which the King
(always a hearty trencherman) endorsed the vegetable. It was a
pity that its potential as a substitute for bread when wheat crops
failed was not realized before the Revolution. Franklin liked
posing as a simple American farmer (which he was not), but
beneath his rustic beaver hat worked a very sharp brain, and he
was successful in persuading the French to send secret supplies
of money and arms to the Americans. The Comte de Ségur
believed that France thought 'it could ruin its rival without
running the risk of a conflict', but 'the English cabinet was too
wide-awake to allow the French government thus to reap all the
advantages of war without incurring its dangers'.[39]

Open conflict held less terrors for the French after the defeat
of the British under General Burgoyne at Saratoga on 17
October 1777. A treaty of commerce and friendship was signed
between France and America on 6 February 1778; Britain retali-
ated by attacking French merchant ships which were carrying
supplies to America, and war between the two European arch
rivals commenced, though not before a curious scene took place
at Versailles. Franklin was presented at Court on 20 March
1778, as the recognized representative of the thirteen states of
America, in a costume which threw all Court etiquette to the
winds. No dress coat, no sword, no tricorne; he milked his
image as a kindly old 'American farmer' to the full. 'His unpowdered hair, his round hat, his brown coat, formed a contrast to
the laced and embroidered coats and powder and perfume of the
courtiers at Versailles,' reported Madame Campan. The ladies at
Court were thrilled by this novel attire, and Franklin was plied
with numerous invitations to 'elegant entertainments'.[40] His
triumph was only to be expected, for in Madame Campan's
words, there was no one in France who 'did not heartily
approve of the support given openly by the French government
to the cause of American independence'.[41]

Ségur's martial temperament delighted in the prospect 'of

retrieving the disgrace of the last war, of taking the field against England, and of flying to the aid of America'.[42] But in 1777, when the French war machine was still uncommitted, it fell to a nineteen-year-old nobleman from the Auvergne, with bright red hair and the spirit to match, to rally support for the American cause. The Marquis de Lafayette was related by marriage to the Comte de Ségur (they had both married into the Noailles family), and together with the Vicomte de Noailles they offered their services to Franklin. Ségur and Noailles were prevented from taking further action by their parents, but Lafayette, 'sole master of his property and his person, and the independent possessor of a hundred thousand *livres* a year', supplied and equipped a ship and set sail for America, where he joined Washington's army and rapidly achieved promotion to the rank of general.[43]

It was news of Lafayette's successes, greeted with wild enthusiasm in Paris, which finally 'urged a regal government to declare itself in favour of republican liberty'.[44] Louis XVI had been reluctant to embroil France in the American War (Lafayette's actions were not universally admired at Court) because 'no instance of aggression had occurred on the side of the English to justify, in his eyes, a hostile measure against the crown of Great Britain', and he may have hoped that the terms of the commercial treaty would be ambiguous enough not to lead to direct conflict in Europe.[45] The ministers responsible for the treaty, Maurepas and Vergennes, knew very well it would be seen as a declaration of war in England – which was of course exactly what they wanted. Louis XV had dismissed the Duc de Choiseul for planning a similar campaign against Great Britain in 1770; his grandson, though a more conscientious monarch, was to be led by his ministers into a war of aggression which ultimately weakened the French crown rather than that of England. Madame Campan reported that the Queen was even less happy than her husband 'about the part France was taking respecting the independence of the American colonies, and constantly opposed it'.[46] Not a profound thinker, she was nonetheless probably well aware of the dangerous absurdity of absolute monarchy giving succour to republicanism, although her letters

to the Empress Maria-Theresa in 1778 show her to have been far more concerned with Austrian claims to Bavaria (which both France and Prussia opposed) than with events across the Atlantic.

A substantial number of French troops and naval forces were despatched to America under d'Estaing and Rochambeau in 1778 and 1780, but the real territorial interest for France lay elsewhere – in the West Indies, Africa, India, and of course, Europe. The Bourbon pact was brought into play in a combined French and Spanish operation to invade England itself in 1779, but notwithstanding much posturing and parading of troops in Normandy and Brittany during the summer, the plan was abandoned. The French troops fell prey to dysentery, the Spanish fleet was unable to cope with Channel storms, and it was 'a lost campaign which has cost a great deal of money', as Marie-Antoinette correctly noted.[47] More modest schemes to seize the Channel Islands also came to naught. It was quite likely that once France saw her colonial objectives being realized, she had no stomach for a European land war which might well take place on French soil.

What is perhaps a surprising feature of the entire American War is the zealous participation of some of the most noble figures in France, including those who were generally regarded as leaders of *anglomanie*. The Duc de Lauzun seemed positively to relish inflicting mortal blows on his English friends. He was on a long visit to England when news of Burgoyne's defeat came through, and as France moved towards open support of the Americans, was asked by Maurepas to extend his stay. The very suave, charming, racing-mad Lauzun quickly made a point of paying calls at all the best London drawing rooms.

> Living much more in society than I had been since my arrival in England, I saw people from all parties who spoke freely in front of me, and without giving myself any trouble, I was soon well informed of all public affairs, and I knew interesting things of which the Marquis de Noailles, our ambassador, could not be aware.[48]

Lauzun returned to Versailles in the spring of 1778 in order to impart his interesting information to Maurepas. A surprise attack on England was then being mooted, in which he fully expected 'to be given a brilliant role'. He also had the charitable idea of bankrupting the Bank of England before hostilities commenced, through the simple expedient of drawing simultaneously on all British banks in Europe; they would be obliged to withdraw funds from the Bank of England in order to meet their liabilities, and in doing so would cause the Bank of England to collapse, for it had low reserves. Lauzun was displeased to find this financial onslaught squashed at Necker's insistence, and even less happy when the daring plan for a pre-emptive military strike was also abandoned. As he had taken the trouble to send Maurepas 'an extended and very detailed report on the state of defences in England and in all English possessions in the four quarters of the world', he felt decidedly snubbed.[49]

He consoled himself by returning to England to gather more intelligence, but there were limits even to his treachery. When England and France recalled their ambassadors in the summer of 1778, Lauzun, at Maurepas's request, asked for permission to remain in London, which was granted; the British government's Sir Charles Thompson told him that he was 'too well known ever to be suspect'. After that, declared Lauzun, 'I could no longer remain honourably in England.'[50]

The duke returned to Paris, and was a keen advocate of the plan to capture the Channel Islands, 'chance having let fall into my hands very detailed and well-written reports on Jersey and Guernsey' – but he was frustrated yet again in his martial ambitions by further ministerial timidity in any direct assault on Great Britain.[51] He then proposed the invasion of the Isle of Wight and the destruction of Portsmouth. Maurepas was not listening. Lauzun was embarrassed at having been excluded from the force commanded by the Comte d'Estaing which sailed for America in April 1778, and he seemed condemned to languish in Parisian boudoirs until one evening a perusal of the *London Magazine* yielded information 'on the state of English possessions on the coast of Africa and their garrisons'.[52]

Nothing could now restrain him. His proposal to capture these poorly defended trading posts was accepted, and despite the entreaties of the Queen (whom he still chose to believe desperately in love with him), he sailed for Senegal, and in 1779 found his brow wreathed in victory laurels as the French flag flew over captured British forts.

Lauzun's desire for glory was not satisfied by this expedition. He was a member of the 6,000-strong French army which sailed for America under Rochambeau in 1780, as was the Comte de Ségur, who found his progress to war considerably slowed by the captain of his ship. When he and fellow officers questioned why they spent ten days tacking about the French coast instead of making full speed for America, it was discovered that the lovesick captain had been paying nocturnal visits to his mistress, who was literally following the fleet in a small coaster!

The surrender of British forces under Lord Cornwallis at Yorktown in 1781 was the turning point in the campaign on the American continent. Attention then shifted to more profitable colony snatching in the West Indies and elsewhere. A preliminary peace treaty between Britain, France, Spain and America, granting America full independence, was signed at Versailles on 20 January 1783, with the full treaty coming into effect on 3 September. British honour had been retrieved by a naval victory over the French at the Battle of the Saintes in 1782, and the singular failure of a combined French and Spanish army to take Gibraltar was a great tribute to British fortitude. On the other hand, perhaps the heroic presence of the dandyish Comte d'Artois (who, it was claimed, was never allowed near the front line unless the British agreed to hold their fire) had something to do with repeated blunders made by the Duc de Crillon, who was in command of the ill-fated assault on the Rock in September 1782.

The French, however, could not conceal their glee at the overall outcome of the war, firmly convinced that they had dealt their enemy a fatal blow. One symbolic result of the peace was the removal, to great public rejoicing, of the British commissioner at Dunkirk, appointed after the Seven Years War to prevent fortification of the port. The Comte de Ségur had no

doubt about who was now the more powerful of the two nations.

> England, deprived of allies, saw herself reduced to her own resources. At length an honourable peace came to crown our glorious labours; it took away thirteen large provinces from our eternal rival, restored to our allies cities, colonies, and islands which they had lost, and restored us to the rank from which the weakness of Louis XV had forced us to descend. . . . The affronts of the peace of 1763 were effaced.[53]

Paris was never more confident and cheerful than in the years immediately following 1783, but the real cost of the American War had yet to be paid. Although France regained colonies in the West Indies and obtained a foothold in Africa, she made little headway in India and failed entirely to reverse the losses she had suffered in North America in 1763. Quebec remained in British hands, and the United States fought shy of a binding alliance with France. Ultimately, the war was a disaster for the *ancien régime*, which not only lent huge sums of money to the Americans (in 1780 alone they asked for 20 million *livres*), but incurred heavy debts at home to meet the costs of a war that yielded little tangible financial benefit. It proved difficult to run the country on *gloire*.

British commercial success, far from being diminished by the war, actually increased. The Americans spurned trading links with France in favour of renewed traffic with Britain, and an Anglo-French treaty of commerce signed in 1786, promoted by those French who sought to undermine the overtly republican aims of some American campaigners, saw British goods flood into France to the great detriment of French industry. According to Madame Campan, it 'annihilated at one blow the trade of Rouen, and the other manufacturing towns throughout the kingdom'.[54]

Where British goods find entry, can British tourists be far behind? One of the most curious consequences of French victory was the resurgence of *anglomanie*, not to mention the folly

of wealthy Englishmen who flocked to Paris to fill the conquerors' pockets with their money. Perhaps it was merely the best way to show off English tailoring, for the vogue for English fashions grew enormousiy during the rest of the decade. The young Comte de Tilly deplored the entire American War. He detested the republican dogma imported from the New World and disseminated by Lafayette (already a *bête noire* of conservative nobles), and was equally appalled to discover that once peace was signed, Paris was 'overrun . . . with English people, who, as usual, were loaded with favours, comforts, and privileges, both at Court and in town'.[55] To his anglophobic mind, the fruits of defeat should have been much more bitter.

The French state, deluded by military glory, was nevertheless blind to the political dangers unleashed by its triumph in America. Parisian high society amused itself by discussing liberty and democracy between anecdotes and risqué jokes. In the words of Talleyrand, 'all young people believed themselves fit to govern. All ministerial manoeuvres were criticised', and political opinions began to be exchanged at balls, 'between *contredanses*'.[56] The *beau monde* was divided; in one camp, anglomaniacs finally made known their opinions on the British constitution and considered how it could be adapted in France, in the other 'the Americans', headed by Lafayette, argued for constitutional reform along American lines.

The government, naturally enough, ignored them all, and 'the heads of the ancient families of the nobility, believing themselves as unshakeable as the monarchy itself, slumbered in perfect security upon a volcano'.[57] They ought to have woken from their feudal torpor if only to see how the younger generation was talking itself inexorably towards revolution. For nearly all the arguments in favour of political reform came initially not from the oppressed underclass, nor even from the bourgeoisie. It was above all the nobility which championed the ideals of liberty and democracy – and the Parisian nobility at that. The *beau monde* had come of age at last. It was to endure a painful maturity.

7

1789: *Year of Reckoning*

In January 1789 Paris was still dancing, Versailles still performed its barren rituals, and the insistent murmur of discontent sweeping through the rest of France seemed utterly irrelevant in the glittering social whirl of the capital. *Cahiers de doléances* were being compiled in every town in the kingdom, detailing the grievances which people hoped would be addressed by representatives to the States General, convened for May 1789: unfair taxation, repressive game laws, restrictions on trade, archaic feudal dues . . . did it matter one iota to the scented dandies who wafted from salon to boudoir, or to the belles who borrowed their carriages in order to gallop to the Opéra, the races, and the gaming table?

Severe storms in the summer of 1788 had caused massive damage to crops, and the price of bread had soared beyond the means of many families: Paris merely shook its head and talked of other things. The budget deficit increased by a few more million *livres*: Paris tut-tutted and continued dancing. Elections to the States General were to be held in the spring: Paris saw its chance to force the pace of political change. Languid *beaux* suddenly grew very prolix on the subject of constitutional reform and hurried off to despised distant provinces to get themselves elected. For high society, the Revolution had already begun. After all, it was fashionable to be avant-garde.

This change of direction for the Parisian *beau monde* was not

just another of its transient whims, despite the novelty of a situation that promised at least a temporary cure for that chronic malady, *ennui*. In 1780, according to Frénilly, old Parisian social life 'was already in ruins . . . but the façade still existed'. By 1787, 'the farce, as they say, was over, the curtain had fallen, and one began to see behind the scenes'.[1] People did not like what they saw, and emboldened by the American War, began to utter aloud their desire for the same liberties they had helped the Americans to win.

Necker's publication of details of French finances in his *Compte-rendu au Roi* of 1781 was an important catalyst for change, producing 'a kind of revolution in the public mind', as the Comte de Ségur explained. 'Hitherto, the nation, a stranger to its own affairs, had remained completely ignorant as to the receipts and expenditure of the public revenue, the debts of the state, the extent of its needs, and the resources it possessed.'[2] It was not long before every salon had an armchair financier ready to pontificate on public affairs, and a class which on principle never paid its bills and spent its way merrily to personal bank-ruptcy now devoted itself to criticizing the government and discussing the dismal progress of the deficit. Young aristocrats were particularly vocal in their opposition to the establishment; they disliked 'the irksome etiquette of the old order', took 'a secret pleasure' in admiring the subversive works of Voltaire and Rousseau, and 'applauded the republican scenes' they found at the theatre. 'We enjoyed our patrician advantages together with the sweets of a plebeian philosophy,' wrote a nostalgic Ségur, and he, like many others, was quite convinced that the approaching revolution was but a prelude to a glorious era of liberty in which power would pass from the King to the nobility.[3]

After the Diamond Necklace scandal and a further exposé of the parlous state of French finances, this time by the disgraced Controller-General Calonne (who found Necker's *Compte-rendu* wildly inaccurate, showing a surplus of ten million *livres* instead of a deficit of forty million!), Parisian salons were dominated by political discussions as never before. Visiting the French capital in 1787, shortly after the publication of Calonne's

Requête au Roi, Arthur Young was amazed by the views being expressed in aristocratic circles.

> One opinion pervaded the whole company, that they are on the eve of some great revolution in the government . . . with a *deficit* impossible to provide for without the states general of the kingdom . . . a prince on the throne, with excellent dispositions, but without the resources of a mind that could govern in such a moment without ministers: a court buried in pleasure and dissipation . . . a great ferment amongst all ranks of men, who are eager for some change, without knowing what to look to or hope for: and a strong leaven of liberty, increasing every hour since the American revolution.[4]

Young was admittedly a guest of the Duc de Liancourt, one of the more enlightened noblemen of the *ancien régime*, and consequently found many liberals at the duke's table. The doctrine of liberty, however, was contagious, infecting even those who would lose everything were it implemented. Alexandre de Tilly, conservative and royalist, had no doubt that many scions of the nobility who espoused the cause of democracy were motivated solely by vanity. In his view, the revolutionary Vicomte de Noailles (the bearer of an illustrious name indeed) suffered from 'an unrestrained craving for celebrity'. Though 'born to be a pillar of the throne', Noailles longed to rival his radical brother-in-law Lafayette, and the only way of attracting attention was to champion democracy and establish his credentials as a reformer.[5]

Louis XVI's failure to intervene on the side of liberty in the Dutch Revolution of 1787 because of the deficit greatly angered veterans of the American War, and the relentlessly hostile scrutiny of the government increased. It was popular to blame the Queen for the financial crisis in France. In addition to her reputation as 'the modern Messalina' she also enjoyed the nickname 'Madame Deficit', although as Bombelles justly pointed out, she was hardly responsible for the huge sums of money swallowed up by the War Department, or the myriad abuses that flourished in other ministries.

Despite its alarming size, the deficit would not have led to catastrophe for the government had ministers been able to force through fiscal reforms before they ran out of money. In 1786, when it was first deemed necessary to raise new taxes to meet the shortfall in revenue, Calonne estimated the deficit at eighty million *livres*; this figure was later revised to 112 million, which makes his criticism of Necker's optimistic arithmetic rather amusing. Gouverneur Morris found that guests at a supper hosted by the Baron de Besenval considered 'that it was not worth while to call the States General for such a Trifle', a view which Chateaubriand shared: 'the application of such a violent remedy to so slight an evil proves that we were being carried towards unknown political regions.'[6]

The deficit became the excuse for a battle to win political control of the country; the States General was the weapon, and the enemy was the Court. Given the arbitrary nature of the King's power, demands for constitutional reform were predictably accompanied by fierce personal attacks on the sovereign, and as the prospect of final confrontation with the Court drew nearer, Parisians grew more vitriolic in their diatribes against all that pertained to Versailles. Bombelles visited the Comtesse de Brionne's salon in January 1789, where he was pained to find 'all the most elegant society of Paris' singing a scurrilous song about the royal family. *Bon ton* was dead, even if gaiety was not, and as revolution approached, high society 'ran laughing and dancing towards the precipice'.[7]

It would be entirely wrong to assume that Louis XVI remained supine in the face of mounting danger. Indeed, his attempt to address the financial crisis rather than to ignore it actually precipitated political upheaval. Although Bombelles criticized 'the cruel care which is taken to keep our masters confined within the Île de France' and the assiduity of courtiers whose 'chief interest' lay in 'preventing the voice of the nation from ever reaching the ears of the King', Louis XVI was never deaf to cries of distress, nor was he unaware of the need to control expenditure, particularly in the royal household.[8] Shortly after his accession in 1774, Marie-Antoinette wrote to

her mother that France could expect a change for the better in the new King: 'what is certain is that he has an inclination towards economy and the greatest desire to make his people happy.'[9] But for all his good intentions, only two months later he was obliged to give the dismissed Duc d'Aiguillon a *traitement*, or golden handshake, of 500,000 *livres* at the insistence of Maurepas.

The structure of the Court and government made economies very hard to find. In 1780 an ambitious programme of cutbacks in the royal household was proposed by the King, but only partially implemented, though a second attempt at retrenchment in 1787, which included abandoning the Court's annual journey to Fontainebleau and the abolition of many posts, did achieve results. The *Grande Écurie* was merged with the *Petite Écurie*, half the lords of the bedchamber were dismissed, the Garde du Corps was reformed, and the King even greatly reduced expenditure on his hunt. Louis XVI finally showed himself capable of restoring order to royal finances; the debts of the nation, largely incurred during the American War, proved altogether more difficult to control.

At Calonne's request, the Assembly of Notables was convened in 1787 to agree to new fiscal measures aimed at cutting the deficit. Though the Notables (including seven princes of the blood) were nearly all land-owning aristocrats, they accepted radical ideas, including the abolition of the *corvée* and noble privileges, which would have made them equally liable with bourgeois and peasant in a new land tax. Not surprisingly, they wanted political advantages in return, and hoping to force the calling of the States General, refused to agree to the implementation of the very measures they had debated (and in some instances, proposed). The Duc d'Orléans, one of the prime agitators for reform, made an English pun on the whole affair: he was, he declared, a 'not-able'.[10]

Loménie de Brienne, who replaced Calonne as Controller-General in April 1787, dismissed the Notables in May; in order to avoid calling the States General, which many saw as inevitably leading to permanent representative government, he opted

to take his reforms to the *parlements*, seats of the magistracy and hotbeds of political opposition. It was only to be expected that they would seize the opportunity to demand a share of government. Like the Notables, they declared themselves incompetent to register the new taxes (which would have affected many of them adversely), and persisted in calling for the convention of the States General.

After exiling the *parlement* of Paris to Troyes, then reaching an unsatisfactory compromise over its reinstatement, the King was eventually obliged to drop the new land tax, reimpose the old and unpopular *vingtième*, and force his refractory magistrates to register the necessary edicts as well as agree to the raising of 125 million *livres* at a *séance royale* on 19 November 1787. In the middle of the proceedings, the Duc d'Orléans got to his feet to denounce the edicts as 'illegal'. Louis XVI, unusually cool and authoritative, gave him a firm reply: 'Monsieur, it is very legal.'[11] He returned to Versailles and issued a *lettre de cachet* exiling Orléans, 'the motor of all this indecent and dangerous opposition', to his estate at Villers-Cotterets. Orléans was later allowed to go to Raincy, nearer to Paris, because according to Bombelles, 'it was cruel for him to be so far away from the prostitutes in the capital'.[12] Exile, of course, merely added to his popularity, and as the deficit increased, so too did the odium heaped on the King and Court. A decree summoning the States General was finally signed on 7 July 1788, just days before storms ravaged crops across France and made bread (or rather the lack of it) such an emotive issue in 1789.

Bombelles, who was to emigrate during that fateful year, had no doubt that France was sailing into very dangerous waters. 'We are taking huge strides towards anarchy, and the more the King demonstrates that he is far from having a despotic will, the more the goodness of this prince is abused in order, at the least, to despoil him of a legitimate authority.'[13] Such was his opinion in September 1788. In January 1789, Madame de Staël, enjoying her father's renewed appointment as finance minister and her own first literary success, was far less gloomy. The French were simply trying 'to form a public spirit in the midst of a thousand

individual interests. They believe that a constitution will arise from the clash of opposing parties.'[14]

Talk of a constitution months before the States General was due to meet shows how far Paris had moved ahead of the Court, which dallied along in blissful complacency. As Madame de La Tour du Pin explained, 'encroachments on royal authority appeared so novel that neither the King nor the Queen discerned any alarming symptom' in the brawls which began to take place outside bakers' shops in Paris. And anyway, although the winter of 1789 was 'disastrous for the people', Parisian social life was still animated by 'pleasure, plays, and balls'.[15]

One of the grandest balls of the season was given by the Duke of Dorset, British ambassador, who was very popular in the Parisian *beau monde*. Madame de La Tour du Pin, exerting an Irish prerogative, dressed in blue rather than white as requested on the invitation. The Baron de Frénilly, who had finally broadened his mind by roaming beyond the walls of Paris, found the same carefree atmosphere at Poitiers. 'I passed the terrible winter of '89 there, of which I recall only balls and fêtes, in the spring came the elections, and the dinners alone remain in my memory.' His only problems, in fact, were his continual losses at the card table of the Marquise d'Asnières; eventually he discovered they were due to his 'immense' highly polished English steel coat buttons, which reflected his cards to his opponents' advantage![16]

Anglomanie therefore had practical drawbacks, although Gouverneur Morris found it in vogue as never before when he arrived in Paris early in 1789. 'Every Thing is *à l'Anglois* and a Desire to imitate the English prevails alike in the Cut of a Coat and the Form of a Constitution.'[17] The British constitution, like the English garden, was imperfectly understood in France, but it was a model for liberal aristocrats because they all wanted to sit in a French version of the House of Lords, something the alternative American constitution would not allow.

Perhaps high society had grown tired of pleasure, perhaps it really was fired by idealism rather than ambition (Madame de La Tour du Pin speaks of 'many good and honourable people,

among them the King himself' hoping 'that they were about to enter a Golden Age'), but its blindness was astounding.[18] With a large class of intelligent, capable bourgeois, and an infinity of angry paupers prowling the streets of Paris, the possibility that political power might be wrested from the crown only to be hijacked by that strange beast 'the Third Estate', ought to have been glaringly obvious. Certainly, neither the monarchy nor the nobility possessed such eloquent champions as the Third Estate, or commons, who succeeded in gaining double representation at the States General (600 deputies as opposed to 300 for the clergy and nobility respectively), and were already pressing their claim to represent the 'nation'. It was a nation from which those nobles and clerics who clung to their positions of inherited superiority were to be excluded – by exile or death.

While the procedural etiquette for this momentous, not to mention archaic gathering was being arranged (the last States General had been held in 1614), the Parisian *beau monde* amused itself by playing politics. Some of its more prominent members, like Talleyrand and Lafayette, travelled to the provinces for the elections. Lafayette, according to a bemused Gouverneur Morris, went to the Auvergne in February 'to get himself elected either for the *Noblesse* or the *Tiers État*'.[19] Morris found that the hero of the American War was not alone in his radicalism, and in a letter to the Marquis de La Luzerne, French ambassador to England, he wrote that:

> As yet the Spectacles hold some share in the Conversation, but I hear as much Politics among the Ladies of Paris as ever you did among those of Philadelphia. Republicanism is absolutely a moral Influenza from which neither Titles, Places, nor even the Diadem can guard their Possessor.[20]

At Versailles itself, where he dined with the Comtesse de Tessé, he found 'Republicans of the first Feather', with whom he felt obliged to disagree. 'The Countess, who is a very sensible Woman, has formed her Ideas of Government in a Manner not suited (I think) either to the Situation, the Circumstances or the

Dispositions of France, and there are many such.'[21] In fact, despite his reputation as a liberal American, Morris found himself advocating a strong monarchy, for he not only believed Louis XVI 'to be a good and honest Man' who 'earnestly desires the Felicity of his People', but also considered the citizens of France totally unfit to govern themselves because of the 'utter Prostration of Morals' they displayed, and their universal 'Indifference to the Violation of Engagements'.[22]

Nothing, however, could avert the headlong slide towards revolution, although three weeks before the meeting of the States General, *le Tout-Paris* as usual went to parade in its finery at Longchamp during Holy Week. Bombelles noted that on the Thursday 'the ladies, in elegant *calèches*, attracted most attention', despite the magnificent cortège of the Duc d'Orléans, who, 'followed by a squadron of outriders more English than those of the Prince of Wales, came to gather tributes to his popularity'. Bombelles was pleased to report that signs of enthusiasm for the duke were muted. On Good Friday a crowd at the Porte Maillot who were watching the procession of splendid carriages on its way from Paris to Longchamp traded insults and blows with the mounted police, but this did not deter Orléans's mistress, the young *intrigante* Madame de Buffon, from appearing that day

> in a *calèche* bearing the livery of her lover, the prince. And, as Madame la Duchesse d'Orléans also came in her carriage, it was necessary for her rival to hasten to an adjacent avenue and for the Duc d'Orléans to alight from Mme de Buffon's *calèche* in order not to commit too excessive an impropriety.

Surely the duchess cannot have been ignorant of this farcical manoeuvre, despite the dignified silence of onlookers 'who kept it secret from a princess too widely respected for anyone to think of disturbing her peace of mind'.[23]

Gouverneur Morris, who first met the beautiful, virtuous and neglected Duchesse d'Orléans at Versailles a month before the parade at Longchamp, soon noticed that 'she has something or

other which weighs very heavy on her Heart', and attributed it to 'the *Besoin d'être aimée'*.[24] He was to become her friend and a regular visitor to her salon at the Palais Royal, where he heard interesting news and rumour from the heart of the Orléanist camp. One of the first disturbances in Paris during 1789, in which the Duc d'Orléans was strongly suspected of involvement, occurred just a week before the States General opened at Versailles.

The destruction of a wallpaper factory in the Faubourg Saint-Antoine might seem relatively unimportant in the light of later revolutionary *journées*, but it was nevertheless an ominous prelude to much more violent and serious unrest which brought the *bas peuple* to the forefront of the Revolution in Paris, and first kindled suspicions that someone was actually employing the mob for political purposes. The target of their wrath on 28 April 1789 was a man of the people, Réveillon, who had built up a flourishing wallpaper business on the rue de Montreuil, employing more than 700 workers. A charitable man, he even provided for 150 men he did not need during the terrible winter of 1788–9, but a false rumour that he intended to cut wages to fifteen *sous* per day led to the complete destruction of his factory and with it the livelihood of many in the Faubourg Saint-Antoine.

Réveillon fled to the Bastille for protection as his house itself was attacked, and a veritable battle broke out between the mob and soldiers sent to stop the looting. Bombelles estimated the number of casualties on both sides at 'more than two hundred'; he was singularly unimpressed to find the Duc de Châtelet and the Baron de Besenval, colonels of the Gardes Françaises and Gardes Suisses who were attempting to end the riot, closeted with the Lieutenant of Police, where they 'agitated rather than acted'. It was soon suspected that the mob had been paid, for most of the looters came from other quarters of Paris and had no connection whatsoever with Réveillon's factory. 'Among the wounded carried to hospital, there were dying men who are supposed to have said that it was dying too cheaply to perish for six francs.'[25] Others put the rioters' pay at twelve francs, and the

provenance of this money was guessed to be the Palais Royal.

The *beau monde* had passed the day pleasantly at Vincennes, where the Duc d'Orléans's horses were racing against those of the Comte d'Artois. Orléans had stopped to speak to the large but inactive crowd gathered near Réveillon's premises as he made his way to Vincennes in the morning, and his theatrical distribution of money provoked cries of '*Vive le duc d'Orléans!*' By the time race-goers returned to Paris, the streets of the Faubourg Saint-Antoine had been spattered with blood, and those who failed to divert their carriages were in for rough treatment.

> Mme de Montagu, wife of the nephew of the Dean of Notre-Dame, passing amidst this horrid scene of butchery, was asked if she belonged to the Third Estate. . . . She replied calmly that she was noble, that she recognized no other master than the King, and, with the same sang-froid, threw to the people who surrounded her coach, not her purse, nor golden *louis*, but a small *écu* for them to toast the health of the King. This firmness saved her. She was allowed to pass, while the Chevalier de La Tourette, having said he belonged to the Third Estate, thought he would be massacred because someone noticed his Maltese cross. He owed his safety only to his swiftness in opening the door of his carriage on the side opposite the bandits who, after pursuing him, seized the vehicle for themselves; no one knows what they have done with it.[26]

The nineteen year old Madame de La Tour du Pin had been offered a ride home from Vincennes by Madame de Valence, whose husband was First Equerry to the Duc d'Orléans, and they too found themselves waylaid by 'four to five hundred people' in the rue Saint-Antoine. Their reception, however, was far from hostile.

> The sight of the Orléans livery worn by Mme de Valence's servants . . . excited the enthusiasm of this rabble. They stopped us for a moment, crying, 'Long live our father! Long live our King of Orléans!' I paid no attention to these exclamations. They

came back to my mind some months later, when I was quite certain of the schemes of this miserable Duc d'Orléans.[27]

Orléans, the 'King of Paris' with his own capital within a capital at the Palais Royal, had possibly staged this bloody *journée* as a demonstration of his power and popularity. It was a gauntlet flung in the very face of Louis XVI. Seven days later, on 4 May, Orléans made a point of walking with the deputies of the Third Estate as he left the church of St Louis at Versailles after the Mass which preceded the opening of the States General. It was to be one of the last splendid processions of the *ancien régime*, with the full panoply of royal and noble magnificence. So hot was the day, even after a night of incessant rain, that Gouverneur Morris got sunburnt as he watched the King, Queen and deputies from all three orders walk slowly from the church of Notre-Dame to that of St Louis.

> The Procession is very magnificent, thro' a double Row of Tapestry. Neither the King nor Queen appear too well pleased. The former is repeatedly saluted as he passes along with the *Vive le Roi* but the latter meets not a single Acclamation. She looks, however, with Contempt on the Scene in which she acts a Part and seems to say: for the present I submit but I shall have my Turn.[28]

The royal family were in full Court dress, the nobility in lace and silk with plumed hats, the clergy in ceremonial robes – and the Third Estate in sombre, menacing black. During the Mass, which was followed by a harangue from the Bishop of Nancy on the plight of the poor, the King and Queen sat in state beneath a canopy of violet satin embroidered with golden fleurs-de-lis. They returned to the palace of Versailles in carriages, and once more, although 'cries of "Long live the King!" were quite loud and frequent, those of "Long live the Queen!" were stifled'. Bombelles, watching from the house of the Maréchal de Duras, overheard disparaging remarks about the Queen from the crowd, and noted sadly that no 'Queen of France has been less

loved, and yet she cannot be reproached with a single act of wickedness'.[29] Gouverneur Morris also pitied the Queen, who was to endure further public mortification the following day at the opening session of the States General, which was held in the inappropriately named *Salle des Menus Plaisirs* at Versailles.

Le Tout-Paris used every means possible to get tickets to the opening ceremony, just as they had leaned from every available window to watch the procession to Mass. Some people, however, had no desire to occupy the rows of benches reserved for fashionable spectators. Madame de Boigne recalls how her father, the Marquis d'Osmond, told the King's aunt Madame Adélaïde that he would not be attending the ceremony. Incredulous, she asked him why not, when many people had travelled huge distances to be there. 'The truth is, Madame,' he replied, 'that I am not fond of funerals, and certainly not when a monarch is to be interred.'[30]

Despite Osmond's forebodings, the cheers which greeted Louis XVI from deputies of the Third Estate showed he still enjoyed much popular support. Mirabeau, monstrous yet magnificent, and elected a deputy for the commons despite his title and his terrible reputation (which had caused the nobility of Provence to reject him), created a stir as he entered the hall alone to take his seat.

> A low murmur – *un sussurro* – but general, was heard. The deputies already seated in front of him advanced one row, those behind drew back, those at the side moved away, and he remained alone in the centre of a noticeable gap. A scornful smile passed across his face and he sat down.[31]

Madame de La Tour du Pin, who witnessed this little drama, attributed the Queen's anxious scanning of the ranks of the Third Estate to a desire to see Mirabeau for herself. Despite her 'great dignity', Marie-Antoinette, seated on the dais just below the King, was far from calm: 'one could see, from the almost convulsive movement of her fan, that she was very agitated.'[32] Morris even thought he detected tears in her eyes, particularly

during the applause which followed the King's speech, by all accounts a well-delivered and sensible discourse. Its brevity must surely have been appreciated, considering what followed.

The *Garde des Sceaux* (Keeper of the Seals), Barentin, spoke next, in a voice 'so feeble that one could barely hear it in a third of the hall', before the stage was taken by the Controller-General, Jacques Necker.[33] Unquestionably intended to be the star of the show (both he and the Duc d'Orléans had been loudly applauded by the Third Estate as they made their entrance), Necker nevertheless allowed most of his speech to be read by a professional reader – just as well, in view of his own weak voice and lack of presence. 'He tries to play the Orator but plays it very ill,' wrote a disappointed Morris. 'A bad accent and an ungraceful Manner destroy much of the Effect which ought to follow from a Composition written by Mr. Neckar and spoken by Mr. Neckar.'[34]

Neither monarch, deputies nor spectators were spared a three-hour analysis of the woes of France. Like other ladies-in-waiting, Madame de La Tour du Pin was forced to maintain an elegant posture throughout with nothing to support her back, and consequently found this monologue unbearable. 'I believe I have never felt so much weariness as during M. Necker's speech, which his supporters praised to the skies.'[35] Bombelles, similarly bored, was highly relieved that the King prevented further speeches by leaving the hall as soon as Necker's was over. It was five o'clock, and the marquis, who had been seated on a bench reserved for the Duc de Normandie since nine in the morning, was surely not the only man who was dying of hunger! Morris was pleased to be able to record some public show of affection for the Queen as she left the dais. 'The Queen rises, and to my great Satisfaction she hears for the first Time in several Months the sound of *Vive la Reine*! She makes a low Curtsey, and this produces a louder Acclamation, and that a lower Curtsey.'[36]

Unfortunately for Marie-Antoinette, it was only a transient display of warmth. The following day, the three orders took possession of separate debating chambers in the Hôtel des Menus Plaisirs; the Third Estate perhaps significantly occupied

the great hall used during the opening ceremony, while the nobility and clergy were 'kicked upstairs' to the first floor. The Duc d'Orléans, meanwhile, attempted to explain why he had declined to walk with the King in the processions, and put it about that he had been insulted when he made his apologies. This was hotly denied by Bombelles who, as a conscientious Court journalist, declared he had the truth from 'a sure and close source'. He was able to note a great revolution in Court life the next day (7 May), when the King did not retire until 1.30 a.m. – a worrying change in the habits of Louis XVI, who for years had gone to bed promptly at 11 p.m. The States General were already disrupting the hitherto immutable routine of Versailles and, as if to prove they meant business, members of the Third Estate insulted several high-ranking Court ladies, among them the Duchesse d'Uzès, on the terrace of the palace itself on 8 May.[37]

Although Madame de La Tour du Pin found that 'nothing materially changed in the web of etiquette which surrounded the Court', she noticed that salon conversations became increasingly sharp and ill-humoured – not to mention tedious, for political discussions bored her.[38] Morris recorded that political argument so bedevilled Parisian salons, women could not even make their voices heard, let alone influence policy as they had done in the past.

> They will have more of this if the States General should really fix a Constitution. Such an Event would be particularly distressing to the Women of this Country for they would be thereby deprived of their Share in the Government; and hitherto they have exercised an Authority almost unlimited, with no small Pleasure to themselves tho' not perhaps with the greatest Advantage to the Community.[39]

The need to reduce the deficit was gradually forgotten as the States General became mired in quarrels over voting procedures, and Paris was inundated with political pamphlets 'whose tendency is absolutely to overturn the present government'.

Arthur Young criticized the 'blindness and folly' of the King's ministers in allowing these seditious publications to be carried into the provinces in state-owned vehicles.[40] It was no secret that most pamphlets were issued from the Palais Royal, whose cafés were filled night and day with table-thumping government critics and impromptu orators. 'The people look very much to the Duc d'Orléans as to a head,' wrote Young, 'but with palpable and general ideas of distrust and want of confidence.'[41]

Their lack of confidence was justified. Orléans's abilities fell far short of his ambitions, and his patriarchal munificence was suspect in its very ostentation. Both personally and through the government, the King and Queen did as much as they could to alleviate the misery caused by the shortage of bread in Paris, but their charity was seldom praised beyond the walls of Versailles. The Duc d'Orléans, however, was a complete master of public relations; in this sense, he was truly a consummate politician. The Court, locked in feudal magnificence which never deigned to explain itself, had no weapons against the malevolent pens of Paris, and no pamphlets of its own to counter those produced in the Palais Royal. Manipulation of the media as a means of gaining political advantage was perhaps used successfully for the first time by the Duc d'Orléans.

His friends fiercely denied his role in bringing down the monarchy, but in retrospect there seems little doubt that Orléans was up to his neck in treason. He had a long history of disagreements with the crown, stemming back to Louis XV's refusal to recognize his father's second marriage to Madame de Montesson. Indeed, the cadet branch of the royal house had always been known for its recalcitrance; but what demon drove Orléans into active involvement in the Revolution, and finally into republicanism and regicide?

Tilly considered that the duke possessed a great deal of 'vanity as a prince . . . though he had far too little pride as a man', and he certainly enjoyed the advantages of his wealth and rank.[42] In Paris, he played the king burdened with none of the cares that kingship imposed. But did he really want the crown? Grace Elliott, his one-time mistress, thought not. 'I am certain that the

Duke never at that time had an idea of mounting the throne, whatever the views of his factious friends.' Tilly, however, felt that Orléans was led into the Revolution 'through the bait of a throne on which he would have been alarmed and astonished to be seated'.[43] Certainly, as a man of pleasure, had he ever succeeded in becoming king he would most probably have opted for a constitutional monarchy which would have enabled him to leave the difficulties of government to others.

Whatever the opinions of his supporters, it seems highly unlikely that Orléans participated in the Revolution purely from a disinterested desire to liberate the people. There was talk of offering him the throne after the flight to Varennes in 1791, or at least a role as regent during the minority of the Dauphin, were Louis XVI to abdicate; and the activities of his son, the usurper Louis-Philippe, would seem to offer conclusive proof of the regal ambitions of the House of Orléans – ambitions which are nurtured to this very day.

Grace Elliott blames the Court for Orléans's revolutionary activities. The repeated snubs inflicted on him by Louis XVI pushed him towards the opposition, and his money was used by 'the horrid creatures who surrounded him' to ferment unrest. 'I am certain', she wrote, 'that the Duke knew little of what was going on in his name.'[44] This is a pretty theory, but hardly bears close scrutiny; living in the Palais Royal, Orléans could not have remained ignorant of the multitude of plots which were hatched there. One strong motive for his machinations against the Court was his deep hatred of the Queen. Grace Elliott declared that 'although I never heard him speak with disrespect of the King, I certainly have heard him very, very, violent against the Queen'.[45]

It was a hatred common to the *frondeurs* of the Palais Royal; but what caused it? According to Madame Campan, Marie-Antoinette 'always excluded' Orléans 'from her private society' because Louis XVI disliked his character, while Madame de La Tour du Pin stated that 'the Queen detested the Duc d'Orléans, who had spoken ill of her'.[46] The Queen also rejected Louis-Philippe d'Orléans as a husband for her daughter; yet surely

none of this was enough to cause such bitter enmity unless, like the Duc de Lauzun (who was his close associate), Orléans's vanity led him to hope for political favours from the Queen. Perhaps he wrongly blamed her for Louis XVI's dislike of him. Whatever the reason, the strategy adopted by the Orléanist faction involved a horrendous persecution of the Queen. Recognized Orléanists, at least during the early days of the Revolution, were Mirabeau, Talleyrand, Lauzun, the Vicomte de Noailles, Siéyès, and Laclos; deep political discussions used to take place not only at the Palais Royal, but also at Lauzun's 'folly' at Montrouge on the outskirts of Paris, and at the home of Orléans's mistress, Madame de Buffon, who was closely allied to Laclos.

Despite Grace Elliott's protestations that Orléans was innocent of revolutionary crimes (though even she could not extract a satisfactory explanation from him on his vote for Louis XVI's execution) and Louis-Philippe's assertion that his father's financial difficulties during 1789–90 were entirely the result of debts and a loss of revenue, it seems very probable that Orléans spent large amounts of money in order to discredit the government and buy popular support. The profusion of pamphlets alone must have been expensive. Arthur Young visited the bookstalls of the Palais Royal on 9 June 1789, where 'every hour produces something new. Thirteen came out today, sixteen yesterday, and ninety-two last week', even though printing costs had doubled in two years from twenty-seven to thirty *livres* to between sixty and eighty *livres* per sheet. Someone must have been subsidizing these diatribes, nearly all of them 'in favour of liberty, and commonly violent against the clergy and nobility'.[47]

Fireworks could be bought very cheaply from boutiques in the Palais Royal, in Young's opinion in order to keep the people in 'a continual ferment'. Money was also believed to have been employed speculating in grain to keep Paris short of bread, for no rational explanation could be found for the difficulty in obtaining flour in Paris when supplies were theoretically being brought in both from other parts of the country and abroad. A hungry mob, however, was a useful weapon, and it is hard to see

how it benefited the Court. Courtiers were convinced that
enemies of the crown were disrupting supplies in order to turn
Paris against the government, and Orléans was the chief suspect.

His financial embarrassment at this period is not readily ex-
plicable. In 1788, Orléans raised eight million *livres* through the
sale of his art collection (much of it came to England), and his
income was enormous. Yet in November 1789 Morris heard
from a banker, Mr Richard, that 'the Duke of Orléans offered
Beaumarchais 20pc for a loan of 500,000 *ff* and that he has since
applied to their House for a loan of 300,000 *ff*, but in both Cases
without Success'.[48] The Duchesse d'Orléans's lady-in-waiting,
Madame de Chastellux, was in no doubt that the duke was
'plunging himself into Debts and Difficulties to support the
present factious Temper' – so much so, that the duchess intended to demand 'an Appropriation of Revenue for her separate use'. Another member of the Orléans household, the
Vicomte de Ségur, claimed that the British government paid
'two Millions Sterling' to 'make Mischief' in France, an assertion
which Morris stoutly contested. He was supported by Madame
de Ségur, who was firmly of the opinion that the Duc d'Orléans
was 'the Distributor of the Money given for these wicked
Purposes'.[49]

It was not necessarily money wisely spent, for Orléans had a
rival in Paris who (without bankrupting himself) managed to
achieve even greater popularity – Lafayette. The hero of the
American War was a natural leader of the movement for reform,
and though every bit as vain as Orléans, was fired by genuine
idealism and a desire to set the world to rights. His main aim was
to give France a democratic constitution, and success seemed
assured when the King gave way to the strength of the Third
Estate and agreed to the formation of a National Assembly on
27 June after the famous Tennis Court Oath by liberal deputies.

Paris soon enlarged its political vocabulary: *'making a constitution'*, wrote Young, 'is a new term they have adopted; and
which they use as if a constitution was a pudding to be made by
receipt.'[50] It was a pudding with British and American ingredients. Lafayette and his supporters wanted 'an American

Constitution with the exception of a King instead of a President', while other *constitutionnel* nobles favoured a British model.[51] Getting the mixture right was the problem, and for months it was seasoned and stirred. So many cooks were, of course, disastrous. The constitution proved to be an indigestible pudding forced down the throat of a reluctant King, and had a very short life indeed – as did many of the cooks.

Constitutional pudding was no food for a Paris which daily demanded more bread. While earnest men toiled over elegant pages of political rhetoric, Paris lived on a diet of rumour, slander and gossip. The main thrust of it was that, one way or another, the Court would attempt to regain its authority by destroying Paris. One scents propagandists at work, whispering tales of impending doom to keep the populace frightened and agitated. Morris was solemnly assured by two noble deputies from the National Assembly that on the day the Bastille fell, the royal family were 'tampering' with regiments at Versailles in a plan 'to reduce Paris by Famine and to take two hundred members of the National Assembly Prisoners' – a day which was in fact so quiet at Versailles that Madame de La Tour du Pin set off on a visit to a friend at Berny, two hours' drive away, without any suspicion 'that there was the least disturbance at Paris'.[52] She was forced to return to the palace because her friend had been unable to leave the capital to meet her, and it was not until the following day that she and other courtiers knew exactly what had happened. Arthur Young also heard the wildest rumours, one being 'that the Queen has been convicted of a plot to poison the King and Monsieur, and give the regency to the Count d'Artois; to set fire to Paris, and blow up the *Palais Royal* by a mine!'[53] From the Queen's point of view, the last suggestion had definite potential!

Given such an atmosphere of fevered speculation, it was little wonder that the arrival of military reinforcements in Paris early in July should have caused trouble. The Gardes Françaises stationed in the capital were in a mutinous state, and the Maréchal de Broglie's decision to prevent riots in the city following the abrupt dismissal of the Parisians' adored Necker on 11 July by

the deployment of Swiss and German regiments was a mistake. Foreigners and loyal to the crown, they were naturally seen as part of a plot to crush Paris by military force. The Gardes Françaises defected to the enraged populace, and gunsmiths' shops and arsenals all over the city were broken into as citizens armed themselves for battle. They also began to demolish parts of the detested customs barrier and looted food depots.

The storming of the Bastille was only undertaken after the people had provided themselves with sufficient weaponry and were assured of the inertia of the dreaded soldiers. Not one infantryman camped on the Champ de Mars prevented the mob from breaking into the Invalides and seizing a large quantity of arms. In the event, little of this firepower was needed. July 14th was to witness the beginning of both the French Revolution and its myth, in the storming of an impregnable fortress by an army of intrepid citizens intent on releasing the victims of oppressive state terror. . . . The truth was too prosaic. Paris needed her theatrical Camille Desmoulins, her red and blue cockade, her pride. Who wanted to know that a mere seven prisoners were released in an incompetent assault which resulted in more casualties on the numerically superior attackers' side than among the handful of defenders? Gouverneur Morris, unaware of the battle because he lived at the other end of town, justly noted that 'the carrying of this Citadel is among the most extraordinary Things that I have met with'.[54] Its effects, both symbolic and political, far outweighed the military significance of the operation.

The fall of the Bastille marked the triumph of Paris over the Court. Unable to rely on his army, dissuaded from leaving the country, Louis XVI found himself obliged to recall Necker to office, and on 16 July, accompanied by deputies of the National Assembly, he drove to Paris to acknowledge defeat. He accepted the good wishes of the nation at the Hôtel de Ville, pinned a revolutionary cockade to his hat, and assented to the formation of the largely bourgeois Garde Nationale commanded by Lafayette. That very night it became known that the Princes de Conti and Condé, and the Comte d'Artois and his children,

accompanied by high-ranking members of his household, had
left France. The Polignacs also fled, doubtless terrified for their
safety after the horrible murders of Launay (Governor of the
Bastille) and Flesselles (Prévôt des Marchands) on 14 July.

Parisian society was changed irrevocably from that moment.
Emigration became fashionable, and people began to raise
money from their estates in order to leave France in greater
comfort. Their motives, as Madame de La Tour du Pin discovered, were diverse. Some genuinely believed in the possibility of staging a counter-revolution from abroad, many clearly
feared for their lives, but not a few young people emigrated
merely to be *à la mode* – or to escape their creditors![55] For those
who remained in Paris, there were still salons to visit, amours
and intrigue, although the Garde Nationale made itself officious
by stopping carriages and demanding patriotic words from the
occupants.

One sign of future repression appeared in the need to obtain a
passport to visit the Bastille, which rapidly established itself as a
tourist attraction. Modern authorities would probably have pre-
served the fortress and charged admission; revolutionary Paris
ordered the demolition of the hated landmark and sold an
enormous quantity of souvenirs made with stone from its grim
walls. Gouverneur Morris and his friend, an *abbé*, had 'some
Difficulty in getting through the Guards' surrounding the former prison just a week after its capture, despite their passport,
for it was already being systematically dismantled. 'We meet an
Architect employed in the Demolition, an old Acquaintance of
the Abbé, who is glad to be useful. He shews us every Thing.
More than I wish to see, as it stinks horribly.'[56]

Morris was happy to return to Adèle de Flahaut's cosy salon.
He was disenchanted with the progress of the Revolution, and
even more disappointed in Lafayette, whose ambition and vanity blinded him to the very real danger of unleashing uncontrollable popular violence. Four days after Louis XVI's pilgrimage to
the capital, Lafayette (who loved prancing about on a white
charger) boasted of his success to Morris, who wrote: 'he has
commanded absolutely an hundred thousand Men, has marched

his Sovereign about the Streets as he pleased, prescribed the Degree of Applause which he should receive, and could have detained him Prisoner had he thought proper.'[57] The hero of the New World was busy drafting a constitution and the Declaration of the Rights of Man, assisted by Thomas Jefferson, then the American ambassador to France. 'Here', wrote Morris of Lafayette, 'is vaulting Ambition which o'erleaps itself. This Man's Mind is so elated by Power, already too great for the Measure of his Abilities, that he looks into the Clouds and grasps at the Supreme.'[58] When he did finally descend to earth, Lafayette was to flee the country and abandon most of his family to the guillotine; imprisoned for five years by the Austrians, he had ample time to reflect on his lack of foresight, though his vanity was incurable.

His great rival the Duc d'Orléans nursed aspirations of a much more sublunary nature, and was widely believed to have instigated the march on Versailles in October 1789, which saw the complete humiliation of the Court. The spontaneity of this 'popular uprising' is questionable, and its necessity even more suspect. After the fall of the Bastille, a certain calm had returned to both Paris and Versailles. The abolition of feudal dues by the National Assembly on 4 August was seen by many people as the culmination of the Revolution, not the prelude to four years of anarchy. On 25 August, the feast of St Louis, the Parisian municipal authorities and Garde Nationale, as well as a group of loyal *poissardes*, went as usual to Versailles to express their devotion to the King. During the summer, Madame de La Tour du Pin found herself entertaining members of the Assembly to dinner twice a week in the War Ministry, to which her father-in-law had been appointed. All deputies except Mirabeau were invited in turn, and she recalled the presence of Robespierre 'in an apple-green suit and with a superior coiffure consisting of a forest of white hair'.[59] Madame de Staël similarly held sway at her father's table in the Contrôle-Général, 'with all the fire of youth', and wit and gaiety were still alive. No one thought of danger.

What prompted the march on Versailles is unclear. Was it

because bread was scarce, as the thousands of women who formed part of the citizens' army claimed? Or was it part of a premeditated plan to capture, and even kill, the royal family? After all, bread had often been scarce before, and nobody imagined that the presence of the King in Paris would materially alter the situation. What is certain is that a banquet at Versailles given by officers of the Garde du Corps to those of the Régiment de Flandre on 2 October where the King, Queen and Dauphin were enthusiastically cheered, was soon translated into an 'orgy' by revolutionary papers at Paris, who claimed that the national cockade had been trampled underfoot. This insult to the nation had to be avenged. Crowds gathered outside the Hôtel de Ville on 4 October and on the 5th, armed with cannon, marched to Versailles.

The events of that day and night have been too well recorded to need detailed repetition: how the women were received kindly by the King and pacified, how Lafayette, who had followed them with the Garde Nationale, assured himself that the palace was secure before snatching an hour's sleep, how, when all was quiet, at six in the morning a determined band of well-armed citizens broke into the palace and headed straight for the Queen's apartments.

It was quite clear that they intended to murder her, and would undoubtedly have succeeded had it not been for the courage of the lone bodyguard outside her doors, Miomandre de Sainte-Marie, who gave Marie-Antoinette warning and held the mob off long enough to allow her to escape through the secret passage beneath the Oeil de Boeuf which connected her bedroom to the King's. Equally certain is that the would-be assassins had inside knowledge of the layout of the royal apartments, were probably let into the locked Cour des Ministres by an accomplice, and were the driving force behind the whole march. The tired and hungry women who took part in it were an ideal cover. Some even claimed 'they had been forced to march, and did not know why they had come', according to Madame de La Tour du Pin, who found them drenched and weeping in the War Ministry's kitchens, where they had been provided with food.[60] She also

swears that the whole plot had been hatched by the Duc d'Orléans, whom her maid Marguerite vowed she saw in the early hours of the morning talking to the assassins in the rue de l'Orangerie.[61] Madame Campan also blames Orléans for the attempt on the Queen's life, though Louis-Philippe, naturally enough, absolves his father from guilt. It is interesting to note, however, that he was himself sent a warning by Madame de Genlis earlier that day to leave Versailles, where he had been to the Assembly, and to go to Passy via Saint-Cloud in order to avoid the army of women on the Versailles road.[62]

It could all have ended very differently had Louis XVI listened to the entreaties of his friends and decided to flee; but his refusal to abandon his household and ministers to the mob led to fatal delay. 'I don't want to compromise anyone,' he kept repeating. By the time Lafayette and the Garde Nationale had arrived, he had no choice but to submit to the will of the people. The entire Court of Versailles, the National Assembly, and the government, escorted by the *poissardes* and thousands of soldiers, entered Paris on 6 October. After the customary speeches and patriotic displays at the Hôtel de Ville, the royal family were allowed to retire to their new residence at the Tuileries.

Gouverneur Morris was given a full account of these momentous events by Adèle de Flahaut, who told him that at Versailles 'the King forbad Resistance. The Queen, in retiring to her own Chamber, told her Attendants that as the King was determined to go to Paris she must accompany him, but she should never leave it.'[63] Marie-Antoinette proved to be uncannily prescient, yet even she heard cries of '*Vive la reine!*' at the Hôtel de Ville, from the very mob which had set out to kill her. She was well aware that henceforth her life was in their hands.

The march on Versailles was a glorious triumph for the capital. Paris was once more the undisputed mistress of France; a capricious, jealous and vengeful mistress, she nevertheless smiled and wore her brightest colours in victory. While 'a dreadful solitude already reigned at Versailles', where nothing could be heard except the clang of shutters being closed for the

first time since the days of Louis XIV, Paris chattered and laughed and danced as usual.[64] But she had little in common with the city that had existed at the beginning of 1789.

Morris took a stroll around the capital on Christmas Day, and sensed an unhappy change in streets which had been soiled with blood. 'It has been a very fine Day but Paris on this great festival of the Nativity shews how much she is fallen by the Revolution. Her Gayness and her Gilt are all besmirched.'[65]

Biographical Notes

Christian names in italics indicate the name used in preference to the first name.

Artois, Charles-Philippe de Bourbon, Comte d', later *Charles X* (1757–1836). Youngest brother of Louis XVI, a fop and a womanizer. Strongly opposed to constitutional reform, he emigrated in 1789, and was the head of the reactionary nobility (the 'Ultras') at the Restoration in 1814. Crowned king after the death of Louis XVIII in 1824, he pursued right-wing policies which led to the July Revolution of 1830 and his renewed exile. He was married to Maria-Theresa of Savoy (d.1805), from whom he lived apart for many years. His abdication in favour of his grandson, the Duc de Bordeaux, was thwarted by Louis-Philippe's seizure of the throne.

Beaumarchais, Pierre-Augustin Caron de (1732–99). The son of a Protestant Parisian watchmaker, Beaumarchais followed his father's profession before buying a Court post and title, and becoming a successful financier. His first play, *Eugénie* was performed by the Comédie Française in 1767, with *The Barber of Seville* and *The Marriage of Figaro* following in 1775 and 1784. He supplied arms to the Americans during the War of Independence. Imprisoned by the Jacobins in 1792, he escaped to Holland, but later returned to Paris, where he died. He married three times.

Bombelles, Marc-Marie, Marquis de (1744–1822). Soldier, diplomat, courtier, bishop, the Marquis de Bombelles was also an indefatigable

diarist, although only a small portion of his immense journal has been published. After a successful military career, Bombelles entered the diplomatic service under the protection of the Baron de Breteuil, serving at The Hague and Naples before becoming ambassador to Ratisbon (Regensburg) in 1774, Lisbon (1785–8), and finally Venice (1789–91). He refused to accept the Constitution, resigned, and lived as an *émigré*. After the death of his wife in 1800 he became a priest in Germany, and returned to France in 1814. He was Bishop of Amiens from 1817 until his death.

Cagliostro, Alessandro, Comte de, (b.1745) more generally supposed to have been Giuseppe Balsamo, a Sicilian mountebank. Whatever his origin, his psychic abilities were widely believed to be genuine. Implicated in the Diamond Necklace Affair, he was acquitted, but expelled from France in 1786. The founder of 'Egyptian' Freemasonry, he was also known as 'Grand Coptha', and it was as a Freemason that he was found guilty of heresy by the Inquisition. Imprisoned at Rome, he is presumed to have died in 1795.

Calonne, Charles-Alexandre de (1734–1802). Son of a magistrate, Calonne held various legal posts before becoming Intendant of Metz (1768) and Lille (1774). Appointed Controller-General in 1783, he convened the Assembly of Notables to discuss fiscal reform, but was dismissed from office in 1787, after allegations that he had enriched himself at public expense. He was a counter-revolutionary during his exile in England, and died soon after his return to Paris in 1802.

Campan, Jeanne-Louise-Henriette, née Genet (1752–1822). After an initial Court appointment as reader to the daughters of Louis XV, Madame Campan joined the household of Marie-Antoinette, whom she served until the Court no longer existed. Married to the Queen's valet, Campan, she separated from him in 1790, and lost other members of her family in the Revolution. She later established a popular school for young ladies near Paris.

Frénilly, François-Auguste Fauveau, Baron de (1768–1838). Born into a wealthy Parisian bourgeois family, Frénilly studied law before the Revolution swept away the official post he had been destined to occupy. He remained in France throughout the Revolution, but as an ardent supporter of Charles X, emigrated in 1830.

Joseph II von Habsburg, Holy Roman Emperor (1741–90). Co-ruler with his mother Maria-Theresa after his father's death in 1765, Joseph was an 'enlightened despot' at home, reforming the Austrian legal, medical, fiscal and educational systems. He also suppressed hundreds of monasteries in an attempt to curb ecclesiastical power. His foreign policy, however, was largely unsuccessful, and his territorial ambitions led to costly wars. He married twice, but both his wives died of smallpox and he had no children. He was very fond of his sister Marie-Antoinette, and like his mother, bombarded her with advice.

Lafayette, Marie-Joseph-Paul-Yves-Roch-*Gilbert* du Motier, Marquis de (1757–1834). Married young to Adrienne de Noailles, and consequently a member of one of the most prestigious families in France, Lafayette nevertheless hankered after military glory. He arrived in America in 1777 and joined Washington's army as a volunteer, distinguishing himself in action. He was promoted *maréchal de camp* in 1782. A Freemason and close friend of Washington, he espoused the cause of liberty during the Revolution. His Declaration of the Rights of Man was accepted by the National Assembly in August 1789, by which time he was also commander of the Parisian Garde Nationale. Lafayette was instrumental in keeping the royal family confined in the Tuileries until his resignation in 1791. After the collapse of the monarchy in August 1792 he fled across the frontier, and was imprisoned by the Austrians until 1797. He sat in parliament during the reign of Louis XVIII, and his last political act was his open support for Louis-Philippe in 1830.

Lamballe, Marie-Thérèse-Louise, Princesse de, née de Savoie-Carignan (1749–92). The Princesse de Lamballe was widowed at nineteen after barely two years' marriage to the son of the Duc de Penthièvre. She was a close friend of Marie-Antoinette, and her appointment as Superintendant of the Queen's household in 1774 caused an outcry. She left Versailles when Madame de Polignac became the Queen's confidante, but the Queen often visited her in Paris and their correspondence continued unabated. Their friendship grew stronger during the 1780s as the Polignacs' influence waned. Loyal and steadfast to the end, Madame de Lamballe returned from a brief exile in 1791 to be with the Queen, was captured after the assault on the Tuileries on 10 August 1792, and massacred on 3 September at the prison of La Force after refusing to swear an oath of hatred to the King and Queen.

La Motte, Jeanne de, née de Saint-Rémy de Valois (1756–91). Descended from a bastard branch of the royal house of Valois, Jeanne de La Motte was brought up in abject poverty. After gaining the protection of the Marquise de Boulainvilliers, she was granted a royal pension of 800 francs (later raised to 1500 francs), but her claims to family lands in Champagne were unsuccessful. Her liaison with Cardinal de Rohan from 1783 brought her money, and he was deeply implicated in the Diamond Necklace Affair. Jeanne de La Motte was found guilty of the theft of the magnificent necklace in 1786, and imprisoned for life. She escaped from prison in 1787 and fled to London, where she died after falling from a window in 1791. Her memoirs, published in 1789, protested her innocence and slandered Queen Marie-Antoinette.

La Tour du Pin, Henriette-*Lucie*, Marquise de, née Dillon (1770–1853). After her marriage in 1787, Madame de La Tour du Pin took up her post as lady-in-waiting to the Queen. She resigned for health reasons in 1790, but she and her husband did not emigrate until 1794, when both their fathers were guillotined. After exile in America and England, they returned to France in 1802. Madame de La Tour du Pin later accompanied her husband on various diplomatic and administrative postings. They went into exile after the revolution of 1830 when their only surviving son had to flee from a death sentence imposed because of his support for the grandson of Charles X. Madame de La Tour du Pin died in Pisa.

Lauzun, Armand-Louis de Gontaut, Duc de (1747–93). Duc de *Biron* from 1788. Courtier, soldier, roué, revolutionary, Lauzun was at one stage a member of Marie-Antoinette's circle. After his fall from favour, he took part in the American War and later joined the Orléanist faction. Elected to the States General in 1789, he became an ardent revolutionary. He served as a general in the republican army, but was guillotined in 1793.

Ligne, Charles-Joseph, Prince de (1735–1814). A prince of the Austrian Netherlands, Ligne was a chamberlain at the Imperial Court in Vienna and a field-marshal in the Austrian army, but spent much time in France before the Revolution. Greatly attached to Marie-Antoinette, he refused to return to France after her death; the Revolutionary Wars also led to the loss of his magnificent estates in Belgium. He wrote amusing memoirs, having retained his quirky sense of humour despite his misfortunes. He died in Vienna.

Louis XVI, Louis-Auguste de Bourbon (1754–93). He became Dauphin in 1765, and succeeded his grandfather Louis XV as King of France in 1774. Although married to Marie-Antoinette of Austria in 1770, no children were born until 1778, by which time incalculable damage had been done to Louis XVI's prestige and the Queen's reputation. Of their surviving children, the first Dauphin died in 1789, the second Dauphin was imprisoned during the Revolution and is presumed to have died aged ten in 1795, and only Marie-Thérèse (b.1778) reached adulthood. She married her cousin, the Duc d'Angoulême, and was childless. Louis XVI, though well-intentioned, was indecisive and inevitably fell victim to a revolution he never foresaw. He was guillotined on 21 January 1793.

Marie-Antoinette-Josèphe-Jeanne von Habsburg, Archduchess of Austria and Queen of France (1755–93). The Queen was highly popular initially, but her failure to produce heirs to the throne and her frivolity soon angered the populace – as did her favourite, the Duchesse de Polignac. Resolute where Louis XVI was weak, Marie-Antoinette was encouraged by the Austrians to intervene in French politics, with calamitous results. She advocated strong counter-revolutionary action, but remained with the King even when all was lost. Sentenced to death for a string of 'crimes against the nation', she died on the scaffold on 16 October 1793.

Maria-Theresa von Habsburg, Queen of Hungary and Bohemia, Holy Roman Empress (1717–80). The eldest daughter of Emperor Charles VI, Maria-Theresa became heir to the Habsburg crown after the death of her brother. Her accession in 1740 sparked off the War of the Austrian Succession, and her reign was marked by several conflicts with her neighbours, particularly Frederick the Great of Prussia. She married Francis of Lorraine (Emperor Francis I) – for love – had sixteen children, including Marie-Antoinette, and was admired as a humane and practical ruler.

Mercier, Louis-Sébastien (1740–1814). A Parisian bourgeois, Mercier wrote plays and articles for newspapers as well as his *Tableau de Paris*, and was awarded a royal pension. He supported the Revolution, edited a Girondin journal, and as a deputy for Seine-et-Oise, voted against the execution of Louis XVI. He was imprisoned by the Jacobins, but escaped the guillotine.

Mesmer, Franz Anton (1734–1815). An Austrian physician, Mesmer founded 'mesmerism', the forerunner of modern hypnotism. He was forced to leave Vienna in 1778 after being accused of magic as a result of seance where he 'magnetized' patients. He moved to France, where he had a highly successful practice despite an unfavourable royal commission on his activities in 1784. Later he travelled throughout Europe, and died in Meersburg.

Morris, Gouverneur (1752–1816). Morris was born in New York and educated at King's College (now Columbia University). He became an attorney at the age of nineteen, was a member of the New York Convention in 1775, and strongly supported the cause of independence. He lost part of one leg after a carriage accident in Philadelphia, where he practised as a lawyer before being sent on private and state business to France in 1789. He succeeded Jefferson as American ambassador in 1792, a post he held throughout the Terror, and left France in October 1794.

Necker, Jacques (1732–1804). A Swiss banker and darling of the Parisians, Necker also represented the city of Geneva in France from 1768. He was appointed Controller-General by Louis XVI in 1777. Forced out of office by Maurepas, he was recalled twice (1788, 1789) before his final resignation in 1790. He published several works on the administration of French finances, though his talents as a banker did more to enrich Swiss banks than reduce the French deficit.

Orléans, Louis-*Philippe*-Joseph de Bourbon, Duc d', (1747–93). Duc de *Chartres* until 1785. A perennial thorn in the King's side, Orléans's hatred of the Queen was one reason for his machinations against the Court. He plunged eagerly into politics when the States General met in 1789, supported revolutionary policies from the outset, and joined the Jacobins in 1791. After the fall of the monarchy in 1792, he dropped his title to become 'Philippe Égalité'. As a member of the National Convention he voted for the execution of his cousin Louis XVI, a move which prompted his son, the future King Louis-Philippe, to defect to the Austrians. Arrested in April 1793, Orléans was guillotined on 6 November that year.

Polignac, Gabrielle-*Yolande*-Claude-Martine-Jeanne, Duchesse de, née de Polastron (1749–93). Intimate friend of Marie-Antoinette from 1775. Her husband, Comte Jules de Polignac (duke from 1780), was

made the Queen's equerry so that the duchess could remain at Court. In 1782, Madame de Polignac was appointed governess to the royal children. She resigned and emigrated in 1789, but did not long outlive the Queen, and died in Austria after a long illness in 1793.

Provence, Louis-Stanislas-Xavier de Bourbon, Comte de, better known (as the King's eldest brother) as *Monsieur*, later *Louis XVIII* (1755–1824). Not altogether trustworthy, Monsieur took a more liberal political line than the Comte d'Artois, and did not emigrate until 1791. However, once across the frontier he threatened counter-revolutionary action which jeopardized the safety of the King and Queen, and he was quick to style himself Louis XVIII after the reported death of his nephew in prison in 1795. He ruled France from the Restoration in 1814. As king, he was a moderate constitutional monarch, though he had to combat 'Ultras' in parliament. He married Josephine of Savoy in 1771 and was childless.

Rohan, Louis-René-Edouard, Prince de (1734–1803). Rohan was a member of one of the most important noble families in France. His furious pursuit of women, passion for hunting, and interest in the occult did nothing to bar his promotion in the church. Bishop of Strasbourg, Grand Almoner (1777), and finally Cardinal (1778), he nevertheless failed in his efforts to gain high political office. His role in the Diamond Necklace Affair was never completely clarified during his trial in 1786, though he was acquitted of both fraud and theft. Exiled from Paris after his release from prison, he mended his dissolute ways to become an exemplary churchman during and after the Revolution, feeding and housing thousands of dispossessed priests at his see in Germany.

Ségur, Joseph-Alexandre-Pierre, Vicomte de (1765–1805). Younger brother of Louis-Philippe de Ségur, the vicomte was generally acknowledged to be the son of the Baron de Besenval (courtier, roué, and Colonel of the Swiss Guards), whom he was to rival in amorous adventures. He published Besenval's memoirs, wrote songs, epigrams, books, and plays, and was very much in fashion before the Revolution. Officially he was Colonel of the Régiment de Noailles and First Lord of the Bedchamber to the Duc d'Orléans.

Ségur, Louis-Philippe, Comte de (1753–1830). Son of the Maréchal de Ségur who brought in unpopular army reforms in 1781, the Comte de Ségur pursued a military career before becoming a diplomat. He was

ambassador to both Russia and Prussia, remained in France through-out the Revolution, and accepted important Court posts under Napo-leon. He was an academician from 1803.

Staël, Anne-Louise-*Germaine*, Baronne de, née Necker (1766–1817). A woman of letters, passion, and politics, the headstrong daughter of Jacques Necker displayed a formidable intelligence from an early age. Unhappily married in 1786 to the Swedish ambassador, the Baron de Staël, she had numerous love affairs and produced equally numerous literary works, from novels and criticism to political tracts. Her diplo-matic immunity enabled her to help many friends in Paris escape the Terror, and she was also instrumental in securing Talleyrand's return from exile in 1796. Napoleon disliked her, and she spent the years 1803–14 travelling, or writing at her home in Switzerland, where she also entertained those Parisians who were daring enough to brave the French secret police to visit her.

Talleyrand, Charles-Maurice, Prince de (1754–1838). One of France's most eminent politicians, Talleyrand was appointed Bishop of Autun in 1788. As a deputy to the States General he allied himself to the revolutionary cause, promoting the nationalization of church property and the Civil Constitution of the Clergy. He emigrated in 1792, and was expelled from England to America in 1794. After his return to Paris in 1796, he devoted himself to politics. Foreign Minister under Napoleon, Louis XVIII and Louis-Philippe, his greatest achievement was the establishment of an independent Belgium, and his greatest political asset was his flair for abandoning lost causes (and kings) at the right moment.

Thrale, Hester Lynch, née Salusbury (1740–1821). Mrs *Piozzi* from 1784. A leading London society hostess during the reign of George III, Mrs Thrale lived until the death of her first husband at Streatham Park, which was home for many years to Dr Johnson. Her choice of second husband, the Italian tenor Gabriele Piozzi, alienated many of her friends. Her opinions on Paris as Mrs Piozzi in 1784 are much in keeping with those of Mrs Thrale in 1775.

Tilly, Alexandre, Comte de (1764–1816). Born in Le Mans, Tilly became a page to Marie-Antoinette at the age of fourteen. A man of means, he dabbled in literature, gambled, and womanized until the Revolution led to emigration. He travelled to England, married (and divorced) in America, and spent several years attached to the Prussian

Court in Berlin. The reason for his suicide in Brussels in 1816 was a mystery, although a woman he deeply loved had taken her own life in Berlin in 1803. His memoirs were dedicated to the Prince de Ligne.

Young, Arthur (1741–1820). An English 'gentleman farmer', Young wrote prolifically on agriculture and travelled widely to gather information. A friend of the Duc de La Rochefoucauld-Liancourt, he stayed with the duke on his visits to France in 1787, 1788 and 1789, and much material relating to the Revolution appeared in his popular *Travels in France and Italy*, published in 1792.

Notes

Full details of all works cited are to be found in the Bibliography

1   Life in Paris

1 Mercier, *The Picture of Paris*, p. 36
2 Frénilly, *Souvenirs du Baron de Frénilly*, p. 41
3 Tilly, *Memoirs of the Comte Alexandre de Tilly*, p. 235
4 Frénilly, op.cit., p. 42
5 Young, *Travels in France and Italy*, p. 75
6 Gaxotte, *Paris au XVIIIe siècle*, p. 56
7 Now rue Denfert-Rochereau
8 Castelot, *Paris: the turbulent city*, pp. 9–10
9 A census in 1801 put the Parisian population at 547,856. Allowing for the Revolution, emigration, and wars, 700,000 in the 1780s seems a reasonable estimate.
10 Mercier, op.cit., p. 16
11 Thrale, *The French Journals of Mrs. Thrale and Dr. Johnson*, p. 93
12 Rétif de la Bretonne, *Les Nuits de Paris*, p. 178 and Mercier, op.cit., pp. 80–1
13 Morris, *A Diary of the French Revolution*, vol. 1, p. xlv
14 Thrale, op.cit., pp. 100–1
15 Mercier, op.cit., p. 30
16 Rétif de la Bretonne, op.cit., p. 146
17 Frénilly, op.cit., p. 3
18 Thrale, op.cit., p. 95. Hampstead was then a country village.
19 Cole, *A Journal of my Journey to Paris in the Year 1765*, pp. 41–2
20 Young, op.cit., p. 85
21 Thrale, op.cit., p. 138

22 Cole, op.cit., p. 39; Bombelles, *Journal*, vol. 2, p. 138
23 Mercier, op.cit., p. 51
24 Thrale, op.cit., p. 148
25 Mercier, op.cit., p. 47; Cole, op.cit., p. 42
26 Mercier, op.cit., p. 13
27 Young, loc.cit. Kennels were gutters.
28 Mercier, op.cit., pp. 91–2
29 Thrale, op.cit., pp. 93–4; Morris, op.cit., vol. 1, p. 65; Cole, op.cit., p. 46
30 Morris, op.cit., vol. 1, pp. xliii–xliv
31 Much of the collection was sold by the Duc d'Orléans in 1788 for eight million *livres*, and many of its finest paintings came to England.
32 Morris, op.cit., vol. 1, pp. xxix, 45
33 Maxwell, *The English Traveller in France 1698–1815*, p. 42
34 Thrale, op.cit., p. 91. Orgeat was a drink made from barley and almonds.
35 Cole, op.cit., p. 97; Young, op.cit., p. 83
36 Thrale, op.cit., p. 210
37 Mercier, op.cit., p. 81
38 Bombelles, op.cit., vol. 1, p. 119
39 Thrale, op.cit., p. 93
40 Mercier, op.cit., p. 17
41 Frénilly, op.cit., p. 24
42 Young, op.cit., p. 128
43 Tilly, op.cit., pp. 405–6
44 Elliott, *During the Reign of Terror: Journal of my life during the French Revolution*, pp. 38, 40
45 'All tastes, all caprices, all peculiarities which the senses, at first domineering, then subdued, require to be sated or excited, were employed by M. le Duc d'Orléans.' Commissioners from the Convention Nationale who searched the Palais Royal in 1793 also found 'secret apartments containing all the equipment for skilled debauchery'. Cf. Dard, *Un acteur caché du drame révolutionnaire: le général Choderlos de Laclos*, p. 137
46 Frénilly, op.cit., p. 25
47 'He has done nothing which is not to be praised/to let.'
48 Mercier, op.cit., p. 135
49 ibid., p. 136
50 Bombelles, op.cit., vol. 2, p. 75
51 Thrale, op.cit., p. 137
52 ibid., p. 95
53 Gaxotte, op.cit., p. 38
54 Young, op.cit., p. 162
55 Mercier, op.cit., p. 25

2   *The Court of Versailles*

1 Mercier, *Picture of Paris*, p. 108

2 The *noblesse d'épée* (nobility of the sword) had the right to be presented at Court, and had to prove by letters patent that their nobility extended back further than 1400. The *noblesse de robe* (nobility of the gown) acquired its titles through the purchase of offices – magistrate, tax-collector etc., and was consequently considered very inferior. These titles were still hereditary. Titles were also conferred by the ownership of certain plots of land.

3 Young, *Travels*, pp. 15–16

4 Cole, *Journal*, pp. 235, 239

5 Ducros, *French Society in the eighteenth century*, pp. 25–6

6 Bombelles, *Journal*, vol. 1, p. 173

7 Campan, *Memoirs of Madame Campan on Marie-Antoinette and her Court*, vol. 1, p. 166

8 Ducros, op.cit., p. 45

9 Campan, loc.cit.

10 Tilly, *Memoirs*, p. 262

11 La Tour du Pin, *Journal d'une femme de cinquante ans*, vol. 1, p. 119

12 Boigne, *Memoirs of the Comtesse de Boigne*, vol. 1, pp. 13–14; Ligne, *Fragments de l'histoire de ma vie*, vol. 2, p. 38

13 La Tour du Pin, op.cit., vol. 1, p. 72

14 Campan, op.cit., vol. 1, p. 268

15 Bombelles, op.cit., vol. 1, p. 157

16 ibid., vol. 2, pp. 204–5

17 Boigne, op.cit., vol. 1, p. 45

18 Cf. Olivier Bernier (ed.), *Imperial Mother, Royal Daughter: the Correspondence of Marie-Antoinette and Maria-Theresa*, (London: Sidgwick & Jackson, 1986), letter from Joseph II to the Grand Duke of Tuscany in 1777, p. 215

19 Stryienski, *The National History of France: the Eighteenth Century*, p. 251

20 Frénilly, *Souvenirs*, p. 86

21 Campan, op.cit., vol. 1, pp. 182–3

22 Tilly, op.cit., p. 67

23 La Tour du Pin, op.cit., vol. 1, p. 114

24 Ligne, op.cit., vol. 1, pp. 289–90

25 ibid., p. 82

26 ibid., p. 115

27 Thrale, *French Journal*, p. 125

28 Morris, *Diary*, vol. 1, p. 69

29 'The modern Messalina' was a common way to describe the Queen, and is recorded by both Mercier and Frénilly.

30 Isherwood, *Farce and Fantasy: Popular Entertainment in Eighteenth Century Paris*, p. 139

31 Mossiker, *The Queen's Necklace*, p. 29
32 Ségur, *Memoirs*, pp. 21–2; Tilly, op.cit., p. 68; letter from Horace Walpole to the Countess of Upper Ossory, Stryienski, op.cit., pp. 238–9
33 Thrale, op.cit., pp. 98, 125
34 Tilly, op.cit., pp. 68–9
35 Bombelles, op.cit., vol. 2, p. 208
36 Campan, op.cit., vol. 1, p. 166; Tilly, op.cit., p. 68
37 Campan, op.cit., vol. 1, p. 173
38 ibid., p. 166
39 Elliott, *During the Reign of Terror*, p. 52; Tilly, op.cit., p. 280
40 Thrale, op.cit., p. 133
41 Campan, op.cit., vol. 1, pp. 121–2
42 Girard (ed.), *Correspondance entre Marie-Thérèse et Marie-Antoinette*, p. 45
43 ibid., p. 128
44 Campan, op.cit., vol. 1, p. 288
45 Girard, op.cit., p. 151
46 Stryienski, op.cit., p. 230
47 Tilly, op.cit., p. 279
48 Campan, op.cit., vol. 1, p. 162
49 Stryienski, op.cit., p. 237
50 Besenval, *Mémoires de M. le Baron de Besenval*, vol. 1, pp. 93–4; Girard, op.cit., p. 150
51 Besenval, op.cit., vol. 1, pp. 102–3
52 Campan, op.cit., vol. 1, p. 240
53 Lauzun, *Mémoires de Armand-Louis de Gontaut, Duc de Lauzun, Général Biron*, pp. 178, 185
54 ibid., pp. 184–5
55 ibid., pp. 188–90
56 Campan, op.cit., vol. 1, p. 226
57 Lauzun, op.cit., pp. 218, 249–50
58 Lauzun inherited the title Duc de Biron on the death of his uncle the Maréchal de Biron in 1788.
59 Ligne, op.cit., vol. 1, p. 79
60 ibid., pp. 113–14
61 ibid., p. 116
62 Campan, op.cit., vol. 1, p. 223
63 Girard, op.cit., p. 136
64 ibid., p. 166
65 Stryienski, op.cit., p. 253
66 Girard, op.cit., pp. 212–13
67 Campan, op.cit., vol. 1, p. 243
68 ibid., pp. 245–6

69 Bombelles, op.cit., vol. 1, p. 196
70 Tilly, op.cit., p. 280; Campan, op.cit., vol. 1, p. 287
71 Tilly, op.cit., p. 127
72 Stryienski, op.cit., p. 234
73 Ségur, op.cit., p. 98
74 Ligne, op.cit., vol. 1, p. 81
75 Bombelles, op.cit., vol. 1, p. 168
76 Campan, op.cit., vol. 2, pp. 307–8
77 Tilly, op.cit., p. 128
78 The Diamond Necklace Affair will be discussed in Chapter 5.
79 Tilly, op.cit., pp. 281, 283
80 Bombelles, op.cit., vol. 1, p. 220
81 Tilly, op.cit., p. 281
82 Söderhjelm, *Fersen et Marie-Antoinette: correspondance et journal inédits du Comte Axel de Fersen*, p. 204
83 ibid., p. 317
84 ibid., p. 315
85 La Tour du Pin, op.cit., vol. 1, p. 232

3 *Le Beau Monde*

1 Tilly, *Memoirs*, p. 130
2 La Tour du Pin, *Journal*, vol. 1, p. 8; Frénilly, *Souvenirs*, p. 105
3 Tilly, op.cit., p. 184
4 Besenval, *Mémoires*, vol. 4, pp. 270–4
5 Morris, *Diary*, vol. 1, p. 45
6 Boigne, *Memoirs*, vol. 1, pp. 17–18
7 ibid.
8 Frénilly, op.cit., p. 29
9 ibid., p. 10. Frénilly would have been eighteen in 1786.
10 ibid., p. 5
11 ibid., p. 4
12 La Tour du Pin, op.cit., vol. 1, p. 74
13 Vigée-Lebrun, *Memoirs*, p. 313
14 Frénilly, op.cit., p. 80
15 ibid.
16 ibid.
17 ibid., pp. 80–1
18 ibid., p. 82
19 ibid., pp. 28–9
20 ibid., pp. 25–6
21 ibid., p. 27
22 Young, *Travels*, p. 78

23 Thrale, *French Journal*, p. 126
24 Tilly, loc.cit.
25 ibid., p. 130
26 La Tour du Pin, op.cit., vol. 1, p. 134
27 Staël, *Correspondance Générale*, vol. 1, pp. 17–18
28 Morris, op.cit., vol. 1, p. 21
29 ibid.
30 Frénilly, op.cit., p. 26
31 Young, op.cit., p. 35
32 Ségur, *Memoirs*, p. 33
33 ibid., pp. 33–4
34 Tilly, op.cit., p. 354. Fanny de Beauharnais was related to the Empress Josephine's first husband, Alexandre de Beauharnais.
35 Morris, op.cit., vol. 1, pp. 3–4
36 Mercier, *Picture of Paris*, p. 32
37 Staël, op.cit., vol. 1, p. 103; Boigne, op.cit., vol. 1, p. 43
38 Talleyrand, *Mémoires du Prince de Talleyrand*, vol. 1, p. 44
39 Staël, op.cit., vol. 1, p. 113
40 Boigne, op.cit., vol. 1, p. 48
41 ibid., p. 163
42 Ségur, op.cit., pp. 120–1
43 Bombelles, *Journal*, vol. 1, pp. 62–3; vol. 2, p. 309
44 Morris, op.cit., vol. 1, p. 86. Morris says: 'Madame, when one is cut to the quick one feels it for a long time.' The matron adds: 'And especially in the foot.'
45 Thrale, op.cit., p. 84
46 Morris, op.cit., vol. 1, pp. 111–12
47 Cole, *Journal*, p. 14
48 Morris, op.cit., vol. 1, p. 61
49 La Tour du Pin, op.cit., vol. 1, p. 201
50 ibid., p. 3
51 Boigne, op.cit., vol. 1, pp. 31–2
52 La Tour du Pin, op.cit., vol. 1, p. 27
53 Mercier, op.cit., p. 31
54 Staël, op.cit., vol. 1, p. 69
55 ibid., p. 142
56 Lauzun, *Mémoires*, pp. 218–25
57 Bombelles, op.cit., vol. 1, pp. 156–7
58 ibid., p. 159
59 ibid., p. 172
60 ibid., p. 180

4   *Tryst and Tragedies*

1 Gaxotte, *Paris au XVIIIe siècle*, p. 258
2 Mercier, *Picture of Paris*, p. 87
3 Lauzun, *Mémoires*, p. 66; Ligne, *Fragments*, vol. 1, p. 51
4 Rétif de la Bretonne, *Les Nuits de Paris*, pp. 184–6
5 Mercier, op.cit., p. 156
6 ibid., p. 101
7 Boigne, *Memoirs*, vol. 1, pp. 31–2
8 Ligne, op.cit., vol. 1, p. 7
9 La Tour du Pin, *Journal*, vol. 1, p. 204
10 Morris, *Diary*, vol. 1, p. 292
11 Frénilly, *Souvenirs*, p. 207
12 Morris, op.cit., vol. 1, p. 112
13 Tilly, *Memoirs*, p. 235
14 ibid., p. 78
15 Morris, op.cit., vol. 1, pp. 93–4
16 Mercier, op.cit., p. 190
17 Morris, op.cit., vol. 1, pp. 22–3
18 ibid., p. 84
19 ibid., p. 58
20 ibid., p. 17
21 ibid., p. 163
22 Staël, *Correspondance*, vol. 1, p. 102
23 Tilly, loc.cit.
24 La Tour du Pin, op.cit., vol. 1, pp. 136, 30
25 Bombelles, *Journal*, vol. 1, p. 137
26 Boigne, loc.cit.
27 Tilly, op.cit., p. 278
28 Morris, op.cit., vol. 1, p. 276
29 Tilly, op.cit., p. 265
30 ibid., p. 210
31 ibid., p. 140
32 ibid., p. 239
33 Ségur, *Memoirs*, p. 42
34 ibid., p. 39
35 Mercier, op.cit., p. 65
36 Lauzun, op.cit., p. 42
37 Tilly, op.cit., p. 63
38 ibid.
39 ibid., p. 71
40 Ligne, op.cit., vol. 1, p. 30
41 Lauzun, op.cit., p. 54
42 Chateaubriand, *Mémoires d'Outre-tombe*, vol. 1, p. 236

43 Morris, op.cit., vol. 1, p. 364
44 ibid., p. 249
45 Ligne, op.cit., vol. 1, p. 167
46 Lauzun, op.cit., p. 204
47 Ligne, op.cit., vol. 1, p. 165
48 Boigne, op.cit., vol. 1, pp. 46–7
49 Tilly, op.cit., p. 118. The whole encounter, pp. 110–20.
50 Bombelles, op.cit., vol. 1, p. 145
51 Tilly, op.cit., p. 211
52 ibid., pp. 197–8
53 ibid., pp. 212–13. The 'Marquise de L.T.D.P.M.' is suggested as the Marquise de La Tour du Pin de Montmort, and is not to be confused with the Marquise de La Tour du Pin who appears elsewhere in this book.
54 Elliott, *During the Reign of Terror*, p. 38
55 Tilly, op.cit., pp. 214–15
56 Morris, op.cit., vol. 1, p. 102
57 Mercier, op.cit., pp. 82–3
58 Morris, op.cit., vol. 1, pp. 104–5
59 Staël, op.cit., vol. 1, p. 101
60 Tilly, op.cit., p. 235

5   *Age of Miracles?*

1 Morris, *Diary*, vol. 1, p. 38
2 Bombelles, *Journal*, vol. 1, pp. 261–2
3 Staël, *Correspondance*, vol. 1, pp. 40–1
4 Ligne, *Fragments*, vol. 2, pp. 29–31
5 Bombelles, op.cit., vol. 1, pp. 315–16
6 Dard, *Un acteur caché du drame révolutionnaire*, p. 136
7 ibid., p. 153
8 Campan, *Memoirs*, vol. 1, p. 34
9 Staël, op.cit., vol. 1, p. 37
10 Bombelles, op.cit., vol. 2, pp. 49–51
11 Ségur, *Memoirs*, p. 187
12 Boigne, *Memoirs*, vol. 1, p. 35
13 Ligne, op.cit., vol. 1, p. 217
14 Cf. Mossiker, *Queen's Necklace*, pp. 96–101 for Madame d'Oberkirch's account of her meeting with Cagliostro.
15 Bombelles, op.cit., vol. 1, p. 66
16 ibid., p. 67
17 ibid., p. 194
18 Rohan's motto: 'I cannot be king, a prince I scorn to be: I am a Rohan.'
19 Frénilly, *Souvenirs*, pp. 86–7

20 Girard, *Correspondance*, p. 107
21 ibid., p. 203
22 Beugnot, *Mémoires du Comte Beugnot*, vol. 1, p. 11
23 Mossiker, op.cit., p. 114. The building is now part of the Archives Nationales.
24 ibid., p. 155
25 ibid., pp. 208–9
26 ibid., pp. 366–8
27 Frénilly, op.cit., p. 88
28 Staël, op.cit., vol. 1, p. 65
29 Beugnot, op.cit., p. 29
30 Staël, op.cit., vol. 1, pp. 66–7
31 Mossiker, op.cit., p. 417
32 Bombelles, op.cit., vol. 2, p. 179

6   *Towards the Precipice*

1 Thrale, *French Journal*, p. 206
2 Gaxotte, *Paris au XVIIIe siècle*, p. 344
3 Frénilly, *Souvenirs*, p. 39
4 Tieghem, *Beaumarchais par lui-même*, p. 32
5 Girard, *Correspondance*, p. 133
6 Thrale, op.cit., p. 200
7 Bombelles, *Journal*, vol. 2, p. 33
8 Cole, *Journal*, p. 96
9 Launay & Mailhos, *Introduction à la vie littéraire du XVIIIe siècle*, pp. 29–30
10 Ségur, *Memoirs*, pp. 13, 33–4
11 Cole, op.cit., p. 151
12 Mercier, *Picture of Paris*, pp. 116–17
13 Bombelles, op.cit., vol. 1, p. 100
14 Staël, *Correspondance*, vol. 1, p. 100
15 Ségur, op.cit., p. 71
16 ibid., pp. 73–4
17 Mercier, op.cit., p. 75
18 Thrale, op.cit., p. 99
19 Tilly, *Memoirs*, p. 232
20 Campan, *Memoirs*, vol. 1, p. 281
21 Tilly, loc.cit.
22 Ségur, op.cit., p. 22; Mercier, op.cit., p. 74
23 Frénilly, op.cit., p. 20
24 Bombelles, op.cit., vol. 2, p. 14
25 Tilly, op.cit., p. 239

26 La Tour du Pin, *Journal*, vol. 1, pp. 130, 165
27 Mercier, op.cit., p. 74
28 Young, *Travels*, p. 72
29 Vigée-Lebrun, *Memoirs*, pp. 336–7
30 Frénilly, op.cit., p. 7
31 Staël, op.cit., vol. 1, pp. 107–8
32 Tilly, op.cit., pp. 239, 183
33 Ségur, op.cit., p. 70
34 ibid., p. 173
35 ibid.
36 ibid., p. 45
37 Thrale, op.cit., p. 81
38 Bombelles, op.cit., vol. 1, p. 53
39 Ségur, op.cit., p. 55
40 Campan, op.cit., vol. 1, p. 273
41 ibid., pp. 274–5
42 Ségur, op.cit., pp. 55–6
43 ibid., p. 58
44 ibid., p. 76
45 ibid.
46 Campan, loc.cit.
47 Girard, *Correspondance*, p. 290
48 Lauzun, *Mémoires*, p. 238
49 ibid., pp. 241–2
50 ibid., p. 245
51 ibid., p. 247
52 ibid., p. 251
53 Ségur, op.cit., p. 165
54 Campan, op.cit., vol. 1, pp. 280–1
55 Tilly, op.cit., p. 183
56 Talleyrand, *Mémoires*, vol. 1, p. 61
57 Ségur, op.cit., p. 15

7 1789: Year of Reckoning

1 Frénilly, *Souvenirs*, p. 79
2 Ségur, *Memoirs*, p. 103
3 ibid., pp. 25–6
4 Young, *Travels*, p. 80
5 Tilly, *Memoirs*, pp. 200–1
6 Morris, *Diary*, vol. 1, p. 22; Chateaubriand, *Mémoires*, vol. 1, p. 193
7 Bombelles, *Journal*, vol. 2, pp. 276–7; La Tour du Pin, *Journal*, vol. 1, p. 160

8 Bombelles, op.cit., vol. 1, p. 61
9 Girard, *Correspondance*, p. 11
10 Bombelles, op.cit., vol. 2, p. 255
11 Louis-Philippe d'Orléans, *Mémoires*, vol. 1, p. 35
12 Bombelles, op.cit., vol. 2, p. 194
13 ibid., p. 230
14 Staël, *Correspondance*, vol. 1, p. 274
15 La Tour du Pin, op.cit., vol. 1, pp. 182, 171
16 Frénilly, op.cit., pp. 121, 113–14
17 Morris, op.cit., vol. 1, pp. xxxviii–xxxix
18 La Tour du Pin, op.cit., vol. 1, p. 160
19 Morris, op.cit., vol. 1, p. xxxix
20 ibid., p. xli
21 ibid., p. 6
22 ibid., pp. xl, 61
23 Bombelles, op.cit., vol. 2, pp. 294–5
24 Morris, op.cit., vol. 1, p. 21
25 Bombelles, op.cit., vol. 2, pp. 300–1
26 ibid., p. 302. The Chevalier de La Tourette was a Knight of Malta.
27 La Tour du Pin, op.cit., vol. 1, pp. 177–8
28 Morris, op.cit., vol. 1, p. 66
29 Bombelles, op.cit., vol. 2, pp. 305–6
30 Boigne, *Mèmoirs*, vol. 1, p. 56
31 La Tour du Pin, op.cit., vol. 1, p. 181
32 ibid., p. 180
33 Bombelles, op.cit., vol. 2, p. 307
34 Morris, op.cit., vol. 1, p. 69
35 La Tour du Pin, op.cit., vol. 1, p. 182
36 Morris, op.cit., vol. 1, p. 70
37 Bombelles, op.cit., vol. 2, pp. 309–10
38 La Tour du Pin, loc.cit.
39 Morris, op.cit., vol. 1, p. 39
40 Young, op.cit., p. 136
41 ibid., p. 128
42 Tilly, op.cit., p. 405
43 Elliott, *During the Reign of Terror*, p. 39; Tilly, op.cit., p. 53
44 Elliott, op.cit., p. 38
45 ibid.
46 Campan, *Memoirs*, vol. 1, p. 162; La Tour du Pin, op.cit., vol. 1, p. 164
47 Young, op.cit., p. 124
48 Morris, op.cit., vol. 1, p. 295
49 ibid., pp. 229, 293
50 Young, op.cit., p. 148

51 Morris, op.cit., vol. 1, p. 136
52 ibid., vol. 1, pp. 150–1; La Tour du Pin, op.cit., vol. 1, p. 187
53 Young, op.cit., p. 178
54 Morris, op.cit., vol. 1, p. 148
55 La Tour du Pin, op.cit., vol. 1, p. 199
56 Morris, op.cit., vol. 1, p. 158
57 ibid., p. 156
58 ibid., p. 306
59 La Tour du Pin, op.cit., vol. 1, p. 198
60 ibid., p. 222
61 ibid., p. 229
62 Louis-Philippe d'Orléans, op.cit., vol. 1, p. 96
63 Morris, op.cit., vol. 1, p. 246
64 La Tour du Pin, op.cit., vol. 1, p. 232
65 Morris, op.cit., vol. 1, p. 344

Bibliography

Place of publication is London unless otherwise stated

Besenval, P.V., Baron de, *Mémoires de M. le Baron de Besenval*, ed. A.J. Ségur, 4 vols., Paris: F. Buisson, 1805

Beugnot, J.C., Comte, *Mémoires du Comte Beugnot*, ed. Comte A. Beugnot, 3 vols., Paris: E. Dentu, 1866

Boigne, C.L.E.A., Comtesse de, *Memoirs of the Comtesse de Boigne*, ed. C. Nicoullaud, 3 vols., W. Heinemann, 1907

Bombelles, M.M., Marquis de, *Journal (1780–1789)*, ed. J. Grassion & F. Durif, 2 vols., Geneva: Droz, 1977–82

Campan, J.L.H., *Memoirs of Madame Campan on Marie-Antoinette and her Court*, 2 vols., Caxton, 1909

Castelot, A., *Paris: the turbulent city*, trans. by D. Folliot, Valentine, Mitchell & Barrie & Ratcliff, 1962

Chateaubriand, F.R. de, *Mémoires d'Outre-tombe*, ed. M. Levaillant, 4 vols., Paris: Flammarion, 1964

Cole, William, *A Journal of my Journey to Paris in the Year 1765*, ed. F.G. Stokes, Constable, 1931

Dard, E., *Un acteur caché du drame révolutionnaire: le général Choderlos de Laclos, auteur des Liaisons Dangereuses*, Paris: Perrin, 1905

Ducros, L., *French Society in the Eighteenth Century*, trans. by W. de Geijer, G. Bell, 1926

Elliott, G.D., *During the Reign of Terror: Journal of my Life during the French Revolution*, trans. by E.J. Méras, T. Fisher Unwin, 1910

Frénilly, F.A.F., Baron de, *Souvenirs du Baron de Frénilly*, ed. A. Chuquet, Paris: Plon-Nourrit, 1909

Gaxotte, P., *Paris au XVIIIe siècle*, Paris: Arthaud, 1968

Girard, G. (editor), *Correspondance entre Marie-Thérèse et Marie-Antoinette*, Paris: Grasset, 1933

Isherwood, R.M., *Farce and Fantasy: Popular Entertainment in Eighteenth Century Paris*, New York: OUP, 1986

Jarrett, D., *The begetters of Revolution: England's involvement with France 1759–1789*, Longman, 1973

La Tour du Pin, H.L., Marquise de, *Journal d'une femme de cinquante ans*, ed. A. de Liederkerke-Beaufort, 2 vols., Paris: Chapelot, 1913.

Launay, M. & G. Mailhos, *Introduction à la vie littéraire du XVIIIe siècle*, Paris: Bordas, 1984

Lauzun, A.L. de G., Duc de (Duc de Biron), *Mémoires de Armand-Louis de Gontaut, Duc de Lauzun, Général Biron*, ed. E. Pilon, Paris: Henri Jonquières, 1928

Levron, J., *Daily life at Versailles in the 17th and 18th centuries*, trans. by C.E. Engel, Allen & Unwin, 1968

Ligne, C.J., Prince de, *Fragments de l'histoire de ma vie*, ed. F. Leuridant, 2 vols., Paris: Plon, 1928

Lopez, C.A., *Mon Cher Papa: Franklin and the ladies of Paris*, New Haven: Yale Univ. Press, 1990

Maxwell, C., *The English Traveller in France 1698–1815*, Routledge, 1932

Mercier, L.S., *The Picture of Paris before and after the Revolution*, trans. by W. & E. Jackson, Routledge, 1929

Morris, G., *A Diary of the French Revolution*, ed. B.C. Davenport, 2 vols., Harrap, 1939

Mossiker, F., *The Queen's Necklace*, Gollancz, 1961

Nougaret, M., *Anecdotes du règne de Louis XVI*, Paris, 1791

Orléans, Louis-Philippe d' (King of the French), *Mémoires*, 2 vols., Paris: Plon, 1973

Rétif de la Bretonne, N., *Les Nuits de Paris ou le spectateur*

nocturne, ed. J. Varloot & M. Delon, Paris: Gallimard, 1987

Ségur, L.-P., Comte de, *Memoirs*, ed. E. Cruickshanks, Folio Society, 1960

Söderhjelm, A., *Fersen et Marie-Antoinette: correspondance et journal inédits du Comte Axel de Fersen*, Paris: Kra, 1930

Staël, A.L.G., Baronne de, *Correspondance Générale*, ed. B.W. Jasinski, 4 vols., Paris: J.J. Pauvert, 1960–64

Stryienski, C., *The National History of France: the Eighteenth Century*, trans. by H.N. Dickinson, W. Heinemann, 1916

Talleyrand, C.M., Prince de, *Mémoires du Prince de Talleyrand*, ed. the Duc de Broglie, 3 vols., Paris: Calmann Lévy, 1891

Thrale, H.L., *The French Journals of Mrs. Thrale and Dr. Johnson*, ed. M. Tyson & H. Guppy, Manchester: Manchester UP, 1932

Tieghem, P. van, *Beaumarchais par lui-même*, Paris: Éditions du Seuil, 1960

Tilly, A., Comte de, *Memoirs of the Comte Alexandre de Tilly*, trans. by F. Delisle, Gollancz, 1933

Vigée-Lebrun, E., *The Memoirs of Elisabeth Vigée-Lebrun*, trans. by S. Evans, Camden Press, 1989

Wolff, J.S., *Historic Paris*, Bodley Head, 1921

Young, A., *Travels in France and Italy*, Dent, 1915

N.^{re} DAME _{de} PARIS

HOTEL DE VILLE